OBSERVING THE LANGUAGE LEARNER

Edited by
Angela Jaggar
and
M. Trika Smith-Burke
New York University

Copublished by the
International Reading Association
800 Barksdale Road, Box 8139, Newark, Delaware 19714

National Council of Teachers of English
1111 Kenyon Road, Urbana, Illinois 61801

Library of Congress Cataloging in Publication Data
Main entry under title:

Observing the language learner.

Includes bibliographies.
1. Language arts (Elementary)—Congresses.
2. Children—Language—Congresses. I. Jaggar, Angela.
II. Smith-Burke, M. Trika. III. IRA/NCTE Committee on the Impact of Child Language Development Research on Curriculum and Instruction.
LB1576.027 1985 372.6 84-12986
ISBN 0-87207-890-6

Contents

Foreword

During times of public insecurity about educational quality in the schools, an uncertainty often emerges about what directions the schools should take. This is particularly true in so critical an area as the teaching of language. Public demands for increased student achievement generally begin with criticism of instruction in the communicative arts–reading, writing, listening, and speaking.

Educators react to public pressure for increased pupil performance in a variety of ways. Those least informed about language learning often respond by centering the language curriculum on a narrow set of language skills thought to be easily defined and measured. Unfortunately, this kind of response almost inevitably leads to an elimination of many goals important to the language curriculum. It may produce assessments that yield trivial and even misleading results and may even restrict good classroom practice. Without question, educators have a responsibility to respond to public concern for student progress. The response is best offered, however, by informed professionals acting in the best interest of long term development of the children they teach.

Fortunately for students and teachers, recent research has added significantly to our understanding of how children learn language. The new research draws upon a diversity of disciplines. Psycholinguistics, sociolinguistics, anthropology, child development, cognitive psychology, and education are among the fields contributing to the emerging theories and methodologies. The new research has extended our knowledge base and changed our understanding of how children develop and use language to make sense of the world around them.

At the heart of these investigations has been the importance of the social and functional nature of language learning. All of the language processes–listening, speaking, reading, and writing–are viewed as means by which learners construct meaning. Students are regarded as active participants in their own learning, and the interdependence of language, thinking, and learning is stressed. Teaching techniques are encouraged that promote genuine student-generated purposes for language use and allow time for free give-and-take among students to solve problems, explore ideas, and confer regarding their work. The importance of process rather than product in the development and use of language is emphasized.

New research points out the importance of a process approach to the evaluation of language growth. Evaluation is viewed as an integral part of language instruction. Assessments of student progress made in isolation from ongoing teacher observations are virtually worthless in gaining information with which to make instructional decisions. Teachers of reading and writing need to be available to students (watching, discussing, responding), gaining insight into the *why* and *what* of language learning.

Research to practice has never been easy. Applying these insights in school settings is even more difficult at a time when teachers may feel discouraged because tests and texts tend to drive curriculum decision making. It is for this very reason that *Observing the Language Learner* is such an important book. Its editors have carefully gathered a collection of articles by leading researchers, representing the best in the current thinking about language learning both in and out of the classrooms.

Although the book is targeted for teachers, its content is equally valid for all persons having responsibility for shaping language policy in the schools. This publication offers readers both a threat and a promise. The threat lies in the potential to upset existing beliefs and habits about the nature of language learning; the promise resides in its ability to offer new ways of working with language learners and to support and confirm the knowledge and practice which teachers have come to value through their own experiences and intuition.

Dorothy S. Strickland
Teachers College
Columbia University

Preface

We know a great deal about how children learn language and become literate. In fact, child language research has expanded so rapidly in the past twenty years that there has been a knowledge explosion. Researchers and theorists from a range of disciplines, including psychology, education, linguistics, psycholinguistics, and sociolinguistics, are having a significant impact on our views of language and of language learning. Their findings are exciting and have far reaching implications for curriculum and instruction. A perennial problem in education, however, is how to get new information to teachers, program planners, and others responsible for classroom practice—that is, how to narrow the gap between theory and teaching. It is clear that professionals who traditionally have not worked closely must now collaborate to provide language programs compatible with the best that we know.

The International Year of the Child, 1979, marked the beginning of a major effort at collaboration among professionals in diverse roles in education. As a means of celebrating the International Year of the Child, NCTE and IRA formed a joint committee on the Impact of Child Language Development Research on Curriculum and Instruction. The committee was charged with bringing together teachers, researchers, and other scholars to explore the significance of the research for language teaching and curriculum. This book grew out of the work of that committee which from 1979 to 1982 sponsored four national and three regional conferences on children's language and learning; these became known as the "Impact Conferences."

The Impact Conferences provided a forum for dialogue among professionals in different roles and with varying points of view. Researchers from the United States, England, Canada, New Zealand, and Australia presented their findings and described their approaches to studying language and literacy development. The participants—

teachers, curriculum specialists, administrators, teacher educators, and other researchers—examined the findings, discussed the implications, exchanged ideas, and grappled with ways to bridge the gap between theory and practice.

The conferences highlighted the dramatic changes that have occurred in child language research. Early studies concentrated on form and described children's language primarily in terms of the product (e.g., number of words used, parts of speech, average length of sentence). These studies provided general indices of linguistic development, milestones, that allowed comparison among individuals and groups of children, and were important. But they did not explain differences in children's behavior or describe how language develops. Dissatisfaction with this approach led to new questions and to more fruitful ways to study children's language.

For example, the earlier concentration on form has been replaced by growing interest in the *process* by which children acquire oral and written language, and in the conditions which facilitate learning. Form is not being ignored; the issues are simply different. Instead of focusing on words and sentences, researchers are analyzing whole discourse: children's stories, conversations, letters, narrative, and expository writing in order to understand better the relations among the different aspects of form, between form and content, and between spoken and written discourse. Similarly, where once researchers were primarily interested in how children learn the linguistic system, now they are exploring how children learn the *functions* of language, and acquire skill in using it to communicate, to think, and to learn. Meaning, form, and function are so intertwined in language use that it is virtually impossible to understand one aspect of language development without carefully considering how it is related to other aspects of development.

The study of process and function has led to a growing awareness that context plays an important role in language use and learning. Whatever the aspect of interest, grammar, spelling, language awareness, reading, or writing, children's language should be studied not in isolation but in relation to the context in which it is used, and to the users' social and cultural backgrounds.

As the research focus changed so did the approach. Rather than studying children's language in laboratory settings or in controlled experiments, theorists now draw heavily upon insights from naturalistic research, that is, observations of children at home, in school, and in other natural settings. Informed observation is the most effective way to learn about language growth and development; it is a critical tool for teachers and researchers. By listening carefully to what children say and watching what they do, we can learn a great deal about their concepts of oral and written language, their stages of development, their strategies for processing language, and their uses of language. The importance of observation, or "kidwatching," became a dominant theme of the Impact Conferences.

Participants in the first meeting recognized the value of this approach and requested more information about how to collect, interpret, and use naturalistic data in teaching and in research. As a result, the committee organized kidwatching workshops that were conducted by teams of teachers and researchers; these sessions became an integral part of all subsequent programs. The idea for this book—to provide teachers with theoretically sound, practical ways to observe different aspects of children's oral and written language—evolved from the success of these workshops.

In planning *Observing the Language Learner*, our aims were twofold: 1) to synthesize and translate, where necessary, recent findings on children's language and literacy development into concepts and generalizations that are meaningful to teachers; and 2) to describe and illustrate ways teachers can use the information to observe and interpret children's language behavior in the classroom and other settings. To accomplish these aims, we selected a theoretical framework that provides a coherent picture of language development. Then we outlined the topics and asked people who are skilled observers of children's language to write original articles on these topics.

Readers come to a book with different backgrounds and expectations; they will interpret the material in light of their own experiences. For those who are already avid kidwatchers and hold beliefs about children, language, and teaching similar to those of the authors, we hope the book confirms your beliefs and offers new ideas about how and what to observe. For those who hold different views, we hope the book demonstrates the potential of kidwatching and intrigues you enough to try some of the ideas.

The creation of a book is a story in itself. From the above, you know something of its beginnings. Many people contributed to the development of the final product and we would like to thank them publicly. First, we wish to thank the cochairs of the Impact Committee, Yetta Goodman and Dorothy Strickland (past presidents of NCTE and

IRA, respectively), for their support and encouragement throughout the preparation of the manuscript. We also want to thank the members of the Impact Committee; they helped to shape the book. We especially want to thank the authors who shared their expertise and willingly accepted suggestions for revision. Their professionalism and cooperation made our task much easier than it might have been. We gratefully acknowledge the contributions of Alvina Treut Burrows, Bernice E. Cullinan, Carol Fisher, Julie Jensen, and Rosemary Winkeljohann. They read early drafts of the articles and made constructive criticisms that contributed significantly to the quality of the book. Kathy Tolman Harwood deserves recognition for her speed and accuracy in preparing the final manuscript as does Louise Maestri for her assistance in proofreading the document. Our colleague, Carol Millsom, deserves special thanks for her support and incisive editorial comments. Finally, we wish to thank the children whose spontaneous and creative use of language provided the real life examples used throughout the volume.

AMJ
MTSB

On *Observing the Language Learner:* Introduction and Overview

Angela M. Jaggar
New York University

This book is about children and their language, and about teachers and their roles in developing children's language. It is based on the belief that a teacher's task is not to "teach" children language but, rather, to create an environment which will allow language learning to occur naturally. This is an environment where children use language to talk to each other, pose questions, solve real problems, and learn about the world while the teacher works with the students listening to what they say, watching what they do, guiding, and promoting their learning.

Aim of the Book

Language learning is a complex process. To create a classroom in which learning flourishes, teachers need a thorough knowledge of children, and of language and how it develops within a child. Recent research has expanded our understanding of how children acquire and develop skill in oral and written language. Teachers familiar with this work will find it an exciting and valuable source of knowledge about children's language.

Teachers also can learn from the ideas and intuitions they derive from being skilled observers of children. Observing children in the classroom and in other natural settings, such as the playground and cafeteria, can tell us things about their language that we can learn in no other way.

The central aim of this book is to help teachers to become more effective "kidwatchers." Using informative and often amusing examples, the articles in this collection describe various aspects of language learning, explain why they are important, show teachers what to look for and how to interpret what they see and hear. The writers explain how teachers, with ideas from theory and research to guide them, can develop a greater appreciation of their students' language abilities and, at the same time, build a sound theoretical base for classroom practice.

Both sources—theory and research on the one hand and the teacher's own observations and speculations on the other—provide vital information for planning curriculum and instruction. Let's briefly consider why both are important to good teaching.

Why Knowledge of Research and Theory Is Important

The past twenty years have seen an unprecedented amount of research on how children acquire and use oral and written language. Although much is still to be learned, one thing is certain—many materials and practices in use in our schools today are at odds with what these studies tell us. For example, research confirms that children are active agents in their own learning. Knowledge is not something that exists outside; it is constructed within by the learner. All learning, particularly the learning of language, involves activity and discovery. Children will acquire new knowledge only when they can relate it to existing ideas or language, that is, when it "makes sense" in terms of what they already know.

Children already know a great deal about language when they enter school. They know the linguistic *structure* of their language, including most grammatical patterns of that language. They know language is a way to express *meanings*, a way of sharing their experiences and ideas with others. Most important, they know language is *functional*, that they can use it to get things done—to make friends, to complain, to find out about things, and even to create imaginary worlds through story and drama. As Halliday (1982a) says, children know what language is because they know what language does. The goal of instruction is to facilitate continuing growth in all these areas by enabling children to use their language resources and to build upon them.

A growing body of evidence shows that young children also know much more about written language than we thought. Many can read or write, or are well on the way to learning how, before they enter school. They realize print (a traffic sign, label, storybook) is language in another form, and that it, like speech, carries a message and has purpose. Witness the child who points to a page in a book and asks,

"What does it *say*?" If the conditions are right, children can learn to read and write as easily and naturally as they learn to listen and talk. For them to make progress, literacy instruction must build on children's previously acquired knowledge of written language.

Most important for curriculum and instruction, advances in the field have led to a better understanding of how language is learned and of the role language plays in education. In earlier work, most researchers concentrated on the structural aspects of children's language, such as syntax and vocabulary, in an effort to understand how children acquired the linguistic system. Now more researchers have begun to investigate children's uses for language and are exploring the important relationships among language, communication, and learning.

It is now clear that language development involves much more than learning the forms of the language. Though they may express it differently, most specialists agree with Halliday (1982b) that there are three interrelated facets to language development: learning language, learning through language, and learning about language. He says that from a child's point of view the three processes are all the same. But to understand them properly, we need to consider them separately in order to see how each enters into a child's overall growth and development (p. 7).

Learning language is the process whereby children, in interacting with others, construct the language system, i.e. the meanings and functions of language and the symbols to represent them in oral and written form. At the same time as they are constructing this system, they are also using the system to construct another one, namely their picture of the world. That is, they are using language and *learning through language.* In the course of developing both systems (language and knowledge), they are also *learning about language* itself. They are becoming "aware" of the nature of language, of its forms and functions.

Halliday emphasizes two things. All three processes take place side by side, reinforcing each other, and are largely *subconscious.* All three are *social* processes. They are learned in meaningful communication with others. These principles are illustrated in many ways in this book which is based on Halliday's view of language development. The authors look at children learning language and learning about language, using language and learning through language.

From this growing and exciting field of inquiry, several important generalizations or themes have emerged. They apply equally to oral and written language. Some are new, others have been clarified through research so that we now have a better understanding of their implications for instruction. Taken together, they represent the common perspective from which this book was written.

> *Language learning is a self-generated, creative process.* Children learn language without explicit instruction. They learn it naturally through experience, by listening to others, experimenting and practicing in situations where language serves genuine purposes.
>
> *Language learning is holistic.* The different components of language—function, form and meaning—are learned simultaneously. Children acquire new and more complex forms and functions for language when they want to express new and more complex meanings. In the process they also learn that the forms used to express meaning and intention may vary depending on the purpose and context.
>
> *Language learning is social and collaborative.* Children acquire language in meaningful interactions with others who provide models and support their learning by responding to what they are trying to say and do, rather than to the form.
>
> *Language learning is functional and integrative.* Children do not learn language and then learn to use it. They acquire language and learn to communicate with it simultaneously, and in the process also learn how to use language to think and learn.
>
> *Language learning is variable.* Because language is inherently variable, the meanings, the forms and the functions of children's language will depend on their personal, social, and cultural experiences.

As a source of knowledge, theory and research are important, then, because they provide teachers with a framework—key ideas, concepts, and generalizations—to use as a guide in observing, interpreting, and assessing children's language. As the articles in this collection will show, they also provide valuable suggestions about ways to promote continuing growth and development. But theory, and the research on which it is based, is descriptive, not prescriptive.

Why Observation Is Important

In education we often mistakenly assume that good teaching is a matter of "knowing the research" and "putting theory into practice." But for research and theory to be meaningful, teachers must be able to relate the findings and ideas to their own models of language and to what they know about their students' language and ways of learning. No research, theory, or curriculum guide for that matter, can prescribe what is appropriate for individual students (Eisner, 1979). Only teachers can.

The key to effective teaching is building on what students have already learned. The best way to discover this is to listen and watch closely as children use language—spoken and written—in different settings and circumstances. Careful observations over time will reveal individual styles and patterns of language use. As patterns emerge, teachers can reflect on them, comparing the information to past observations and to their knowledge of language development, to determine what their students know (competence) and can do (skill) with language. When combined with informed reflection, observation becomes inquiry (Amarel, 1980); that is, careful study which leads to sound judgments about children, and to continual learning for the teacher.

Observation, as the diagram illustrates, plays a critical role in teaching. It is the link between theory (knowledge) and practice (teaching).

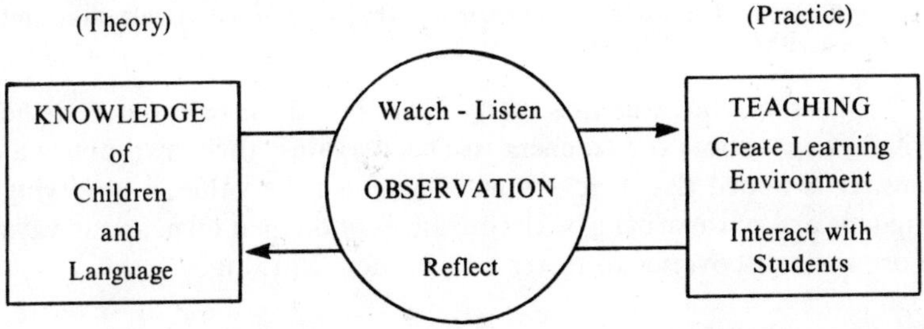

The real value in knowing the research is that it provides a background of ideas against which teachers can compare their own observations and speculations. They can ask, "Do these ideas make sense, given my knowledge of classroom life, children, and language?" If they do, teachers can use them to refine their own classroom procedures. If not, they may think of other interpretations that will help them clarify the reasons behind their instructional choices. (Barr, D'Arcy, & Healey, 1982, p. ii)

Kidwatching, then, is an ongoing purposeful activity. But because language is complex, it is impossible to observe all aspects at once. The first essential in observing children's language is to decide in advance what facet to concentrate on and what to look for. Before deciding, it is important to keep in mind distinctions such as those between form and function, acquisition and use, communication and learning—distinctions that will be made clear in the following articles. Second, it is necessary to decide how, when, and where to observe. No one approach is best; that will depend on the aspect of language observed and the circumstances under which it is observed. (Macaulay, 1980, pp. 53-54)

This book suggests several ways to study children's language behavior. With increased skill and confidence, teachers can devise their own strategies and techniques. The important thing is that teachers think of observation as a form of problem solving; it is a selective search for knowledge to guide instruction.

James Britton (1982) said in declaring this the decade of the teacher:

> There are great opportunities for us, provided we see that interactive learning applies to teachers as well as to those we teach; provided we see our role as helping each other to theorize from our own experience, and build our own rationale and convictions. For it is only when we are theorizing from our own experiences that we can, selectively, take and use other people's theories. (p. 214)

This volume contains many ideas based on research and the writers' experiences for teachers to check against their own observations. It is hoped that teachers will recognize the value in observing language and of theorizing, with colleagues or on their own, about ways to use their discoveries to foster and support learning.

Overview of Contents

The book is divided into four interrelated parts. The two articles in Part One, "Knowing Children and Language," provide the rationale for observing children's language and establish the central theme.

The next two parts comprise the heart of the book. They deal with the different, but overlapping, facets of language development described by Halliday. Both contain sections on observing oral language and written language. Each writer looks at a single aspect of language learning and illustrates through examples of actual language behavior how careful observation can illuminate this aspect of development.

Part Two, "Children Learning Language and Learning about Language," concentrates on what children learn as they construct the symbol system, the strategies they use, and how their behavior reveals their developing awareness of language. Because so much of this learning takes place before formal schooling, the articles in this part of the book focus primarily on children in the early childhood years which have significant implications for teachers at all levels. In Part Three, "Children Using Language and Learning Through Language," the writers focus on school age children, looking at ways in which they use language. Some concentrate on the social nature of language and examine how children use language for communication. Others look at children using language—talking, reading, and writing—to think and learn.

Part Four, "Curriculum and Instruction: The Language Learning Environment," highlights the importance of continually monitoring the effect of curriculum and instruction on children's language use and learning.

This collection is not a comprehensive treatment of children's language, but an overview of the kind of exciting work that is going on in the field. Its primary purpose is to introduce the reader to the use of observation as a window on the language learner's mind.

References

Amarel, M. "The Teacher As Observer," Occasional paper. Harrisburg: Pennsylvania Department of Education, Right to Read Office, 1980.

Barr, M., D'Arcy, P., and Healy, M.K. *What's Going on? Language/Learning Episodes in British and American Classrooms, Grades 4-13.* Montclair, New Jersey: Boynton/Cook, 1982.

Britton, J. "English Teaching: Retrospect and Prospect," in G. Pradl (Ed.), *Prospect and Retrospect: Selected Essays of James Britton.* Montclair, New Jersey: Boynton/Cook, 1982.

Eisner, E.W. *The Educational Imagination.* New York: Macmillan, 1979.

Halliday, M.A.K. "Relevant Models of Language," in B. Wade (Ed.), *Language Perspectives.* London: Heinemann Educational Books, 1982(a).

Halliday, M.A.K. "Three Aspects of Children's Language Development: Learning Language, Learning through Language, Learning about Language," in Y. Goodman, M. Haussler, and D. Strickland (Eds.), *Oral and Written Language Development Research: Impact on the Schools.* Urbana, Illinois: National Council of Teachers of English, 1982(b).

Part One
Knowing Children and Language

Introduction

To plan effective language and literacy programs, two things clearly are essential. One is knowledge of children and how they grow and develop. The other is knowledge of language, what it is, and how children learn it. Part One focuses on how we can enrich our knowledge of both by making informed observation an integral part of our teaching.

In the first article, Goodman develops the rationale for "Kidwatching: Observing Children in the Classroom." She begins by discussing kidwatching as an alternative to testing and explains why informal, naturalistic observation is the most effective way to learn about children's language and their ways of learning. She describes how teachers who know children and language, and are sensitive observers, can play significant roles in their students' language development.

In "Language and Language Learning for Child Watchers," King discusses what we can learn from child language research to guide our observations and interpretations. She presents an overview of current information about children's oral and written language, stressing areas that are vital in understanding how language is learned and how it functions in a child's life. She describes all children as competent, creative language learners.

Kidwatching: Observing Children in the Classroom

Yetta M. Goodman
University of Arizona

Three first graders were grouped around the flotation bowl. They were trying to discover what things could float and why. Elana put a wadded piece of foil in the bowl. Just as it sank to the bottom, Mr. Borton walked up and observed the scene. He noticed a wet, fair sized aluminum boat next to the bowl.

He addressed the group, "What did you just learn?"

Elana responded quickly, "Big things float and small things sink."

Robin reacted, "Uh, uh. I don't think that's always true."

"What might you do to prove the hypothesis Elana just made?" said Borton.

"Well," said Lynn, "Maybe we could make a small boat and a big ball and try those things to see what will happen." As the children got involved in the new tasks they set for themselves, Borton walked on to another group.

Good teachers, like Mr. Borton, have always been kidwatchers. The concept of kidwatching is not new. It grows out of the child study movement that reached a peak in the 1930s providing a great deal of knowledge about human growth and development. Teachers can translate child study into its most universal form: learning about children by watching how they learn. The term kidwatching has caught on among those who believe that children learn language best in an environment rich with opportunities to explore interesting objects and ideas. Through observing the reading, writing, speaking, and listening of friendly, interactive peers, interested, kidwatching teachers can understand and support child language development.

Evaluation of the progress of conceptual and language development for individual children cannot be provided in any useful sense by formalized pencil and paper tests. Evaluation provides the most significant information if it occurs continuously and simultaneously with the experiences in which the learning is taking place. Borton knows a lot about how children conceptualize, develop new insights into the physical nature of the world, and what kinds of language they use and have developed during the activity in which they were involved.

Even in the home, parents are aware of how much their children have grown, whether they have become better ball players or how much more considerate they have become toward other family members. Parents know this by their constant attention to and involvement with size of clothes, the faster and harder return of a pitched ball, or some deed a child does for a parent or sibling. Scales and yardsticks may provide some statistical data for parents to use to verify their observational knowledge, but it is never a lone measure on which they rely.

Unfortunately, especially in recent years, scores on tests have been viewed as more objective than the judgment of a professional observer since test results are often presented under an aura of statistical "significance" which for many people has an unquestionable mystique.

Formal tests, standardized or criterion referenced, provide statistical measures of the product of learning but only as supplementary evidence for professional judgments about the growth of children. If teachers rely on formalized tests they come to conclusions about children's growth based on data from a single source. Tests do provide evidence of how children grow in their ability to handle test situations but not in their ability to handle settings where important language learnings occur. Studies of the role that context plays in how children learn have made it clear that children respond differently in different situations. Teachers who observe the development of language and knowledge in children in different settings become aware of important milestones in children's development that tests cannot reveal.

Kidwatching, the focus of this book, is used as a slogan to reinstate and legitimatize the significance of professional observation in the classroom. Those who support such child study understand that the evaluation of pupils' growth and curriculum development are integrally related. The energies of teachers and other curriculum planners must go into building a powerful learning environment. The key question in evaluation is not, "Can the child perform the specific tasks that have been taught?" Rather, the question is, "Can the child adjust language used in other situations to meet the demands of new settings?" The teacher must be aware that children learn all the time. The best way to gain insight into language learning is to observe children using language to explore all kinds of concepts in art, social studies, math, science, or physical education.

Teachers screen their observations through their philosophy, their knowledge base, and their assumptions whenever they are involved in kidwatching. Following are some of the basic premises which underlie kidwatching notions:

1. Current knowledge about child language and conceptual development must be a part of continuous education for teachers. Such knowledge guides observations. Not only does it help teachers know what to look for as signs of growth and development but it also helps teachers become consciously aware of their knowledge, their biases, and their philosophical orientation.

2. Language and concepts grow and develop depending on the settings in which they occur, the experiences that children have in those settings, and the interaction of the people in those settings. The richer and more varied these settings and interactions, the richer the child's language and concepts will be.

3. Knowledgeable teachers ready to assume responsibility for observation and evaluation of children play a very significant role in enriching the child's development of language and concepts.

Current Knowledge about Language

During the second half of this century a knowledge explosion has occurred in the study of language or linguistics. Much of this knowledge is contrary to the ideas about language which have been taught in the past under the labels of phonics, spelling, vocabulary, and grammar. In addition, there have been enormous gains in understandings about how children learn language. When old beliefs are being questioned and new knowledge is not fully understood, a great deal of controversy is often generated. This is especially true of those who have to apply the knowledge, as teachers do in classroom situations. Since much of the new information that must be considered by kidwatchers will be presented in the following chapters, only a few aspects of language variation and the role of error in language learning will be touched on here.

There are many issues concerning language differences in the areas of both dialect and second language learning which teachers must consider. Too many children have been hurt in the past because of lack of knowledge about language differences. Not only teachers but test makers and curriculum builders often produce materials that reflect myths and misunderstandings. The more knowledge teachers have about language variation, the better position they are in to evaluate materials and tests in order to use them wisely and appropriately. Attitudes such as "these children have no language" or "bilingualism confuses children" are still too prevalent. Kidwatching can help teachers be aware of how such statements are damaging to language growth, if they are armed with up-to-date knowledge. By observing the language of children in a wide variety of settings such as role playing, retelling of picture books, or playing games during recess or physical education, teachers gain many kinds of information that help to dispel myths about language and language learning.

For example, Sorita, age 6, would use the following types of construction often in oral conversations with other children or during sharing sessions:

> "Lots of my friends was at my house. . . ."
> "We was going to the store. . . ."

However, during her narration of "The Three Billy Goats Gruff" which accompanied the acting out of the story by some of her classmates, her teacher heard, "There were three billy goats. . . ." Sorita used this more formal construction throughout the narration.

Retelling a story, about a farmer and his son, a recent 9 year old immigrant from Lebanon said, "They were working at to plant something."

Both examples provide insight into each child's language development. Sorita shows the ability to use the more formal "were" form in storytelling although she uses the colloquial form in the informal settings. She is aware of formal and informal language settings and that each permits different language.

The second child shows growing control over two kinds of complex English structures—the verb plus particle "working at" and the infinitive form "to plant," even though as this child combines the structures, they may sound a little unusual to a native English speaker's ear.

Errors in language and in conceptual development reflect much more than a mistake that can be eradicated with a red pencil or a verbal admonition. What an adult perceives as wrong may in actuality reflect development in the child. Errors, miscues, or misconceptions usually indicate ways in which a child is organizing the world at that moment. As children develop conceptually and linguistically, their errors shift from those that represent unsophisticated conclusions to ones that show greater sophistication. The previous examples are evidence of this kind of growth. Sometimes teachers expect certain responses or "correct answers" because of a school based cultural view of the world. The child's unexpected responses, if observed with understanding, may broaden a teacher's conceptualization about the child's world. "Errors" also indicate interpretations which may in no way be wrong but simply show that the child has used inferences about reading or listening which were unexpected.

For example, a kindergarten teacher gave her class a short talk about what was wrong with wasting milk prior to morning snack time. Tomasa was observed taking a small sip of milk. She then carefully closed the milk carton, wiped her place with her paper towel, and slowly placed the carton of milk in the waste basket, holding it tight until it reached the bottom.

> "Didn't we just talk about not wasting milk?" Miss Dasson asked.
>
> "I ain't waste my milk," Tomasa responded. "I keeped everything real clean!"

Miss Dasson now knows that "waste" has an alternate meaning in the language of Tomasa's community—"to spill." She and Tomasa can now share each other's meanings.

The kidwatcher who understands the role of unexpected responses will use children's errors and miscues to chart their growth and development and to understand the personal and cultural history of the child. There are no tests available which can provide this kind of data to the professional educator. These insights can emerge only from kidwatching based on a sound knowledge of language and language learning.

Individual teachers may not be in a position to keep current about the dynamic information so vital to understanding language learning. However, courses of study or programs can be organized through setting up teacher support groups, working cooperatively with teacher educators at local universities and colleges or with inservice personnel at the district level, and holding discussion groups. Although courses in linguistics, the science of language, may in themselves be helpful, it may be more useful if teachers encourage and participate in the development of programs which have an applied orientation for the classroom.

Variations of Setting, Function, and Material

Thoughtful observation of children takes place in a rich, innovative curriculum in the hands of a knowledgeable teacher who demands and accepts responsibility for curriculum decision making. With such teachers, children are involved in exciting educational experiences and make the greatest growth in language learning and conceptual development.

Curriculum becomes sterilized when it is based on pupils' results on standardized tests or progress on "criterion referenced" behavioral checksheets. In order to achieve appropriate gains, curriculum experiences must narrow to those safely entombed in the test itself. Curriculum becomes repetitive practice with the same kind of "skills" on workbooks and worksheets as in the test. The only individualization is how much practice each pupil must endure.

Where kidwatching is an integral part of the curriculum, the teacher's focus is on providing rich learning experiences for children. There is an awareness of the dynamic relationship among the teacher, the children, and the experiences. Evaluation is ongoing. Although teachers should certainly be expected to document and discuss the growth of their children, the most important role of the teacher is involving children in learning through the richness of the curriculum. Only when children have a variety of materials available to read and many good personal reasons to want to learn about new ideas and concepts will they read various genre, write for different purposes, and grow in their ability to use written language effectively.

As functions and purposes for learning new concepts change, so will the settings, the language, and the materials needed for the learnings change. These broadened experiences enrich language learning for children and provide many opportunities for kidwatching to occur. Children must go to the library to solve certain problems, to the principal's office to solve others. They interview some people orally, read about others, or write letters as it serves the purposes of their explorations. Language learning reaches out to meet new challenges and teachers can evaluate the flexibility with which children can expand language use.

For example, keeping copies of children's letters written to different people over the course of a few months provides evidence about: 1) the appropriateness of the language of the letters, depending on their purposes; 2) the degree to which children change the language and style of the letters, depending on their audience; 3) the increase of conventionally spelled words over time; 4) changes in the complexity of grammatical structures; and 5) concern for legibility.

Teacher's Role Is Significant

Concepts from three scholars in different fields of child study provide a jumping off place from which to explore the significance of the teacher's role. Jerome Bruner talks about "scaffolding"; M.A.K. Halliday, about "tracking"; and L.S. Vygotsky, about the "zone of proximal development." Each of these concepts is used to express the significance of communicative interactions between adults and children which are basic to the expansion of language and the extension of learning in children. If parents play as significant a role in a child's language development as these scholars suggest, it seems logical that a teacher with understandings about how children learn language might capitalize on their ideas and be even more effective than parents in supporting child language growth and extending it once the child comes to school.

Focusing on mother/child interaction, Bruner (1978) defines scaffolding by quoting Roger Brown:

> A study of detailed mother/child interaction...shows that successful communication on one level is always the launching platform for attempts at communication on a more adult level. (p. 251)

Bruner continues:

> The mother systematically changes her BT (Baby Talk) in order to "raise the ante" or alter the conditions she imposes on the child's speech in different settings. (p. 251)

According to Bruner (1978), the adult always takes the child's ideas seriously, thinking through what the child is trying to communicate, allowing the child to move ahead when capable of doing so, and supporting the child only when the child seems to need help.

> Once the child has made a step forward, she (the mother) will not let him slide back. She assures that he go on with the next construction to develop a next platform for his next launch. (p. 254)

Halliday (1982) uses a similar notion about language learning in children which he calls tracking. From his extensive study of language development, Halliday concludes that the adults and older siblings who live with the child "share in the language-creating process along with the child" (p. 10). He suggests that teachers take on a similar role when the child comes to school, helping children find new ways to say or write things as children find new reasons to express themselves or to understand.

Vygotsky (1962) who adds additional perspectives on the significance of child/adult interaction, believes that educators can make use of cooperation between adult and student and "lead the child to what he could not yet do" (p. 104) by himself.

Vygotsky defines the "discrepancy between a child's actual mental age and the level he reaches in solving problems with assistance" (p. 103) as the child's zone of proximal development.

> With assistance every child can do more than he can by himself.... What the child can do in cooperation today, he can do alone tomorrow. Therefore, the only good kind of instruction is that which marches ahead of development and leads it, it must be aimed not so much at the ripe as at the ripening functions. (p. 103-104)

Although there may be some theoretical differences among these scholars, there is little disagreement about the significance of the role of the teacher or other adults involved in children's growth. Teachers who continually observe children using knowledge about language and cognition can ask the appropriate question, or pose a specific problem, or place an object in front of children so that learning is extended. As they observe, they also gain information for planning new experiences or instructional activities, leading the child toward new explorations. Observation, evaluation, and curriculum planning go hand-in-hand.

Teachers can develop a variety of ways to keep records of these developments for reporting to parents, to remind themselves of children's growth over the year, to involve students in self-evaluation, and to leave records for continued school use. However, the records of kidwatchers are not simply statistics used to compare children nor to have them compete with one another. Whether they are anecdotal records of children's interactions; selected writing samples of students' letters, logs, and stories; or tapes of children's reading or oral reporting, their purpose is to provide profiles of the children's language growth in different settings, with different materials, and through different experiences.

Where to Start? What to Do?

My own observations of outstanding kidwatching teachers are reflected in the following suggestions:

1. *When a child achieves success in some communicative setting (including reading and writing), the teacher may find a number of ways to extend this to a new and different setting.* For example, a child who is responding orally to a patterned language book such as "I Know An Old Woman Who Swallowed A Fly" can be encouraged to write a book either alone, with the teacher, or a peer entitled "Johnny Swallowed a Bumblebee." This would extend the holistically remembered oral reading of a book to writing a book to share with others using similar language structures but personalizing characters and experiences in writing. But don't expect the new use of communication to look as successful as the one previously achieved. When a child tries something new it is bound to seem less sophisticated at first than something the child does which is familiar.

2. *When children are involved in exploratory activities, the teacher might raise questions such as "I wonder why this is so?" or "What do you think is happening here?"* The questions may help children reflect on their own thinking and see contradictions in their hypotheses.

3. *When children are observed to be troubled with an experience, the teacher can move in and talk about the situation with them and lead them to what they cannot yet do by themselves* (Vygotsky, 1962). It is at a moment of frustration that a kidwatching teacher can help children resolve conflictive situations a la Piaget (1977) and move on to expand their language and conceptualization.

4. *Teachers need to trust in children's learning and in their own ability to learn along with their children.* Language learning involves risk taking. When teachers believe in their own professional judgment and respect the children's ability, success occurs as part of the curricular experiences. With such a sense of security teachers can become kidwatchers and with the children build a community which contains many launching pads from which the children and the teacher can reach the next level of language learning together.

References

Bruner, J.S. "The Role of Dialogue in Language Learning," in A. Sinclair, R.J. Jarvella, & W.J.M. Levelt (Eds.), *The Child's Conception of Language*. Berlin: Springer-Verlag, 1978.

Halliday, M.A.K. "Three Aspects of Children's Language Development: Learning Language, Learning through Language, and Learning about Language," in Y. Goodman, M. Haussler, & D. Strickland (Eds.), *Oral and Written Language Development Research: Impact on the Schools*. Urbana, Illinois: National Council of Teachers of English, 1982.

Piaget, J. *The Development of Thought: Equilibration of Cognitive Structures*. Translated by A. Rosin. New York: Viking Press, 1977.

Vygotsky, L.S. *Thought and Language*. Translated by E. Hanfmann and G. Vakar. Cambridge, Massachusetts: M.I.T. Press, 1962.

Language and Language Learning for Child Watchers

Martha L. King
The Ohio State University

Those who embark on child watching follow a long line of brilliant predecessors who have enhanced our knowledge of children by careful observation of what they did and said. In writing the foreword to Chukovsky's *From Two to Five* (1971), Frances Clarke Sayers stated that there is a world of fellowship of those who:

> having an intuitive kinship with children, fortify and extend it by observation, by scientific and psychological studies, and so increase our sense of wonder and delight in children and cast across the divergent theories of education a long shadow of universal wisdom. (p. vii)

The fellowship that Sayers mentions includes not only the poets and writers (such as Chukovsky, Paul Hazard, and Walter de la Mare whom she lists) but also, psychologists, physicians, and educators (such as Piaget, Vygotsky, Montessori, Susan Isaacs). What each observer saw and reported was influenced by his or her special interests and expertise; but they all approached their work with tremendous sensitivity to, and great appreciation for, what children could do.

As readers of this book join this long standing fellowship of child watchers, sensitivity to children and appreciation for their abilities are assumed. The purpose of this chapter, therefore, is to bring together some information that will sharpen perceptions and help "watchers" to see. Generally, those who observe children need two kinds of information—that which provides the tools needed to make precisely focused observations and that which informs the vision and provides the background information leading to insightful observations. This latter sort of knowledge, the domain of this paper, not only focuses the observations, but also frames the interpretations.

Language and Language Learning

Certainly a great number of our problems in education can be traced to failure of some sort in language, at some place in the educational process. Sometimes it is the failure of teachers to understand and/or accept children's language (and culture); sometimes it is failure in communication in the classroom; sometimes children fail to make the transition from spoken language to literacy; and frequently children fail in subject matter areas, i.e., in science or mathematics, because they are unable to disembed the meaning of the subject from the language in which the content is framed. Language plays a complex and crucial role in schooling because it pervades the entire process. It is much more than the medium for conveying the message; it helps to form the message.

Fortunately, the research in language of the past two or three decades has provided an abundance of information about children's language learning that has implications for education. A great deal of this information, particularly that which concerned the way children learn various language structures, already has been made easily available to teachers (Genishi, 1979; Moskowitz, 1978). This chapter will focus on areas that seem to be especially vital in understanding the role of language in school; namely, how language functions for the child and how language is learned through social interaction.

Language serves children essentially for two global purposes—to *communicate* with others and to *learn*. These categories of major function emerge during the second year of life when children discover that they can use language to interact with people and their environment, and at the same time talk about the experience (Halliday, 1975). These two superordinate functions stem from combinations of specific language functions that children have developed during their first year and emerge when children discover that language can serve them to talk about things that aren't in the immediate context.

Language Learning Is an Interactive Process

Children are born into a social world of activity in which talk is a vital part of experiences; they become part of the activity, explore with their eyes, turn their heads, and begin to make distinctions about the important things and people around them. They participate in the daily routines associated with family attention and care—all accompanied by talk—and gradually begin to build a system of meanings shared between themselves and their parents. The mother or principle caretaker feeds and bathes the baby; caresses and plays with him or her;

and in the process talks, sings, or recites nursery rhymes. Routines are built up with movements, changing facial expressions, and vocalizations. The patterns of the activity are soon learned and the baby begins to anticipate the sequence of events. Once the routines are learned, the baby begins to initiate the action and seeks the participation of the adult. The process is one of parent-child interaction and its success rests on the shared interests (i.e., a finger or toy to grasp) between the participants. The relationship is unequal, but each is sensitive to the other. The infant shows an awareness of the intentions of the parent who in turn follows the baby's path of interest and responds with the appropriate actions and words. Language develops in these social interactions involving people, objects, and routines that are a part of the infant's world. What children learn in these encounters is more than words and principles for making grammatical constructions: they learn a system for *making and sharing meaning*. The purpose of these conversation-like exchanges is to communicate, to exchange meaning, rather than to deliberately teach or learn language. There is evidence that children make less progress in learning when parents try to teach them to talk by selectively reinforcing correct usage and rejecting incorrect forms, or when parents pursue a topic of conversation of their own choice beyond the interest of the child (Nelson, 1973; Wells, 1981). Successful parents listen to *what* the children say and respond to them. They interpret the child's language attempts and reply with related action accompanied by words and sentences. Learning is greater where children are supported by caring adults who share their world with them and enter into the children's worlds of play and talk, tuning in to their feelings and experiences. The essential element is the intimacy between child and adult who share a common environment which fosters the understanding of meanings intended.

Learning to Use Language

Language experiences within the family may vary, but the learning process—the meaning sharing and interaction—remains the same across children. They learn very early to use their linguistic system in different situations to fulfill their own purposes.

During the first year, even before they have learned words, infants use a repertoire of sounds to convey their needs and relate to others. They begin to learn their mother tongue by mastering certain basic language functions and developing a range of meanings within each. First, they use particular sounds to 1) get what they want, an *instrumental* function; 2) regulate behavior of themselves and others, a *regulatory* function; 3) relate to others, an *interactional* function; and 4) reveal self, a *personal* function. The infants *intend* to convey meaning and they use the language resources they have to do so. Words and grammatical structures develop within the context of these meanings (Halliday, 1975).

Toward the end of the first year and well into the second, children use words to make language serve them in new ways: 1) to find out what things are, a *heuristic* function; 2) to pretend, an *imaginative* function; and 3) to tell someone something, an *informative* function. This last function develops during the second year and signals a big language leap for children. They discover that they can use language to tell someone something, to *refer* to experience of another time or place. This is a difficult function for the child to master because it requires a fair amount of word knowledge.

With rapid growth in vocabulary during the second year, there is a consolidation of the early functions into the two major functions mentioned above. Children now use language to relate to others, a pragmatic function, and to learn, a mathetic function. Uses of language within these two categories continue to expand as talk becomes a major channel of communication between children and adults. The adult extends the child's meanings and language as together they pursue common interests. This important adult support is illustrated in the following example[1] of Mark (2:3) and his father who are sharing a picture story book. Mark stops to look at a picture:

M: That? in the plane now.
F: That's them all flying in the plane now. Yes. Because the little baby is pretending he's flying in his plane.
M: —gone. Gone up.
F: Yes. It's gone up. What will happen when it comes down?
M: Land.
F: It'll have to land, yes.
M: Landed now.
F: Yes. It's landed now. Who is standing next to it?
M: Boy.
F: Yes, that's the little boy, Louis. It's landed where he used to live.
M: (pointing)—aeroplane. Mark been on that. (repeats) Mark been on that.
F: Yes. Mark's been on one of those.
M: (pointing to the picture and laughing) Mark been on moon.

F: You haven't been on the moon. (said jokingly)
M: (pointing) Gone up.
F: Yes. You can see the people waving goodbye.
M: Going home.
F: Yes. He's going home now.

The success of this dialogue between Mark and his father arises from the way they respond to each other, collaborate and negotiate meanings to be shared. They make and maintain a common frame of reference around the picture book. Mark chooses to talk about the airplane and his father, as the more skilled participant, responds to his meanings in such a way that Mark, as he takes his turn, can either continue the conversation or initiate another direction. Note that Mark does change direction when he moves away from talking about the boy in the picture to talking about his own experience of flying. His father follows his lead, laughing with him about "Mark been on moon." Such collaboration and negotiation of meaning in conversation is an extremely important aspect of all that children have to learn as they progress toward the adult system of language.

The ability to construct an oral *text* with another person is an essential part of the adult linguistic system which entails the ability to attend to words out of immediate context, to use appropriate grammatical forms, and to participate in dialogue. The adult system incorporates in more abstract form the two categories of function, i.e., communication and learning, of the earlier grammar and also includes a third, a *textual* function. The communicative or *interpersonal* function incorporates all of those uses of language for doing and relating to others. This global function is interperson oriented and represents those functions in which a speaker uses particular communication rules to express personal values and attitudes, to seek to influence actions and attitudes of others, and in various ways reveals self (Halliday, 1975). The learning or *ideational* function of the adult grammar, on the other hand, incorporates language uses for thinking, organizing, and expressing experience—experience of both the real world and of the inner world of one's own consciousness (Halliday, 1975). The textual function, demonstrated so well in the example above, refers to the language resources one has for creating oral or written texts to represent meanings intended by the speaker or writer. It represents the ability to use words, sentences, and other language options to construct texts which are coherent within themselves and within the context of the situation.

The text created by Mark and his father clearly shows the functions of language operating in an integrated way. Each participant attends to the ideas expressed by the other and together they create an oral text. Such extended dialogues between parent and child were found by Evans (1977) to be related to children's later success in reading in school. Evans concluded that it was the quality of the adults' contribution to the conversation—the kind of feedback they gave and the length of the sequence of talk that seemed to make a difference. She expressed the opinion that such sustained dialogue helps children to develop comprehension skills which are needed in reading. Certainly, maintaining a substantial piece of dialogue requires the child to develop skills in predicting the direction the conversation will take, skills which are an important part of comprehension.

Extending Uses of Language

Children meet new demands for language use when they move into neighborhood play groups and attend day care centers or nursery schools. They need to make themselves known to friends and teachers outside the family. They need to compete and maintain status among people who don't know them very well. These situations require children to use language to tell about themselves, their families, and past experiences without support of an adult or the environment in which the experience occurred. Some children are much better able to do this than others.

Joan Tough (1977), who has studied children's language at home and after entry into school, claims that most children can use language for such purposes as 1) maintaining their status in a group, 2) directing their own actions and the actions of others, and 3) talking about things in the present. They differ, she claims, in the ability to 1) recall their own relevant past experiences; 2) to make associations, to analyze events, to anticipate and predict; 3) to collaborate and to sequence possible events; and 4) to move away from the immediate concrete play situations and project into the perspectives and experiences of others.

This latter range of language uses is the kind children need for success in school because a great deal of the learning activity is carried on through language. Children are expected to link into the experiences of other children, the teacher, and the instructional materials. Further, their success in reading is extensively dependent on their ability to sequence events and predict what is to come next.

While it is important for teachers to accept and appreciate the language children have when they enter school, it is their responsibility to provide conditions whereby children can increase their range of competence. Dialogue with a more skillful language user plays an important role in this process. Such encounters give children the opportunity to express their inner thoughts and to have them tested against or supported by another person. To carry on a conversation with a partner requires that each person must project into the meanings of the other and reflect on the meanings each is offering.

Talk facilitates learning in a number of ways as it is used to find out "what things are" and "what things mean." It helps children to refine and reorganize concepts as they sometimes try to express in words certain concepts or explanations which they think they know very well. This process is illustrated very well in the example[2] of a discussion of a group of nine- and ten-year-olds given below. It shows how very difficult it can be for some children to express their understanding of very ordinary things. The teacher had finished reading a selection from a book, *Train to Yesterday* (Jennings, 1974), when the discussion occurred. The children (for some, English was a second language) tried to show how they would explain to a boy who lived in the 19th century some of the inventions they enjoy in the present century. They attempt to describe television first and Paul says (It's)...

Paul: Like magic...Like it...a thing...when you turn it on you have a picture, and people speak on it.

Ch: Yeah.

Paul: As if you were magic.

D: Miss, do you think it might be real people inside the telly?

...

Paul: You might. Then you'd have to go inside the telly.

D: Miss. My Mum...um. There was an advert on the telly. And it was horse racing or something, when someone went to go and fix the telly there was people coming out the back. And my mum told me to go down and look at the back of the telly to see if someone was coming out.

Teacher: Tony what were you going to say?
(Tony tries to describe a car.)

Tony: I could...in a car. It's with four wheels and its on...on a...ermm...like a shape, a shape.... And there's a door. And inside the door there's umm three chairs....

Paul: Four.

Tony: Three.

Paul: Four. And a long one in the back. Four. There's one big one at the back and two out front. And at the front there's a steel wheel. Um a round wheel. And you drive it. And you have to have a key....

Teacher: How does it go?

Tony: By engine.

Paul: By engine. You (meaning "he") might not know what an engine is.

Ch: Miss, Miss, he would know what an engine was because of the steam engine....

The talk continued with the children explaining that a boy from the previous century would know about engines, but not about gasoline engines. They also discussed the fact that he would know about wheels, but not about rubber tires. One child thought that they could convey their ideas more clearly by drawing pictures, suggesting that they thought they knew more about televisions, cars, and airplanes than they could put into words. Clearly some children had better control of the language needed to express concepts than others, but together they were able to construct descriptions of the inventions. The talk gave them the opportunity to translate the global and perhaps vague concepts and images they had of these common inventions into surface level linear syntax, and thereby to make a text.

Language and Learning

Young children use speech-to-self first to gain mastery over their physical surroundings and then to control their own behavior. Vygotsky (1978) described situations in which young children, three to four years of age, use talk-to-self to solve practical problems and to extend the range of possibilities for action in reaching desired goals. Having learned language in conversation with others, they then use talk-to-self to guide their actions, just as they had previously experienced being guided by the talk of others. In Vygotsky's view, children's use of self speech in play helps them to sequence actions, to become more flexible in ways of solving problems, and to be more effective both in controlling their own behavior and in manipulating the objects of play. With young children, the speech accompanies the action, but as they grow older speech takes on a planning function and children decide in advance what they will do next. Subvocalized speech is often heard when they are planning what they will draw or write, as well as when they are actually engaged in producing a text or a picture.

Vygotsky maintained further that speech-to-self turns inward and becomes internalized silent speech, which, he hypothesized, is a highly abbreviated idiosyncratic form of language that serves thinking with no communicative function. It is the language one uses to reflect on experience, to reorganize and shape it to fit into what one already knows and wants. Once experience has been represented to self in some symbolic form—through talk, play, dance, drama, painting—language is the means by which one goes over it, to reexperience what has happened. Or, as Rosen & Rosen (1973) explain it,

> Life is more than a vast anthology of unedited narratives. We impose narrative on it; we pluck the tale out of the whirl of experience, and with words marshall it into narrative line and make it something whole and ordered. (p. 57)

Events in life are framed in verbalizations which people create about "the way things are." It is through such re-creations of experience that one builds up a system of knowing that brings order into the environment of both the physical world and the inner world of one's thoughts. Meaning and language are entwined as children struggle "to know," as is illustrated in the discussion about the television and car. Individuals build up a personal construct system or a "representation of the world in the head," by which they live their lives—i.e., predict future actions, create expectations for actions and events, and modify behavior on the basis of what occurs. In the ongoing process language plays a vital role: it allows the individual to reflect and generalize about experience and to recode it in different forms so that it can be assimilated into one's existing knowledge (Kelly, 1955; Britton, 1970).

Language Is Deeply Personal

It is easy to see why language is so deeply personal and why direct attacks on their speech ("for improvement") can be perplexing and often devastating to children. Developing as it does in the caring supportive environment of the home, language is "part and parcel" of all one knows and *is*. A frontal attack on one's speech touches the innermost self.

The transition from home to school is difficult for many children, but especially troublesome for those whose home experiences are least like those offered and valued by the school. Too often children are expected to fit into the ongoing curriculum of the school with very little attention given to, or appreciation of, what they already know and can do.

Children Are Competent, Creative Language Learners

Normal children have demonstrated before school that they can learn and use language creatively. Chomsky recognized this language competence when he described children's ability to generate sentences never heard before as a "creative act." Earlier in the 20th century, Chukovsky came to the same conclusion after observing children's language in natural situations. He noted some of the amusing remarks ("Can't you see? I'm barefoot all over." and "Put your glasses on or you will catch cold.") and concluded that children were "creative geniuses."

Such linguistic powers continue to intrigue and sometimes dismay researchers and teachers as children show in many different ways how clever they are. For example, they learn many of the important features of their language system without being directly taught. There is substantial evidence in both oral and written modes that children invent their own unique system of rules to guide their language use before they learn the adult system. As illustrated earlier, infants develop a grammar of sounds and language functions during the first year; then in the second year, when they have more words, they shift to a grammar of two major functions before moving to the adult system which is composed of three integrated functions. The point is that children use what they have and know and make language work for them! In their early attempts to write, for example, preschool children invent a system of spelling that follows logical and predictable rules before they learn the conventional forms. They omit particular letters, especially vowels (e.g., ws, wash; frns, friends; mostr, monster), rely on letter names where useful (e.g., DA, day; KT, Katie) and use a number of other techniques (as one letter representing a word, RU DF: Are you deaf?) or substitute a tense vowel for a lax one (FES, fish) [Read, 1971; Henderson & Beers, 1980; Bissex, 1980]. To an informed teacher, these spellings are not errors, but evidence of the kinds of assumptions children are making about how the sounds they hear can be translated into visual symbols.

As they seek to understand and to use the writing system, children again operate on the assumptions they make from their observations of the writing and writers around them. They assume that visual signs say something; they differentiate between visual marks that are pictures and those that represent messages; and they believe that a longer message can be written by repeating and reorganizing the letters and signs they already know. Once they can distinguish letters from signs and numbers, children begin to reveal their assumptions about how to segment their strings of signs and symbols into words, including their thoughts about the number of letters required in a word (Clay, 1975; Ferreiro, 1982; Ferreiro & Teberosky, 1982).

Development is highly individual, influenced by environmental factors in both the home and the school, and often extremely uneven within a particular child. The avenue to writing for one child may be by the way of copying letters and words found in the home or classroom; for another, it may be through using known letters to construct a message or a story, if the situation requires it. When one class of children early in grade one were asked to write a story, one child produced the example shown in Figure 1. Letters are used to represent words and syllables and lines to segment parts of the text.

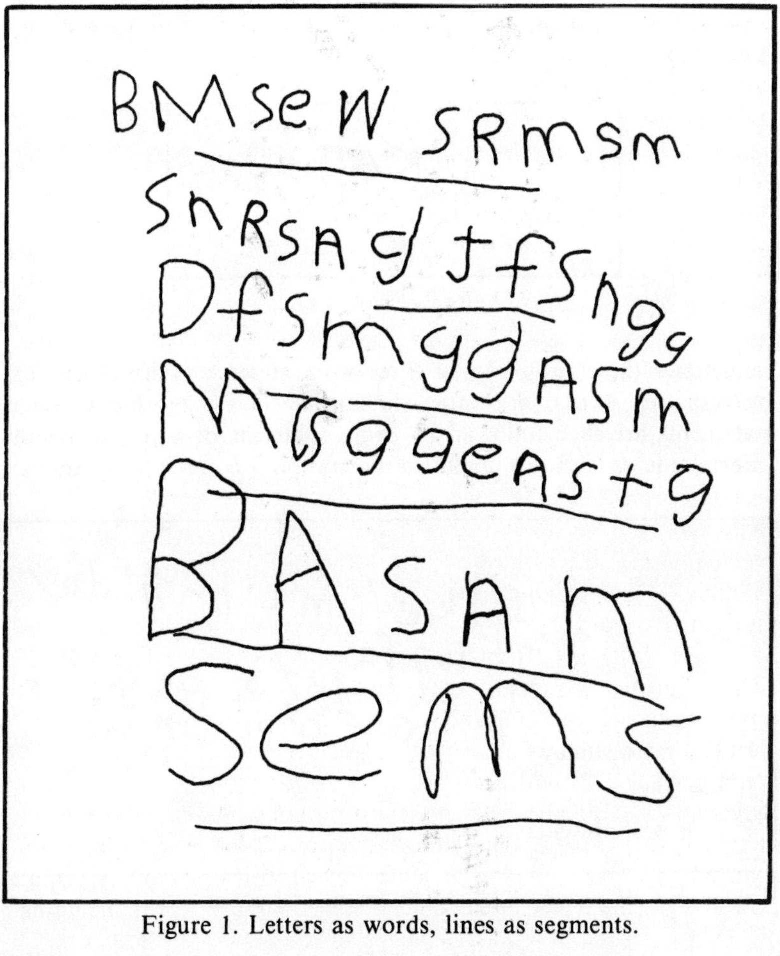

Figure 1. Letters as words, lines as segments.

When asked to read the text, the child produced the following story:

> One day there was a little turtle. It was getting in the water and it was going down the street. Then the little girl came and picked it up and the mother said to her it was time for bed. That's the end!

When children have the opportunity to write freely and for purposes that are meaningful to them, they go about the process in a systematic way and use whatever they know to convey meaning. Adelia, for example, wrote four separate letters above a picture of a little girl (g b m d) and read, *girl, boy, mom*, and *dad*, indicating that it was a message about her family. Several days letter she created a message of three words to accompany a picture of a kite with a very long string (Figure 2).

Figure 2. I saw a kite.

Sometimes these early two or three word statements are labels for pictures (*My house*) or simple statements: *This is my horse*. Such statements are then followed by some comment or a second bit of information as is shown in a third illustration (Figure 3) from Adelia:

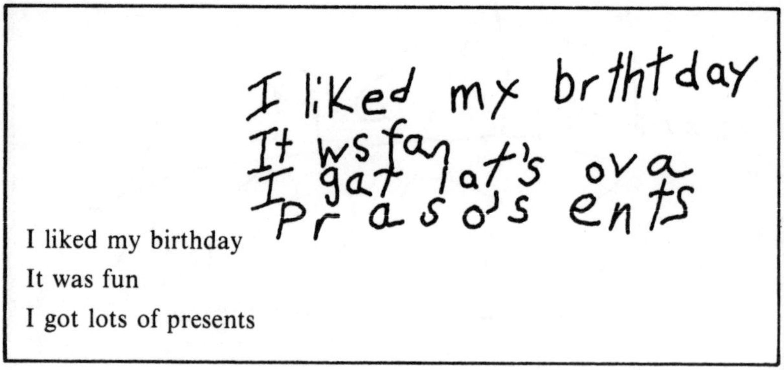

Figure 3. Adelia's statement and comments.

Children show considerable ingenuity in these early efforts to understand and use the alphabetic nature of the language around them. Despite some limitations, their efforts clearly show that children perceive visual language in a wholistic way and as meaningful and related to another *whole*—an object or whatever in the real world.

Writing for Varied Purposes

From this point on children's texts continue to develop and to fulfill a wider range of purposes. Their writing, like their talk, is expressive, closely tied to the context of their personal experiences and most meaningful to those who share their context. It develops more rapidly of course when children have reasons for writing and someone to respond to what they have to say. The above texts and the following one (Figure 4) written by Adelia in the spring of her kindergarten year are all expressive. They "signal self," share recent happenings, and express personal feeling. Her intentions are clear and strong, overcoming any reticence she might have about spelling or other writing conventions. Obviously, Adelia has purposes clearly in mind and uses what she knows about the writing and spelling system to construct her texts. She has discovered the apostrophe some place and overgeneralizes its use in several places. She uses the exclamation mark appropriately, but has tremendous difficulty when she tries to sound out Soeu in Figure 2 and Pras o's ents in Figure 3. While she considers wsfn (was fun) one word, her sounding out to spell *presents* causes her to represent it in two parts.

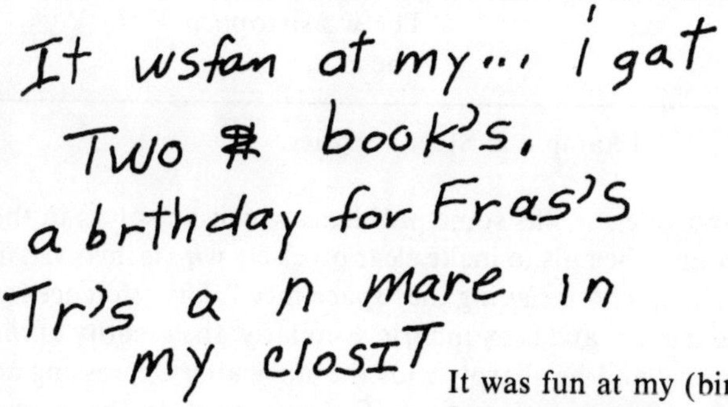

It was fun at my (birthday)
I got two books.
A Birthday for Frances
There's a Nightmare in My Closet

Figure 4. Adelia's expressive writing.

The next examples produced by Steve in March of first grade show how writing develops from expressive recounting of personal experience to attempting to recapture and shape vicarious experiences in story form. The first text (Example 1) with pictures was written in Steve's journal. It reads as though Steve were expecting a response to each segment, as occurs in interactive speech. (The punctuation is Steve's.)

> I had a throat infection. I had to stay in bed for five days. and it was boring. staying in bed. I got some comic books. I had a "zinger."

Example 1. Entry from Steve's journal.

The next two texts (Example 2), written about one week apart, show Steve's first attempts to write a *story*. He gives both stories a title and clearly shows in the way he begins each one that he intends to construct a story.

Space Flight	The War
A long time ago they had a space race the astronaut complained that they shouldn't have a race. The end.	A long time ago There was an entrance that nobody knew about during the war. But one person knew about it The wars stopped The end.

Example 2. Steve's stories.

In the first tale, he has some problems which he solves in the second. For example, he fails to make clear precisely *who* is involved in the story action, i.e., who is having the "space race." The reference for *they* lies outside the text and is exophoric. Similarly, the identity of *the* astronaut is unclear and he sharply ends the story after expressing an initial action (complaint) by the unidentified astronaut. In the second story, which ends abruptly too, he makes the meanings clear within the text itself, a signal that Steve is learning an important feature of written texts. This story is slightly more elaborate, too, with an element of complication added to the plot—"one person knew about it/the war stopped"—implying a resolution to the problem and the restoration of equilibrium. In these three pieces of writing Steve demonstrated that he was learning to control the written mode, *and* to make his texts explicit within themselves and to attend to some of the conventions and obligatory elements of story.

While expressive writing continues throughout life—in diaries or in letters to close friends—children extend their writing competence to write for a variety of purposes that increasingly are less context bound. Generally, their writing develops in two directions: 1) toward communicative or *transactional* functions where writing is objective and concerned with reality, and 2) in the opposite direction, where writing is more subjective and less concerned with directly influencing ongoing events. The writer's goal in this instance, rather, is to recapture, to savor and reformulate events, and to shape them into a verbal construct. In this *poetic* domain (Britton, 1971), writing functions through all of its artistic forms of story, poetry, and so on. The next examples show how children's writing can develop from expressive toward both transactional and poetic purposes when conditions are facilitating. The following texts by Vevene (8 years) were produced in a classroom in which much of the writing was embedded in the ongoing learning experiences of the classroom in which writing is used to learn. Vevene's class, while on a walk near their school, collected some clumps of nettles bearing eggs which they later placed in a classroom vivarium to hatch. Naturally, the children observed and discussed the action as it occurred in the vivarium. Vevene wrote two brief records (Example 5) of her observations which shows her growth in writing and in knowledge of caterpillars as well as some imagining and analogizing about them.

My Catepillar

My caterpillar has got big and long. He doesn't like the sun so he puts the leaves together and goes to sleep and curls himself up.

A Caterpillar

I have got two caterpillars. One is brown, I drew the brown one. The brown one is a looper, it has two sucker feet at the back and three at the front of the caterpillar. He pretends that he is a twig and his face looks like a human being's face. He has not got any feet in the middle of it. It is getting very big. It is very hairy and he looks very lumpy.

Example 5. Vevene's records of her caterpillar observations.

The first record is brief but includes both Vevene's observation and inferences; on the other hand, the second gives much more information including some (The brown one is a looper) that came from the teacher or a book. The purpose of these texts is to be objective, to record reality, and to communicate it. The next example (Figure 6) came later after considerable observation of the caterpillar and hearing a story about a caterpillar. Note the authentic information in the story as well as Vevene's tacit knowledge of traditional stories:

> There was once a caterpillar. He was a very sad caterpillar, he wanted to have wings, he wanted to talk to a bird but he didn't because he didn't want to be eaten up. One day the caterpillar went in a pupa. He was in it for a long time, he stayed there till June and one morning when nobody was up and the sun was about to come up the pupa opened. A big tortoise shell butterfly came out and went away.

Example 6. Vevene's caterpillar story.

This is a different order of writing; the purpose is not to convey objective information or to affect reality; but rather to enjoy and reshape events, to create a particular artistic form.

The Learning Context Is Crucial

The total learning situation has a powerful influence on whatever talk or writing occurs in the classroom. When children spend hour after hour in isolated tasks working on ditto sheets or filling in blanks in workbooks, they have little opportunity to talk or write for real purposes or to use language as it is used in the real world. The dialogue between Mark and his father illustrates how the situation impacts on the kind of talk that is produced. The "text" they created together was influenced not only by the book and the illustrations, which provided a starting point for the talk, but also by the relationship between the father and son and the father's sensitivity to his son's interests. The shared physical context facilitated the construction of a collaborative "text" or sustained conversation between the two, as occurred also among the older group of children in the classroom discussion following the book, *Train to Yesterday* (1974).

In a recent article, Hasan (1980) makes the point that it is the relevant factors in the environment that influence the language used. In the two oral examples above, a book and the relationships between the adult and the children were certainly relevant factors, but the physical situation where the talk occurred was not so important. But in the case of Vevene's records of the caterpillar, the physical environment played a vital role. Her teacher organized the entire learning environment of the classroom—the time, space, materials, and working procedures—to facilitate a learning process which involved using firsthand experience. The room was rich in concrete learning resources with numerous collections and displays to challenge children's interests and curiosity. Specimens of insects and plants were regularly brought into the classroom for children to observe closely and repeatedly, to discuss or write about as the teacher and pupils deemed necessary. There were both fiction and nonfiction books easily available in the classroom. These not only brought children information and enjoyment, but also provided them with varied models of written language.

A serious problem in extending language and literacy in schools arises from the fact that so much of the content of learning has been decontextualized. That is, reading, writing, and various other skill and content areas have been removed from the real world of experience, and practice exercises put in their places. Children find that they are expected to deal with abstractions of knowledge before they have had an opportunity to understand the real thing. Ironically, those children who have the greatest need for special help in reading in the first years of schooling are given reading experiences that are least like those in the real world. They often are drilled in letter names and sounds—abstractions of written language—that are extremely remote from stories and books, the kinds of experiences their more successful peers had received in the home.

Sometimes even the very ordinary, everyday events of life go unnoticed in the child's environment until someone or something calls attention to them. Life in the immediate environment of the school or the neighborhoods where the children live, traffic rolling along the highways, or children waiting for parents to come home from work are all subject matter for thinking, talking, and writing in school. Example 7, a poem by two girls (10 years), came from a classroom where the teacher tried to make the children sensitive to, and appreciative of, their environments and the lives they were living at the moment. She also tried to share with them her love of poetry. She read quantities of poetry to them and encouraged the children to talk about their own images and to share their observations and feelings about events around them.

The school was located on a slight knoll rising above a housing project consisting of townhouses and blocks of apartments, all low rent or subsidized housing. Opposite the school on the far side of the project and near the highway was a manufacturing plant called the KLG where some of the children's parents worked. It was customary for many of the children to go down and wait near the gate for their parents and walk home with them. Day after day they would watch the weary workers pouring out of the factory to catch the 85 bus or to walk to their homes nearby. One day Sara and Jo jotted down in a notebook their observations and impressions as they watched and waited. The next day they formed their notes into the following poem:

The KLG

Me and Jo went outside the KLG
We wait for the great race to begin
The big hand goes on six
Now it's half-past four
And the bell goes
And me and Jo says
On your marks
Get set, Go!
And they bumpied out of the building
They all looked tired
But some of them run to get the 85 which is across the road
And they're off
The man in the red hat is in the lead
He does look awfully tired but he's still running
But the man with the blue jacket on is coming up
Then just behind him is a lady with a fur coat on
She reminds me of the bionic woman
Then they get to the finish line
The man with the red hat on came first
The lady with the blue jacket on came second
And the lady in the fur coat come third
The runners-up were everybody
Except for Jo's mom and her friend who were last
They came floating along chatting away

Example 7. Poem by Sara and Jo.

The girls were able in this instance to stand back from their experience, to look on it as a spectator and describe it in terms of something else they knew—a model of discourse they had in their minds. They were writing to savor experience for subjective purposes, in the poetic direction. When asked about their poetry, the girls referred to poetry books and some of their favorite poems. Sara explained further that she had been influenced by watching horse racing on television and tried to make her poem sound like the "man who describes the race."

In Conclusion

As the examples have shown, children are competent, creative language learners and users who arrive at school knowing how to learn. They have learned their language as it has served them in relating to others, in attaining knowledge, and in achieving other goals. Their oral language competence forms the basis for their future growth in literacy which they approach with the same inventive skills they have used in learning to talk. In learning, children rely on interaction with others who share their interests in new experiences. The quality of these experiences, including the relationships with others, determines the knowledge they will gain and the language they will use. It is the obligation of the school to extend the opportunities for children to use language for an ever increasing range of purposes—especially to use it to *learn.*

Notes

1. From M. McKenzie & M. King. *Literacy in School* (in progress).
2. From M.G. McKenzie. *Extending Literacy,* video recordings of literacy programs for Inner London Schools. Inner London Education Authority, 275 Kennington Lane, London, SE 11, 1981.

References

Bissex, G. "Patterns of Development in Writing: A Case Study," *Theory into Practice, 19* (Summer 1980), 197-201.

Britton, J. *Language and Learning.* London: Allen Lane, Penguin Press, 1970.

Britton, J. "What's the Use? A Schematic Account of Language Functions," *Educational Review, 23* (June 1971), 205-219.

Chukovsky, K. *From Two to Five.* Translated by M. Norton. Berkeley, California: University of California Press, 1971.

Clay, M.M. *What Did I Write.* Exeter, New Hampshire: Heinemann Educational Books, 1975.

Evans, J. "The Significance of Adult Feedback on Child Language Development," dissertation, University of Bristol, 1977.

Ferreiro, E. "The Relationship between Oral and Written Language: The Children's Viewpoints," in Y. Goodman, M. Haussler, & D. Strickland (Eds.), *Oral and Written Language Development Research: Impact on the Schools.* Urbana, Illinois: National Council of Teachers of English, 1982.

Ferreiro, E., & Teberosky, A. *Literacy before Schooling.* Exeter, New Hampshire: Heinemann Educational Books, 1982.

Genishi, C. "Young Children Communicating in the Classroom: Selected Research," *Theory into Practice, 18* (October 1979), 244-250.

Halliday, M. *Learning How to Mean: Explorations in the Functions of Language.* London: Edward Arnold, 1975.

Hasan, R. "What's Going On: A Dynamic View of Context in Language," in J.E. Copeland (Ed.), *The Seventh LACUS Forum 1980.* Columbia, South Carolina: Hernbeam Press, 1981.

Henderson, E., & Beers, J. *Developmental and Cognitive Aspects of Spelling.* Newark, Delaware: International Reading Association, 1980.

Jennings, Paul. *Train to Yesterday*. London: Harrap, 1974.

Kelly, G. *A Theory of Personality: The Psychology of Personal Constructs*. New York: W.W. Norton, 1955.

Moskowitz, B.A. "The Acquisition of Language," *Scientific American, 239* (November 1978), 92-108.

Nelson, K. "Structure and Strategy in Learning to Talk," *Monographs of the Society for Research in Child Development, 38* (1973), 1-2.

Read, C. "Preschool Children's Knowledge of English Phonology," *Harvard Educational Review, 41* (February 1971), 1-34.

Rosen, C., & Rosen, H. *The Language of Primary School Children*. Baltimore: Penguin Press, 1973.

Tough, J. *The Development of Meaning: A Study of Children's Use of Language*. London: Allen & Unwin, 1977.

Vygotsky, L.S. *Mind in Society: The Development of Higher Psychological Processes*. Edited by M. Cole, et al. Cambridge, Massachusetts: Harvard University Press, 1978.

Wells, G. *Learning through Interaction: The Study of Language Development*. New York: Cambridge University Press, 1981.

Part Two
Children Learning Language and Learning about Language

Introduction

Part Two focuses on what children learn as they master the intricacies of the symbol system we call language. The authors examine how children, in exploring the world and interacting with others, discover what language is, how it works, and what it is for. Above all they provide insights into the child's intellectual power and unique resources for learning language.

In the section on observing oral language, Lindfors concentrates on helping teachers understand how children acquire their knowledge of the structural components of language—sounds, meaning, and syntax. Using many delightful examples, she describes the course of this development and shows us how children demonstrate their knowledge of language structure in their informal talk, their language play, their questioning, and their comprehension of others' talk. In the course of acquiring knowledge of the linguistic forms and rules, children also acquire knowledge of the functions of language. Pinnell argues that form follows function and explains why it is important for teachers to continually monitor what students do with language in the classroom. She describes a category system for recording the functions of language, and outlines ways the information can be used to design instructional strategies and activities which will encourage children to use language for a wide variety of purposes.

In the following section, we see that in a literate society such as ours, where they are surrounded by print, children can and do learn about written language in the same natural way as oral language. Two authors explore the learning that occurs before formal schooling.

Haussler uses observations from a case study of her three-year-old daughter to illustrate how preschool children develop concepts of print and devise strategies to "read" written language which, in context, is functional and meaningful to them. Then Doake examines in detail a feature of early literacy, called "reading-like behavior," which emerges in children who are read to regularly. He explains how this behavior develops, its role in reading development, and why it should be encouraged both at home and in school. In discussing the educational implications of their observations, both writers take issue with the school's concept of "readiness," stressing that early literacy instruction should build on children's previously acquired knowledge of written language.

Bissex and Watson extend this theme by focusing on how teachers can observe what children know about writing and reading. First, Bissex traces the patterns of early writing development. Then, through an analysis of two first graders' work, she demonstrates why we need to give children many opportunities to show us what they know about writing. Watson concludes the section by discussing what we can learn by watching and listening to students before, during, and after reading. She describes techniques that reveal children's concepts of reading, their strategies for processing written texts, and their views of themselves as readers.

ORAL LANGUAGE LEARNING

Understanding the Development of Language Structure

Judith Wells Lindfors
University of Texas at Austin

> "You should say what you mean," the March Hare went on.
>
> "I do," Alice hastily replied, "at least—at least I mean what I say—that's the same thing, you know."
>
> "Not the same thing a bit!" said the Hatter.
>
> (Carroll, n.d., pp. 75-76)

What Is Language Structure?

Little did Alice and her friends realize that they were discussing language structure. The Hatter is right: meaning and saying (overtly expressing) are not "the same thing." But Alice is also right in her realization that meaning and expressing are basic in language and they are intimately related.

It has been a central interest during this century to try to understand how children, universally, acquire without explicit instruction, the structure of their language—that complex and abstract system for relating meaning and expression.

The meaning component of language structure (called the *semantic component*) includes one's knowledge of the conceptual categories of that language and the words—lexicon—that express those concepts. Different languages conceptualize, categorize, and label experience differently. But virtually every child comes, in time, to know how his or her language community does it. This is quite remarkable when you consider the various types of meanings a language encodes. In English we find meanings that get expressed as "table," "virtue," "pretty," "walk," but also meanings like plural, comparative, past, and continuousness that find expression in forms like "tables," "prettier," "walked," "(be) walking."[1] In addition, our semantic knowledge includes elements that serve to change word class: the expression "-er" in "teacher" or "baker" conveys the change from verb to noun; the "-able/-ible" of "likeable" or "resistible" conveys the change from verb to adjective; the "-ly" of "quickly" or "softly" conveys the change from adjective to adverb; the "-ness" of "quickness" and "softness" conveys the change from adjective to noun and so on. But this is only the beginning.

Our language is full of compounds ("football," "flatfoot," "birthday," "boathouse") and idioms ("kick the bucket," "two left feet") all of which we understand as single meaning units. Our semantic system includes a meaning we express as "walk," but also those we express as "limp," "wade," "wander," "stroll," "tiptoe," "stagger," "swagger," "strut," "amble," "trudge." Part of our semantic knowledge involves the combining possibilities for semantic units: I can "wade in a stream" but not "through the woods"; I can "stroll leisurely," but not "rapidly." We do not combine "trudge" with "briskly" or "tiptoe" with "noisily" unless, of course, our purpose is to deliberately violate semantic combining rules so as to produce the special effect of metaphor. It is no wonder that this component of language continues to expand throughout our lifetime. The wonder is that children acquire this aspect of language—as they do all aspects—so effortlessly, out of their own experiencing of their world.

Not all of the meaning in language is elemental. Much of it is relational. The *syntactic component* of language structure includes our knowledge of the relationships among the items within sentences and how to express those relationships. It is not enough to know the individual meanings expressed by "girl," "boy," "hit," "big," "rock," "with." We also are able to associate relational meanings like actor (does), action, object, modifier, instrument, with their expressions and thus we can differentiate among sentences like the following:

> The girl hit the boy with a big rock.
> The girl with a big rock, hit the boy.
> The big girl hit the boy with a rock.
> The big boy hit the rock with the girl.
> The boy hit the big girl with a rock.

All of these contain the same individual meaning units yet have quite different total meanings because of the different relations among the units. Our semantic knowledge also includes our recognition that the "with" phrase in the sentences has two meanings. Does the "with" phrase indicate an instrument of destruction or simply "in the company of"?

Alice is aware that language is not only a matter of meaning but also a matter of "saying," of knowing how possible meanings and possible expressions relate. The basic universal way of expressing meanings in a language is through strings of verbal sounds, but not just any old sounds in any old combinations. Our knowledge of the sound system of our language (the *phonological component*) is, like our knowledge of the semantic and syntactic components, orderly and systematic. Some sounds and sound combinations occur in our language and others do not, and we recognize which are occurring and nonoccurring ones. We know how the various "tunes" of our sound system relate to meanings—the significance of expressive devices like alterations in stress (emphasis), pause, intonation (rise and fall patterns of the voice).

In summary, then, to know a language is, among other things, to have an abstract and complex knowledge system of the semantic (elemental meaning), syntactic (relational meaning), and phonological (sound system) components of our language and how these components relate to one another. Typically this knowledge is intuitive, unconscious. We are no more aware of it than we are aware of the air we breathe. Yet it is no less real. This knowledge provides the basis for our understanding the expression of others (relating their sounds to meanings) and for our own expression of meaning (relating our meanings to sounds). Our language behavior—understanding and producing—is not random but, rather, orderly and systematic in accordance with the meaning-expression relations we consciously know. Above all, this knowledge enables us to endlessly create novel sentences—sentences that we have not spoken or heard before. We endlessly (though without conscious awareness) communicate through novel sentences which, because they are organized in accordance with meaning-expression principles which our listeners share, are immediately comprehended by our listeners, though those sentences are as novel to them as they are to us. We might well wonder how children—virtually ALL children—acquire such complex and abstract systems without direct, explicit instruction (which most adults could not possibly provide because they themselves lack conscious awareness of their own complex knowledge).

What Is the Course of Development of Language Structure in Children?

Infants communicate intentions. They request to be picked up by raising their arms and later by saying "up" as they do so: they request to be fed by whimpering and later by saying "milk" or "juice"; they request the adult to wind up a toy by handing the toy to the adult, perhaps with an accompanying vocalization. But over time a child's intentions "become grammaticalized" (Halliday, 1977), that is, the child comes to mean and to express more in accordance with the adult system. The child's early system which guides comprehending and producing is modified over time until, eventually, it closely matches the adult's and thus the resulting understandings and productions come to match the adult's also. It is important to recognize that the difference between adult and child language is not that adults have a system of language structure and children do not but, rather, that adults and children both have systems of language structure that govern their language behavior; their systems are different and thus give rise to different ways of comprehending and expressing. Clearly, the adult's system is relatively stable while the child's undergoes continuous expansion, revision and change in the early years. It is possible to describe some of the major changes in terms of basic dimensions.

Nonverbal → verbal. The child moves from a more generalized to a more refined system of nonverbal expression during the first year. Then vocalizations, which become progressively more stabilized as word forms, gradually take over as the major means of expressing meaning (though nonverbal support continues to be important).

Shorter → longer utterances. There is a predictable move from single word utterances to progressively longer sequences. For example, children might early request juice by saying "juice." Later, they are likely to say "more juice" or "want juice," and still later "I want more juice."

Building blocks → "ivy". The child's earlier, shorter utterances are comprised of heavy content words (nouns, verbs)—"building blocks" which carry a lot of meaning. One important factor accounting for the increased length of children's utterances over time, is the child's gradual inclusion of "ivy" (Brown, 1973)—the bits and pieces of language that don't carry as much specific content as nouns and verbs, but make the utterance more fluent (prepositions, articles, auxiliaries).

Simple → complex (embedded/conjoined) structures. The child's earliest sentences express single propositions rather than combinations. There is a single verb/action at the core of each utterance (though it may be unexpressed as, for example, when a child says "Mommy ball" meaning "Mommy is throwing the ball"). But the child soon moves from single proposition sentences like "want juice" and "watch me" to proposition combinations like "I want you read this book" (I want something + You read this book) and "watch me draw circles (watch me + I draw circles). Children also show an earlier preference for joining two equal propositions (sentence + "and" + sentence) and later join propositions of unequal status using words like "before," "after," "because."

Initial negative element → inserted negative element.[2] In developing negative structures, the child moves from simple sentences with "no" or "not" at the beginning ("No do that," "No the baby crying"), to sentences including a negative word within ("I no want that," "I can't find that," "I don't see you"). Later still the child's negative sentences show "negation spread," suggesting the child's awareness that negative meanings must be expressed in sentences ("I don't see nothing," "You never have none").

Unreversed interrogative → reversed interrogative forms. After an initial period of asking simple "what" and "where" information questions without any auxiliaries ("What that?" "Where kitty go?" "Where book?"), children typically expand their set of question words ("why," "which," "who") and begin using auxiliaries in their questions, but they don't reverse the auxiliary and subject as the adult does. This results in questions like "Where *I can* put it?" "Which way *they should* go?" "How *he can* make one?" Interestingly, at the same time that children do not reverse subject and auxiliary in information questions, they do reverse these elements in yes/no questions ("*Will you* help me?" "*Did I* caught it?"). In time the child begins to reverse subject and auxiliary in information questions as well as in yes/no questions. Note that the child's sequence in information questions reflects increasing cognitive as well as syntactic complexity, with concrete "what" and "where" questions (identification and location) preceding more complex and abstract "why" and "how" questions (cause and explanation).

Regular patterns → exceptional cases. It is quite typical to hear children as old as nine or ten use forms like "brang" (for "brought") and "putted" (for "put"). Children acquire and use (*overuse* in many cases) the regular patterns of the language rather early and only gradually work out the specific, irregular, idiosyncratic cases.

More → less reliance on immediate situation. The young child's language is very much embedded in and dependent on the immediate concrete situation. In fact, it is often the situation itself that enables us to understand the child's verbalization at all. But over time the child's language becomes less dependent on the immediate context of its occurrence. The expression becomes more able to stand on its own and the child is able to talk about other locations, past experiences, people not present at the moment of speaking. Further down the road the child will be able to talk about hypothetical situations and impossible situations and eventually even about language itself.

How Do Children Demonstrate Their Knowledge of Language Structure?

The simplest answer to this question is "In many and various ways." However, some of the clearest demonstrations of children's knowledge of language structure are to be found in children's informal talk, in their language play, in their questioning, and in their comprehension of others' talk.

Informal talk. As we listen to children talk informally with one another (on the playground, at lunch, at centers) or with us, we hear which semantic domains are more elaborated for each child. I think immediately of the kindergartners I know whose vocabularies about dinosaurs, superheroes, and monsters far exceed my own. There was a time when educators said of children whose vocabularies were well elaborated in domains other than the school's preferred ones: "That child's vocabulary is limited in some areas and expanded in others because the life experiences that give birth to it are uneven." Every time I consult my auto mechanic about my ailing car or listen to the sportscaster on the evening news talk about "bogies" and "birdies" and other such mysteries, I am reminded just how limited my experience and —necessarily—my vocabulary are in these areas. And so it is with children. Their semantic domains are differentially developed and their informal talk tells us in which semantic areas each child's language is well developed and in which areas we would hope to extend the child's experience and the language that lives in it.

Our children's informal talk often tells us about their *meanings* for particular words. Consider these examples.

1. While caring for her three year old grandson, a grandmother found crayon marks on the wall:

Grandmother: Oh, Chris. Look at this! How did this get here?

Chris: I did it, Grammy.

Grandmother: *You* did it?

Chris: Yes, but it was a accident. I couldn't find a piece of paper.

(Lindfors, 1980, p. 169)

2. A mother had this conversation with her three year old daughter.

   Mother: People are always telling you to share aren't they, Brenda? What does "share" mean?

   Brenda: It means I get to play with somebody else's toys.

   (Lindfors, 1980, p. 169)

3. A four year old had found his one shoe and was looking for the mate. He asked his father, "Where is the other shoe that rhymes with this one?"

   (Lindfors, 1980, p. 52)

It would be easy to simply say that these children don't know what "accident," "share," and "rhyme" mean. But clearly this would be an error. Each child does have a meaning for the word in question and, what is more, that meaning matches the adult's meaning in some important aspects. The first child, like his grandmother, sees an accident as a situation which is out of your control and which you therefore do not bear responsibility for. He and his grandmother simply differ on which areas they consider to be within one's control and responsibility. The second child and her mother would agree that "sharing" involves one individual using —legitimately— what belongs to another; they simply disagree as to whether "share" focuses on the giver or receiver of the action. The third child and his father both know that things that "rhyme" go together; the father has narrowed the "going together" dimension to one of word sounds; his son has not. These children's meanings for these difficult terms are substantial and revealing of what the child has figured out. "Knowing what a word means" (i.e. having a word-meaning connection that matches the adult's) is not a simple all-or-nothing affair. We would probably say that these same children know what "table" and "chair" mean, though the meanings "table the motion" and "chair the committee" are probably not part of their semantic knowledge.

Sometimes we hear semantic overextensions in our children's informal talk. For example, a child may refer to cats, dogs, sheep, and goats as "doggies." On the other hand, we sometimes hear a child underextending. When told to "get off the furniture," one two-year-old answered, "That's not the furniture, it's a chair." (Wells, 1981, p. 82). These semantic overextensions and underextensions show us important ways our children's semantic knowledge is evolving. Further experience of animals which are and are not dogs, and furniture which includes chairs and other objects as well, and the talk which is embedded in these experiences, will help the child restructure these semantic categories and labels into closer matches with those of the adult language.

The *word forms* children create and use in their talk tell us a great deal about their linguistic knowledge. Here are some examples from informal adult-child conversation.

4. A teacher asked a four year old who was sweeping the nursery school floor, "Are you mopping?" The child replied, "No, I'm brooming."

(Lindfors, 1980, p. 52)

5. A four year old had been put to bed by someone else in her mother's evening absence. In the middle of the night she came to her mother's bed, woke her, and requested that the mother put her to bed properly, saying, "I need to get good-nighted."

(Lindfors, 1980, p. 52)

In examples 4 and 5, the children create verbs they have not heard before. These are not simple imitations. Rather, the children demonstrate here, by creating novel forms that conform to basic patterns in the language, that they have discerned those patterns and use them to guide their language behavior (present continuous "-ing," past participle).

The children in examples 6 and 7 are telling stories for wordless storybooks.

6. A first grader said this about actions in Mercer Mayer's *Bubble Bubble* (1973): "And then he buyed the bubbles. Then the man went off. He blowed bubbles. Bubbles, bubbles, bubbles. He blew a rabbit bubble. Then he blew a lot of more bubbles....And the snake almost bited him."[3]

7. A five year old told his mother the following about the events in Mercer Mayer's *Hiccup* (1978): "...The drink accidently got on her, and she was mad at him. But she forgived him....And they hollered at each other and they keeped on hiccupping....And she kicked him into the water. And she was a 'laughing' at him—and sticked her tongue out at him."

Here the children have taken common verbs that they hear daily in adult irregular past tense forms, and they have restructured them according to the knowledge they are constructing about the expression of past tense in English. Notice in example 7 the logic of "kicked" and "sticked," and the ease with which alternative forms "blowed" and "blew" live within the language system of the child in example 6, much as alternative forms (e.g. "can't" and "cannot") live in ours.

8. A three and one-half year old, sitting at the table in a booster chair, finished her lunch and wanted to get down from the chair. Unable to push her chair back from the table, she said to her mother, "Mommy, will you unpush me?"

(Lindfors, 1980, p. 52)

9. A six year old was looking at a picture in which a fat mouse that had been blown with magic bubbles had suddenly disappeared. He pointed to the visual representation of the poof where the mouse had been, and said, "It's a deblown mouse."

(Lindfors, 1980, p. 52)

10. A four year old asked a nearby adult to give her the sifter by saying, "Give me that big winder. I'm going to wind and wind."

11. A five year old, describing a character from outer space that had just fallen into the ocean, said, "But when he was in here he was afraid, but then he lost his fraidness...."

Examples 8-11 show the children's grasp of various meanings and their expression as affixes: the negative meaning expressed as "un-" ("unpush"); the undoing meaning expressed as "de-" ("deblown"); the doer meaning expressed as "-er" (the "winder" is something that winds); and the change from adjective to noun expressed as "-ness" ("fraidness").

12. A second grader was describing a picture of a pony with a boy on his back flying over a weather vane: "He was flying over the southwesteast thing."

13. A fourth grader said of a picture of story characters getting out of a boat: "And then they got off-board."

In examples 12 and 13 the children demonstrate their understanding of compound forms. In "southwesteast thing" the child has created a combination form which names as a single label; in "off-board" the child has created a compound analogous to "onboard." This shows deep level understanding of compound forms. What the child does not know (that these particular forms don't happen to exist in English—at least, not yet) is insignificant, merely a matter of simple memory, in comparison to what the child does know—what compound forms are, how they are structured, how they are interpreted—a matter of understanding significant semantic processes in the language.

Language play. Often we hear children play with language, using language as a toy. In example 14 two five year olds are playing with *word forms*, using the -y suffix to express a change from noun to adjective.

14. C-1: 'Cause it's fishy too. 'Cause it has fishes.

    C-2: And it's snakey too 'cause it has snakes and it's beary too because it has bears.

    C-1: And it's. . .and it's hatty too 'cause it has hats.

(Garvey, 1977, p. 70)

The children in examples 15-17 are playing with *semantic aspects* of their language.

15. Several five year olds are playing. C-1 is a boy; C-2 is a girl.

    C-1: (pointing to boys) You're a girl; you're a girl; you're a girl. (pointing to C-2 who is a girl) You're a boy. (Laughs)

    C-2: If I'm a boy, you're a girl!

    C-1: On no! We mixed it all up! I'm a girl! (Speaks in a high voice) I'm a girl! I'm a girl!

16. Two four year olds are conversing.

C-1: I eat milk.
C-2: I drink chicken. (Both laugh)

17. The teacher of a kindergarten-first grade classroom has just explained that "the gold beads" and "the decimal beads" refer to the same objects. An assistant teacher doublechecks with the assembled group of children:

Assistant teacher: (to children) Did everybody catch that? The gold beads and the decimal beads are the same thing.

First grade child: (Quietly, to another child) I didn't catch that. I'm not a very good football catcher.

The children in example 15 demonstrate their knowledge of semantic categories (male child/female child) and the expression—labels—for them (boy/girl) by deliberately violating those category/label relationships. The joke for the children in example 16 is their deliberate violation of well understood constraints on semantic combining: that "eat" takes only solids and "drink" takes only liquids. In example 17 the children demonstrate their knowledge of two meanings for the word "catch."

Often it is the *sound system* of the language—the children's phonological knowledge—that they play with. The children in examples 18 to 20 all show their knowledge of the basic sounds (and possible sound combinations) of their language as they make sound substitutions in their language play.

18. Two four year olds are talking:
C-1: You're a crazy nut head.
C-2: You're a coo-coo brat head.
C-1: Well you're really a boo-boo bat bed.
C-2: You're a foo-foo fat head.

19. Two four year olds are conversing:
C-1: (Hopping along in a squatting position) Guess what kind of animal I am. Rib-it, rib-it, rib-it.
C-2: A frog.
C-1: No. Rib-it, rib-it, rib-it.
C-2: A toad.
C-1: No. Rib-it, rib-it.

C-2: I don't know, then.
C-1: A rabbit.
C-2: Uh-uh (no).
C-1: Uh-huh (yes). This rabbit says rib-it. (Laughs)

20. Three four year olds are playing with dolls in the housekeeping area:
C-1: (with feather duster) I'm a duster lady.
C-2: (Grabs duster, giggles and starts a chant) Mumadee-humadee, mumadee-humadee, mumadee-humadee, mumadee-humadee. (Giggles)
C-3: (Loudly) I HAVE TO GO TO A PARTY!
C-1: We'll have to share these beebies. (Giggles)
C-3: We are going to the *potty* and then...to the *party* (giggles) but we'll have to take all of them.

To play with a language element, whether semantic, syntactic, or phonological—to manipulate it, turn it upside down, stand it on its head—is the surest possible evidence that one is aware of that element and of its normal functioning.

Questions. Many children ask an abundance of questions. Their questions give us clues about what they are trying to make sense of in their world. Often children's questions reveal their active attempts to make sense out of aspects of language structure. For example, it has been noted that the sharp increase in the one and one-half to two year old's "What dis? What dat?" questions corresponds to a sharp increase in the child's vocabulary. It appears that the child is using these identification questions to find out how various objects are categorized and labelled. Similarly, many three to four year olds suddenly begin asking a high proportion of why questions. [One four year old told his mother "I'm a why'er, you are a because-er!" (Chukovsky, 1968, p. 31)]. The adult because-ers who interact closely with why-ers sometimes remark that the why-er doesn't seem to be particularly interested in the *because* that is offered, but simply jumps in with yet another *why*. Then after some months, this inflated use of why questions drops to a reasonable level and there it stays. It has been suggested that this often observed phenomenon may reflect the child's active attempt to understand those abstract and diverse causal relations expressed as "because X." Every time the child asks "why?" he or she is given an example of a causal relation. Given enough examples, children are apparently able to figure out these relations—what "because" is about—at least enough to satisfy them for the present.

Comprehension of others' talk. Our children's talk tells us a great deal about their ever-increasing grasp of the meanings and expression possibilities of their language. But this knowledge is also evident in their comprehension of the talk of others. One place where this demonstration is particularly apparent is in children's responses to literature that plays with language elements—literature which, like the children themselves, uses language as a toy. *Dr. Seuss's Sleep Book* (1962) is only one of an abundance of such books available for children. When we read this book to children they enjoy the sound play:

> They've talked about laws and they've talked about gauze/They've talked about paws and they've talked about flaws.
>
> or:
>
> Moose juice, not goose juice, is juice for a moose/And goose juice, not moose juice, is juice for a goose./So, when goose gets a mouthful of juices of moose's/And moose gets a mouthful of juices of goose's,/They always fall out of their beds screaming screams. (unpaged)

They also grasp the syntactic relations within the frolicking phrases that they have surely not encountered outside of the context of this particular book. They do not have to be told that the underlying structure of "the time for *night-brushing of teeth* is at hand" is "X brushes teeth at night"; of "old *drawbridge draw-er*" is "X draws the drawbridge"; of "*stilt-walker walkers*" is "X walks on stilts"; of "*Hinkle Horn Honking Club*" is "club for people who honk horns of the Hinkle type"; of "trying to sell *Zizzer-Zoof seeds/ Which nobody wants because nobody needs.*" is "Nobody wants seeds of the Zizzer-Zoof type because nobody needs them." Nor do we have to explain the semantic play—the invented categories that get invented labels—an "Audio-Telly-o-Tally-o-Count" or a "Hoop-Soup-Snoop Group."

When we read such stories to children, we have no way of knowing just how they are relating the created, playful meanings and expressions, how they are making sense of what they hear. But this need not trouble us since, after all, we never can know for sure just what kind of sense the child is making of his or her experience. What we can and do know is that each child is making some kind of sense out of what we read to them, based on his or her unique experience with language in the world. This we know from the fact of the child's attentiveness, interest, engagement when we read.

Our children are active participants in the world of words and their participation both as producers and comprehenders of oral language, externalizes for us their growing sense of how their language is structured, of how they and others say what they mean and mean what they say.

What Is the Nature of the Language Acquisition Process?

Children's demonstrations of their knowledge of language structure are important for the adults who interact with them. Yet far more important for these adults are children's demonstrations of how they are learning in this area of language. The same talk and comprehension that demonstrate *what* the children know, demonstrates *how*—the process involved in the ongoing learning. And because it is the ongoing process that adults foster, it is crucial that we recognize in our children's language behavior the nature of that process. How shall we characterize the process on the basis of the examples we have considered?

Language acquisition is a continuous, dynamic evolving process. This is evident in the children's word meanings that partially match the adult's ("accident," "share," "rhyme"), in overgeneralized word forms that reflect the basic patterns of the language but not the exceptional cases ("blowed," "bited," "keeped," "forgived," "buyed"), in the predictable negative and interrogative structures that show a partial working out of these subsystems ("I don't see nothing," "Why you are doing that?").

Language acquisition is a meaning focused process. Though the child's meanings and expression change over time, the fact that expression of *meaning* is the goal of language remains *un*changing over time. The child is thrusting to mean. For adults who interact with children, one of the most significant and dramatic findings of language acquisition research to date must surely be that language-acquiring children are responded to by adults on the basis of the meanings the children are attempting to convey, rather than on the basis of the forms they use.

> When a child says "He a girl" (referring to her mother), the mother answers "that's right," and when the child says, "Her curl my hair" (again referring to her mother), mother verbally approves the child's comment.
>
> (Brown, Cazden, Bellugi-Klima, 1971, p. 410)

The child is focused on meaning; the caregiver is also responding to the meanings, rather than the forms, of children's nonadult utterances ("unpush me," "Why I can't go?"). And in the context of this meaning-full exchange, expressive forms—as well as meanings—develop.

Language acquisition is an interactive process. A child figures out how language is organized and used by actively participating in real communication events. Britton would call this "practice," but not the rehearsal type of practice that the juggler does before a performance, but rather the engaging in kind of practice that the lawyer and doctor do when they "practice" medicine and law (Britton, 1973, p. 130). Rehearsal doesn't require the participation—or even the presence—of another. But the child's engaging-in practice of language does, for it is interactive in nature as the child uses language to joke ("This rabbit says rib-it."), to explain ("It was a accident. I couldn't find a piece of paper."), to request help ("Where is my other shoe that rhymes with this one?"). And in the context of this "practice" in communicating—producing and comprehending language in real conversation—the child figures out how language is structured (as well as how it is used).

But above all else, language acquisition is *an active process of creative construction.* The old images of children as blank slates to be written on or clay lumps to be shaped by the environment will no longer do. Whether observing, comprehending, producing, questioning, children are actively engaged in figuring out how language works. Out of their language experience they build hypotheses—hunches—about the meanings and expressive devices of the language. In their talk and their comprehension they are acting on their hunches. This is what we hear when they say "I'm brooming," "the southwesteast thing," "she forgived him." And this is what we observe when they make sense out of "old drawbridge draw-er" and "Hinkle Horn Honking Club." These productions and understandings are not the result of environmental "shaping" either by the provision of "reinforcement" for language form or by the provision of models to be imitated. They are the creative constructions of an active language learner who makes and uses hypotheses about language structure and revises those hypotheses over time.

Frank Smith (1973) suggests "one difficult way to make learning to read easy." That one difficult way is as apt for oral language as it is for reading: "Respond to what the child is trying to do" (p. 195). As adults interacting with children, the more we recognize in our children's talk and understanding that what they are "trying to do" is actively and creatively evolve a system of language structure in the context of meaning-full interaction, the more effectively we will be able to "respond to"—and support—those active efforts.

Notes

1. Throughout this discussion I am using written forms. It is important to remember, however, that the expression I am talking about is oral. Thus, the meaning of plurals in the "tables" example is expressed as the sound /z/ and past in the "walked" example is expressed as the sound /t/, etc.
2. The discussions of negative and interrogative are based on Klima and Bellugi-Klima, 1971.
3. I am indebted to Ellis Scarf, Alice Koury, Chris Grannan, Sandra Longoria, Cynthia Postel, Judith Blalock, and Judy Muery for examples 6, 7, 10, 11, 12, 13, 15, and 16.

References

Britton, J. *Language and Learning*. Hammondsworth, England: Pelican Books, 1973.

Brown, R. *A First Language*. Cambridge, Massachusetts: Harvard University Press, 1973.

Brown, R., Cazden, C., & Bellugi-Klima, U. "The Child's Grammar from I to III," in A. Bar-Adon & W. Leopold (Eds.), *Child Language: A Book of Readings*. Englewood Cliffs, New Jersey: Prentice-Hall, 1971.

Carroll, Lewis. *The Complete Works of Lewis Carroll.* New York: Random House, n.d.

Chukovsky, K. *From Two to Five.* Translated and edited by M. Morton. Berkeley: University of California Press, 1968.

Garvey, C. *Play*. Cambridge, Massachusetts: Harvard University Press, 1977.

Geisel, T.S. *Dr. Seuss's Sleep Book*. New York: Random House, 1962.

Halliday, M.A.K. *Learning How to Mean.* New York: Elsevier North-Holland, 1977.

Klima, E.S. & Bellugi-Klima, U. "Syntactic Regularities in the Speech of Children," in A. Bar-Adon & W. Leopold (Eds.), *Child Language: A Book of Readings*. Englewood Cliffs, New Jersey: Prentice-Hall, 1971.

Lindfors, J.W. *Children's Language and Learning*. Englewood Cliffs, New Jersey: Prentice-Hall, 1980.

Mayer, M. *Bubble, Bubble.* New York: Parent's Magazine Press, 1973.

Mayer, M. *Hiccup*. New York: Dial Press, 1978.

Smith, F. "Twelve Easy Ways to Make Learning to Read Difficult," in Frank Smith (Ed.), *Psycholinguistics and Reading*. New York: Holt, Rinehart and Winston, 1973.

Wells, G. *Learning through Interaction.* New York: Cambridge University Press, 1981.

Ways to Look at the Functions of Children's Language

Gay Su Pinnell
The Ohio State University at Lima

> Six year old Andrew has just been to a concert given by a harpist at his school. He is now drawing a harp and talking to himself: "Harperoo. Harperoo. Harperdy dart, harperdy dart, parperdy dart, arp arp, arpity, dart, dart, arpity dart, arpity, dart, arpity, dart, dart, arp, arp, parpity, dart....Ok, this was a fine assembly...but I can tell you something. That harp was about six feet tall! And if you don't believe me, ask the woman that was playing it. Whew! Boy!"

"New, new, new" declares a catalog designed to persuade teachers to purchase the latest materials to help children develop skills in language. Some of the catchy titles include "growth in grammar," "phonics in context," "word attack and comprehension," "spelling for beginners." These materials may indeed help youngsters look at various forms of language and perhaps to perform well on worksheets and tests designed to measure the lessons the materials teach. But most are usually based on assumptions about what children do not know about language while ignoring their competence—what they do know. Such materials fail to recognize and respond to the natural and enthusiastic language play we observe in Andrew's example above. And they are not "new." Most important, they are inconsistent with language research of the past decade which urges us to focus less on the form of language and more on its social function and meaning.

This article will concentrate, therefore, on what teachers can learn about children's language—their ability to communicate and to engage in conversation—through observation and on ways to extend their language for a range of uses in real life situations.

Developing a Functional View of Language

A functional view of language means focusing on how people use language in their everyday lives to communicate, to present themselves, to find out about things, to give information, to negotiate and interact. What is important about language is what we can do with it—how it functions in a world of people. What we can *do* with language is worth assessing and teaching.

Children live in a rich social world of language. They hear language, reorganize it and use it to express their own meanings. As they interact with others, they gradually learn how to share their meanings and, as they do so, construct a set of beliefs and expectations about language. They learn that language can be used to meet their needs, to learn and to communicate with others. The more they use language the more they learn about the forms of language—the words and patterns—that will help them to accomplish their purposes. When we think about children learning language, we can apply the simple principle: form follows function.

As Harold and Connie Rosen (1973) have pointed out, "language is for living with," and we might add, "learning with" (p. 21). Research for at least the past decade supports the idea that function and meaning are the most important, and probably the most neglected, concerns of parents, researchers, teachers, and others who must make decisions about the assessment and development of young children's language (Cazden, John, & Hymes, 1972).

A productive way to monitor language development—and one which will also help teachers to evaluate their own effectiveness in fostering language use—is to observe children in a systematic way to determine the range of language functions used in the classroom. There are several established systems for observing and categorizing functions of language. These systems are useful for assessment and also for devising strategies to extend children's use of language for a variety of social purposes.

One simple and useful category system has already been developed by M.A.K. Halliday (1973, 1975), who maintains that the linguistic system is a "range of possible meanings, together with the means whereby these meanings are realized or expressed" (1975, p. 8). He identifies seven categories for functions of language and stresses the importance of children experiencing the whole range in their homes, communities, and schools. The categories based on Halliday's framework are listed below. The definitions were formulated by Pinnell for use in a study (1975) of language in the classroom.

Function Categories

Instrumental Language

Instrumental language is what we use to get what we want, to satisfy needs or desires. At the early stages it may be to satisfy simple needs or wants; at later stages of sophistication, it may take the form of polite requests or persuasion. Appropriate and effective use of instrumental language in conversation, on the telephone, and in writing is important for the skillful language user. Little intervention is needed to elicit instrumental language. Children use it all the time. As they grow more independent, instrumental language should, in fact, decrease and become more complex, taking on forms of persuasion and argument.

Regulatory Language

The regulatory function means using language to control the behavior of others, or getting them to do what we want them to do. Regulatory language may include giving orders or at more subtle levels, manipulating and controlling others. This kind of language is often used in competitive game situations in which there is a rule-governed "right" answer. Positive regulatory language is one of the "life skills" that every parent, shop owner, foreman, or administrator must know. The student who leads a committee or serves on Student Council will practice regulatory language every day.

Interactional Language

Interactional language is used to establish and define social relationships. It may include negotiation, encouragement, expressions of friendships, and the kind of "maintenance" language all of us use in group situations. The "setting, joking and small talk" adults do before a meeting begins is also an example. Because those who are effective in building informal relationships are likely to succeed, children need to develop a comfortable awareness of their ability to use language to establish relationships with other people, to work cooperatively with them, and to enjoy their companionship.

Personal Language

Personal language is used to express individuality and personality. Strong feelings and opinions are part of personal language. Personal language is often neglected in classrooms and thought inappropriate. Yet, it is through personal language that children relate their own lives to the subject matter being taught, establish their own identities, build self esteem and confidence.

Imaginative Language

Imaginative language is used to create a world of one's own, to express fantasy through dramatic play, drama, poetry or stories. This use of language flourishes in the kindergarten with its house corner, big blocks and toys. Unless it is fostered, it will rapidly disappear in later years. Its importance cannot be underestimated, especially when we consider how difficult some teachers find it to get students to write with imagination. Poetry, stories, drama—all are the result of active use of the imaginative function.

Heuristic Language

Heuristic language is used to explore the environment, to investigate, to acquire knowledge and understanding. Heuristic language is for investigation, for wondering, for figuring things out. It is the language of inquiry and is one of the most important functions.

Informative Language

Informative language is used to communicate information, to report facts or conclusions from facts. It is the language of school. Teachers most frequently use it themselves and require it of children, but informative language is not only recall of facts. Helping children synthesize material and draw inferences and conclusions is also important.

In this article, Halliday's framework will be used to look at children's use of language. But it is not the only system. Tough (1977), Smith (1977), Wood (1977) and others provide different frameworks for looking at the functions of language. Teachers can easily develop their own by thinking about all the ways they use language; these are the functions the child must eventually develop.

Whatever the system, sensitive observation, using a simple category system for language functions, can help a teacher determine children's competence in using language that relates to real life situations. Teachers need ways of assessing language that will help them to monitor the child's growing ability to use language skillfully in the social milieu. Test scores may be part of the assessment, but teachers' judgments of language ability are still the most trusted and reliable assessment. Studies (Black, 1979; Tough, 1977) show that observing and recording children's language behavior is a viable way to look at what they *can* do, thus giving an effective starting point for instruction.

The important thing is that teachers need to think carefully about the social interaction going on in the classroom, perhaps asking themselves questions such as:

1. Does each child use language for a variety of purposes? How is the function of language linked with what the child is doing and who he/she is talking to?
2. What range of language functions do we hear in the classroom? What situations promote different uses for language?
3. How can I extend children's use of language as I work with them?

In order to answer these questions teachers must pay attention to the context in which language is used, in this case, the school and the classroom.

Children learn how to use language within a social context and as they do so, they learn the needed forms of expression. The language context, the environment, and the climate of the classroom and school are important factors that influence how children will use language. Context includes the other people in the situation, the expectations and background knowledge of speakers and listeners alike, as well as the physical surroundings in which the language takes place. As Clark and Clark (1977) have pointed out, the "function of language is intimately bound up with the speakers' and listeners' mental activities during communication, in particular with the speakers' intentions, the ideas speakers want to convey and the listeners' current knowledge" (p. 25).

What Can We Learn from Watching and Listening?

As the following examples will demonstrate, a great deal can be learned by careful watching and listening. In the example below, Anne and Amy, two first graders, are painting clay ash trays they have made.

Anne: Yeah, 'cause my mom really does need a ash tray. She only got three or four ash trays and she smokes a lot. And we always have to clean the ash trays out for. . . .I use the, uh, stuff that you dust the tables with but in the ashtrays and they turn out real clean. Don't you, Amy?

Amy: Mm, hm.

Anne: You're my sister but you had to get adopted by somebody cause mommy didn't like you. You were mean! (She giggles.)

Amy: She liked me, but she didn't wanta have that much children and. . .

Anne: Why? 'Cause she already got five kids now. 'Member, she gave away sister, and brother. We had two brothers until she had to give you and then two. We did have eight kids. Wasn't it? Yea, it was eight kids. (Pause) 'Cause five plus three equal eight.

Amy: I'm done with the inside now. Where's that pretty blue?

Monica: I know.

Amy: Here's that pretty blue on there. See the pretty blue on there, Sue Anne?

Anne: Yeah. (Laughs) Gosh, your ash tray is little. How come you just put it on a straw?

Amy: I'm gonna put some string around it.

Anne: It has tape underneath. I just made a big one because my mom smokes a lot. You know mommy's been smokin' more than she usually does since you've been gone. And she has to sleep with me at night. She thinks I'm you. 'Cause she likes to sleep with you. 'Member, she always did? But you never did wanta clean. I always did.

What do we know about Amy and Anne now that we have listened to them? Using Halliday's categories as a guide, we can identify many skillful uses of language in the girls' conversation. They can readily switch from interactional language (talking about work arrangements, etc.) to regulatory language (giving orders) to imaginative language (playing a role, such as "sisters"). When they switch to imaginative language, there is no verbal signal such as "let's pretend." They simply follow each others' cues. There is a system of subtle signals between the girls which helps them to make these switches smoothly and maintain their conversation. We also notice that they report and utilize knowledge gained from other situations; for example, "five plus three equal eight." They certainly weave some personal language, opinions, sharing of feelings and thoughts, etc., into the conversation. They seem relaxed and comfortable with each other. The work continues productively. Each girl is accomplishing her task while engaged in purposeful talk. The clay/painting situation was a fruitful context for developing both work skills and language skills.

A little later on in the same scene, Anne is still painting her ash tray; Monica is painting at the easel; Amy has been wondering what to do.

Anne: Why don't you paint your ash tray? It might be dry. Mine was dry and now I'm gonna paint it.

Amy: Ok, ok, ok.

Anne: I just said, "Why DON'T you." I didn't say PAINT your ash tray," Amy. I just said "Why DON'T you paint your ash tray."

Amy: (inaudible)

Anne: Well, how come you have to say it when you go "ok"? (She imitates Amy's earlier intonation.)

Monica: I'm going to make mine green!

Anne: I'm doin'...on the outside of mine I'm doin' it dark green but I ain't painting the bottom, girl, 'cause when you set it on a piece of paper to let the paint dry then it, the paint'll get stuck on that and then the paper'll come up with your ash tray and you won't get to take it home. You'll have to spend all your time takin' off that paper. That's why I won't put the, uh, I got to set this thing down. I can't paint with it like that.

What more do we know? Further observation of Anne and Amy shows that Anne can use language to describe, to report prior knowledge, and to project into the future. We also notice Anne and Amy are capable of using language to talk *about* language. Anne, in fact, makes a very fine distinction between an order, "Paint your ashtray," and a suggestion, "Why don't you paint your ashtray?" They are examining language and its meaning as they talk with each other.

During a more formal classroom activity, two first graders, Matt and Brent, are talking as they complete an assigned task, writing numerals. Their talk is casual, but they are using language to describe the work they are doing.

Matt: Ten hundred! That's far isn't it? Ten hundred's far isn't it?

Brett: Nine hundred's farther than ten hundred.

Matt: No, it's not.

Brett: Yes, it is.

Matt: Ten hundred is.

Matt: Oh, I messed up! (He has made a mistake on the paper.) How do you make a ten like, oh, I know how to make a ten.

Brett: You make a one, then you make a zero.

We might be tempted to direct a "shhh..." to the boys above. Yet, looking at it another way, the conversation is actually adding to the learning experience. They are learning to write numerals and learning to talk about math at the same time. Brett and Matt are helping each other understand complicated ideas through language. They are wondering aloud, asking questions and instructing each other. In Halliday's terms, they are using informative, interactive, heuristic, and personal language in a complex interaction while concentrating on the task at hand.

While the teacher's intervention is necessary to expand children's language, peer language is a rich social context in which to try out new language uses and receive feedback. Although teachers often think they must be everywhere doing everything and providing all the instruction, observation of children reassures us that children do encourage, instruct, and help each other effectively. And, in so doing, they develop communicative competence in using language. (For discussions of peer-peer interaction, see articles by Michaels and Foster, and Smith-Burke in this volume.)

The above samples were of conversations between young children in the first year of school, but it is equally important to be aware of and foster a range of language functions with older children. The following group of Canadian fifth graders discussed a problem of national interest.

Graham: If Quebec separates from Canada, the Maritime Provinces will probably go to the United States. The Grand Banks fishing area is important and the U.S. could use it.

Doug: I kinda do hope they separate, 'cept in one way—the Maritimes would be poor! But, I would be glad in another way because they cause so much trouble.

Jeremy: Doug, I don't think they cause all that many problems. They just want to speak their own language there....

Graham: Doug, you have to remember that the French came over and did a lot of exploring as well as the English so it just wasn't the English people who have a right to Canada!

Jeremy: (nodding) I think the Canadians are being selfish to want just one language. There is no reason why we can't speak many languages and live together.

Bob: Yeah, we should be able to speak many languages but the French only want to speak French, Jeremy. They have to be willing to give a little, too!

Doug: Bob's right, they don't have the right to cause so much trouble! Even the labels on the cans have to be written in French. That's why we can't get half the stuff from the states!

Caroline: I think we should have only one main language. The labels cost a lot for the rest of us.

Martine: I would say the same as Caroline.[1]

The children in this example had had much experience in using language in a variety of ways and were accustomed to participating in discussion groups. Here they are using informative and personal language to deal with complex ideas, to make inferences, and to argue skillfully. The students were expressing opinions and backing them up with information. It is in genuine argument that one must muster his or her best command of language in order to be persuasive enough to get the point across. Youngsters need many opportunities to try themselves out in arguments and discussions with peers, older students, and even with adults—teachers, principals, and others in the community. The demands of group interaction are seldom assessed in classroom situations; yet, they are critical language skills and deserve careful attention.

In a study of first graders, Pinnell (1975) found that at least two elements are usually present when children are actively engaged in using language functionally: 1) students are encountering real problems to which they want to find the solutions, and 2) two or more students are working and talking together about the problems. The interactions in the examples above, took place in classrooms with these characteristics. The activities were interesting and challenging so that children had something to talk about, a chance to guess, argue, make predictions and check them out, and a chance to use their imaginations. Rather than seeing talk as distracting, their teachers saw it as valuable. They structured activities and the environment to take maximum advantage of the way children learn. That is, they gave children a great many opportunities to talk. The key is a teacher who is aware of the importance of fostering a wide range of language use and who is a good observer.

Observing Language Use

By observing language use in the classroom, we can make two kinds of assessment:

1. We can assess an individual child's competence by looking at the extent to which he/she uses the various functions of language and how effectively.
2. We can assess the language environment by determining which functions occur and where, and which are being neglected.

For the first kind of assessment, the teacher should observe the same child in several different settings in the classroom and in formal and informal activities in other areas of the school. Observations may be brief (three to five minutes), but they should be recorded and reported periodically so that progress can be noted. For the second kind of assessment, a teacher may observe the entire class or small groups in different areas of the classroom or at different times of the day. The teacher can also combine data from observations of individual students to form a group composite. For both kinds of assessment, simple forms and checklists connected to the teachers' own goals and classroom activities could be used.

Since Halliday's categories are relatively easy to use, a teacher might start with them. Become familiar with the categories and then observe students in several different settings. A simple approach would be to make a list of the seven functions, or use a form like the one in Figure 1, and jot down examples of each type of language. Statements may seem to fulfill several functions at once. That is not surprising since language is complex and the categories are not discrete. What we are looking for is a profile that describes the variety of functions used. While it seems impossible to note all the language that is taking place, teachers will be surprised how much they can record in a short time. And, observations over a period of time provide a good picture of students' language.

This simple system provides a guide for observing language in the classroom and for monitoring student progress. It also provides a framework for teachers—individuals, teams or the whole staff—to use in designing instructional activities that encourage students to use language for a variety of purposes. By examining observational records, the teacher can determine which functions are being used and which are not and plan accordingly. For example, if no personal language is noted over several observations of a child, the teacher may want to make some time for an informal one-to-one conversation or for a home visit to establish a more productive relationship with the child. If little or no heuristic language is used by the children, the teacher might need to introduce materials or plan problem situations that stimulate curiosity and question asking. If most of the talk in the classroom falls into only a few categories, the teacher may want to reexamine the whole environment and reorganize learning activities so that the use of a greater variety of functions is encouraged.

Listed below are a few instructional strategies for each language function. Teachers can add others to the list. Try them and observe the results.

Figure 1. Functions of language observation form.

Name: ______________________________
(individual, small group, large group observed)

Time: ______________________________
(time of day)

Setting: ______________________________
(physical setting and what happened prior to observation)

Activity: ______________________________
(activity, including topic/subject area)

LANGUAGE FUNCTION	EXAMPLES
Instrumental	
Regulatory	
Interactional	
Personal	
Imaginative	
Heuristic	
Informative	

Note: Check each time a language function is heard and/or record examples.

Instructional Strategies to Promote Language Functions

INSTRUMENTAL LANGUAGE—The teacher can:

1. Be accessible and responsive to children's requests, but teach independence by having children state their requests effectively.
2. Encourage the use of instrumental language with other children, helping them to expand their own language through providing help and direction to peers.
3. Analyze advertising, propaganda, etc., to help children become aware of how language can be used by people to get what they want.

REGULATORY LANGUAGE—The teacher can:

1. Create situations that let children be "in charge" of small and large groups.
2. Find instances in which regulatory language is used inappropriately to teach appropriate regulatory language or the alternative, instrumental language.
3. Attempt to use less regulatory language as a teacher.

INTERACTIONAL LANGUAGE—The teacher can:

1. Create situations that require children to share work areas or materials and talk about how they are to do it.
2. Find ways of having small group (especially pairs or trios) discussions in a variety of subject areas. Through these discussions, students not only learn the subject matter more thoroughly, they practice communication.
3. Let students work together to plan field trips, social events, and classroom and school projects.
4. Whenever possible, mix children of different ages, sexes, races in work groups or discussion groups.
5. Have informal social times and, as a teacher, engage in some talk that is not "all business."

PERSONAL LANGUAGE—The teacher can:

1. Use personal language to give permission to children to share personal thoughts and opinions.
2. Be willing to listen and talk personally during transition times; for example, when children are coming in in the morning. Converse with children while on cafeteria or playground duty.
3. Provide some comfortable, attractive areas in the classroom where students can talk quietly.
4. Encourage parents and family members to visit and participate in classrooms.
5. Read stories or books that prompt a very personal response from students.

IMAGINATIVE LANGUAGE—The teacher can:

1. Create situations that naturally elicit spontaneous dramatic play; for example, house corner, dress up, blocks for younger children, and drama and roleplaying for older children.

2. Read stories and books which feed the imagination and which are a stimulus for art, drama, and discussion.
3. Provide time for children to talk in groups and/or with partners before they begin their writing or imaginative topics.
4. Encourage "play" with language—the sounds of words and the images they convey.

HEURISTIC LANGUAGE—The teacher can:

1. Structure classroom experiences so that interest and curiosity are aroused.
2. Create real problems for children to solve.
3. Put children in pairs or work groups for problem-solving activities.
4. Use heuristic language to stimulate such language in children. Saying "I wonder why" often promotes children to do the same. (This should, however, not be contrived; it should be an honest problem.)
5. Try projects which require study on the part of the entire class, including the teacher. Find some questions that no one knows the answer to.

INFORMATIVE LANGUAGE—The teacher can:

1. Plan activities which require children to observe carefully and objectively and then to summarize and draw conclusions from their observations (field trips are a good opportunity).
2. Require children to keep records of events over periods of time and then to look back at their records and draw conclusions; for example, keeping records on classroom pets.
3. Use questioning techniques to elicit more complex forms of information giving.
4. Instead of having tedious classroom reports, have children give their reports to small groups and encourage feedback and discussion of those reports.

Once teachers have increased their sensitivity to the range of language functions used in their classrooms and in the school, several things happen:

1. They have good information on children that can be used to support and defend instructional strategies to develop language.
2. They can talk more specifically and persuasively to parents and others about each child.
3. They are more aware of language functions so they can informally and constantly perform assessment without using the checklists and only occasionally making records.
4. They can more effectively plan educational experiences.

Getting Started: Suggestions for Two Faculty Meetings

Studying language development in your own classroom is often difficult. Observing, recording, and teaching at the same time can be tricky. And sometimes questions come up—how to categorize a particular statement, how to interpret a puzzling remark, how to help a certain child use regulatory language more effectively. It is much more exciting and much easier when there are others to hear your ideas and to make suggestions. The following guide could be used by a school staff or student teachers to get started in assessing and fostering the uses of language.

Meeting #1

1. Ask the group to "brainstorm" all of the uses of language they can think of. (In brainstorming, every idea is accepted and written down on the chalkboard or chart paper so everyone can see). You will come up with a long list, including joking, gossip, lecturing, giving directions, etc.
2. With their own list before them, have the group examine the categories established by Halliday. Provide an introduction to the idea of functions of language.
3. In small groups or as a whole group, ask participants to generate examples from their own experiences for each of Halliday's categories. For each example, try to specify elements of context: where the language occurred, the topic, who was speaking, who the speaker was addressing, what the people were doing at the time.
4. The group should then develop a plan for observing in the school. They can observe classrooms—their own or each others'—and someone should observe on grounds, in the library, in the cafeteria, and in the hallways. They should specify times of day so that a variety of observations can be collected.
5. Each person leaves the meeting committed to observing for a designated period or periods of time during the next week and recording examples, with full contextual information, on the observation form.

Meeting #2

1. Staff members work in small groups or (if there are not too many) in the large group. They share and compile their observations from the previous week. They note the range of language observed and try to relate context to kinds of language. They come up with some summary statements about the language environment.
2. Using a checklist of the functions of language, the group discusses and generates a list of strategies for extending children's language.
3. Each group selects one or two language functions that they particularly want to observe for and foster during the next week. For each function they make a list of strategies to try. They specify the action plan they will follow.
4. Each person leaves the meeting committed to an action plan for extending children's language. They are to report on their success at the next meeting.

Meetings need not be as formally structured as the ones described above. The central goal is for school staff members to explore children's language together and to help each other become more aware. The greater a teacher's sensitivity to language, the less formal assessment tools will be needed.

Note

1. Example from Mary Louise Skinner, Deep Cove Elementary School, Sidney, British Columbia.

References

Black, J. "There's More to Language than Meets the Ear: Implications for Evaluation," *Language Arts, 56* (May 1979), 526-533.

Cazden, C.B., John, V.P., & Hymes, D. (Eds.). *Functions of Language in the Classroom.* New York: Teachers College Press, 1972.

Clark, H., & Clark, E. *Psychology and Language: An Introduction to Psycholinguistics.* New York: Harcourt Brace Jovanovich, 1977.

Halliday, M.A.K. "The Functional Basis of Language," in B. Bernstein (Ed.), *Class, Codes, and Control, Volume 2. Applied Studies Toward a Sociology of Language.* London and Boston: Routledge & Kegan Paul, 1973.

Halliday, M.A.K. *Learning How to Mean: Explorations in the Development of Language.* London: Edward Arnold Ltd., 1975.

Pinnell, G.S. "Language in Primary Classrooms," *Theory Into Practice, 14* (December 1975), 318-332.

Rosen, H., & Rosen, C. *The Language of Primary School Children.* London: Schools Council Publication, Penguin Books Ltd., 1973.

Smith, F. "The Uses of Language," *Language Arts, 54* (September 1977), 638-644.

Tough, J. *Talking and Learning: A Guide to Fostering Communication Skills in Nursery and Infant Schools.* London: Schools Council Publications, 1977.

Wood, B.S. (Ed.). *Development of Functional Communication Competences: PreK-Grade 6.* Urbana, Illinois: Eric Clearinghouse on Reading and Communication Skills, 1977.

WRITTEN LANGUAGE LEARNING

A Young Child's Developing Concepts of Print

Myna M. Haussler
Tucson Unified School District, Arizona

Children are surrounded by print. They see it every day—as they are driven past traffic signs, watch television, attend day care or nursery schools, and shop in local stores. How many times have you heard parents asking very young children to bring them a specific brand of cereal from a shelf at the supermarket? Children usually respond by running over to the shelf and pulling off the right brand. How are they able to do this?

In a print oriented society such as ours, children naturally become aware of print. They always have. Back in 1908, Huey wrote about the naturalness of learning to read at home:

> The child makes endless questionings about the name of things, as every mother knows. He is concerned also with the printed notices, signs, titles, visiting cards, etc., that come in his way, and should be told what these "say" when he makes inquiries. It is surprising how large a stock of printed or written words a child will gradually come to recognize in this way. (p. 314)

However, we as teachers, parents and researchers have not, until very recently, begun to focus on this remarkable developmental process.

For the past twenty years, researchers in the field of psycholinguistics and sociolinguistics have demonstrated that children learn oral language naturally as they interact with their family and other members of their speech community. According to Halliday (1977), the motivation for learning to speak is the desire to interact with others and to make sense out of one's surroundings. For these same reasons, young children become aware of the print around them. It is the need to communicate with others and to make sense out of printed language which motivates young children to begin reading. A growing body of evidence indicates that very young children in our society, prior to formal schooling, are aware of print, understand the functions of written language, and are naturally beginning to develop reading strategies.

A case study of the developing awareness of print in one three year old child, Anna, provides the basis for this article. A case study is an indepth analysis of one child's development. Case studies are invaluable for teachers to use in learning more about their students. They provide developmental information for planning instruction and reporting progress to parents. As we observe and question individual children, patterns emerge and we become even more knowledgeable about how children are learning. Samples of children's reading and writing are collected, observational notes are made, and responses to interviews are used in doing case studies like the one carried out by this parent-researcher.

Observation of one child's interactions with written language helps us raise and answer questions about that child's learning. It also provides information to begin answering the more general question, "What do three year olds know about written language?" In this chapter, Anna's developing concepts of written language are described and illustrated through examples of her responses to print. In addition, other research is discussed in terms of what this may mean for understanding written language development in other preschoolers. Knowledge of the process of how reading develops allows both teachers and parents to focus on meaningful ways to support and extend this learning.

Understanding the Functions of Print

As Anna interacts with the myriad of print in her environment, she learns that written language can be functional for her. She is surrounded by print in a home where a variety of reading and writing activities occurs during each day. Anna uses reading strategies when the print situation is functional and has meaning for her. An example is seen when Anna's father is leaving on a business trip. He travels on TransWorld Airlines and for the next two months, Anna can read TWA no matter where or in what form it appears. After a period of time, when the business trip is forgotten, she no longer can read TWA.

Anna also exhibits graphophonic correspondence for the initial consonants of family members' names and reads their first names functionally. Whenever her father's name, Martin, is presented, Anna reads it as Daddy, Martin, or Martin Smith (his last name). The same is true for her mother's first name which also begins with M. At no time does Anna ever confuse the names of her parents which both begin with M.

Halliday's ideas (1977) about language functions are revealed in Anna's written and oral language use. She particularly uses the instrumental, personal, and interactional functions when she is involved with print. Halliday states that these, along with the regulatory function, develop first in oral language. Here are some examples of Anna's functional responses to environmental print. When Anna is presented with a two-dimensional Lucky Charms box and is asked, "What does this say?" she responds by saying the name, Lucky Charms. When asked "How do you know that says Lucky Charms?" her response is, "Because I want to buy Lucky Charms." (Halliday's instrumental or "I want" response.) Other responses to "How do you know it says TWA, Trix, or another item?" include:

> It's yucky. I don't like it! (personal statement)
>
> TWA. Dad went at [sic] his trip to Germany. (interactive relationship to another)
>
> Is that Trix? (heuristic questioning)
>
> We have it at home. (informative statement)

Two other of Halliday's functions, the regulatory (control) and imaginative (pretend) functions are least used by Anna while she reads. However, Anna does use both of these functions of language when she is frustrated by questions her mother is asking her. Anna, who generally is very cooperative, uses oral language to try to manipulate the communication situation when she is not succeeding in the print task. For example, she uses these functional language strategies to handle the following difficult reading situations.

> Mother: What else do you know about this? (Fed Mart Milk)
>
> Child: This is the end! (to regulate the behavior of others)
>
> ---
>
> Mother: Have you seen this before? (Trix)

Child: Nay-no. On sco sco.

Mother: What does it say?

Child: Noah.

Mother: Show me what says Noah.

Child: No Noah means no! (imaginative use of language to show that she will not continue)

(And so ended the interview.)

Goodman and Goodman (1979) suggest that children learn written language when it is functional to them. Smith (1976) also notes, "Children probably begin to read from the moment they become aware of print in any meaningful way" (p. 299).

When children interact with meaningful print, they learn that it is functional and find ways to "read" it. When it is not meaningful children find ways to avoid dealing with it.

Using Context in Reading

Anna is reading in her environment. At the supermarket, in her home, and in the car, she relies on the context of the situation for reading cues. She indicates that packaging and signs are saying something. Anna knows this because she interacts with print in many meaningful situations—writing shopping lists, reading cereal and milk cartons, and reading signs from the backseat of her mother's car. During the following exchanges, Anna indicates that she does indeed use the context of the situation to cue her reading:

Mother: What are you looking at? (showing Anna a two-dimensional McDonald's hamburger wrapper)

Child: A "Hang-ge-burg."

The picture of the hamburger wrapper may carry the McDonald's message to her; however, it also held a hamburger at one time. Although it is difficult to state which aspect of this complex situation she focuses on, it is possible to see that Anna is using contextual cues, other than print, to read McDonald's.

Another example of Anna's use of context in reading occurred when her mother showed her a napkin from Dunkin Donuts.

Child: It's a Dunkin Donut napkin.

Mother: How do you know?

Child: It is. (looking at napkin)

Mother: What are you looking at?

Child: At this. (pointing directly to the coffee cup emblem on the napkin)

Smith (1976) describes the observation of another three year old who responded to print in a department store. Smith took the child on an excursion through a department store and asked him questions about print in many areas of the store. Smith was convinced that the child was reading in his environment and that no one had specifically taught him how to do it. "My brief case study tells me that children learn a great deal about reading without adult assistance or even adult awareness" (p. 322). Smith concludes that the child he observed was not responding to sound symbol relationships, but to his own personal responses to the context of print around him. In the same way other children, like Anna, use the situational context to cue their reading.

Using Print Cues

Anna uses a variety of graphic strategies to construct meaning for the printed signs around her. These strategies include using print to name and using the cues of configuration and graphophonic correspondence to respond to written text.

This three year old often reveals that print "says something," even when she does not verbalize which cuing system she is using. She uses print to name as in the following example.

Mother: What does this say? (Fed Mart Milk)

Child: Milk.

Mother: What says milk on here?

(Child points to Fed Mart, then to Milk.)

The child sweeps her hand across the print from left-to-right and from top-to-bottom, showing that at three years of age she understands how English is read, even though she does not show exactly where it says milk. She does, however, point to print—using print to name.

The shape or configuration of the printed signs also aids in Anna's reading. When reading the sign LEVY'S, a local department store, the child points to each letter and also to the apostrophe.

Mother: What is this word? (LEVY'S)

Child: It say, uh, it says, it says LEVY'S things.

Mother: How do you know that?

Child: Cause I love LEVY'S bag.

Mother: It does say LEVY'S. How do you know?

(Child pointed to each letter, L-E-V-Y, her finger moved up to the apostrophe, then down to the S.)

Another aspect of configuration certainly includes the stylized printing on the bag which has become a symbol of LEVY'S.

Anna never indicates that she is using sound and symbol cues to read when other cues are obvious. However, when no other cues are available, she gives us this example.

Mother: Read what this says. (TWA)

Child: It says Tommy.

Mother: How do you know it says Tommy?

Child: Because it is T like Tina. (her sister)

Although the sign was read incorrectly, the child reveals a generalization of the beginning consonant T.

While on a family trip, Anna was focusing on the letter A. As she was driving past Anaheim Stadium in California, she saw a huge A on the front of it. She remarked, "That's Anna." When questioned by her mother, she always read M&M's and McDonald's correctly, even when they were printed in manuscript with no accompanying contextual cues. As mentioned earlier, both of her parents' names begin with M.

Harste, Burke, and Woodward (1982) report that their research reveals young children make several decisions about printed language: 1) they use information of personal value, such as reading the name of their favorite fast food restaurant; 2) they use whatever generalized features they have factored out of the system, that is, letters, linear organization, phoneme-grapheme correspondence, to place hold or intuit the message (p. 129); 3) they maintain their focus on meaning, even when pressed beyond their competence. Ferreiro and Teberosky (1982) also mention that even before children begin reading they have a clear concept of what can be read.

Knowing How to Handle Books

Anna has many books on a low bookshelf in her bedroom and more are available at her nursery school. She uses them daily in play-like situations. She is read to at least once a day by a teacher or her parent and also by her six year old sister.

Anna's book handling knowledge and reading concepts were assessed using Clay's *Sand Test* (1973). The *Sand Test* is an observational guide originally developed by Clay to observe five year olds. The instrument is useful in gathering information about young children's book handling knowledge and their concepts of the print in books. It reveals that Anna knows where the front of a book is, and that she knows English is read from left to right and from top to bottom down the page. She is able to identify certain letters and words, and knows what reading is. By changing voice tone and phrasing as she "reads," Anna also demonstrates that she knows that print can be turned into speech.

Doake (1981) notes that children who have books easily accessible, and who are read to, learn the special language of books, learn how to handle them, and learn how to read them. (See Doake's article in this volume.) Based on her research with five year old New Zealand school entrants, Clay (1977) declares that the most valuable preschool experiences are those which develop a love for books and the language patterns in them.

Implications

Most young children, like three year old Anna, are aware of print in their environment. When they use books for their own personal functions, they also learn about the connected print of books. Three and four year old children who are experienced with reading know: the functions of print, the use of context in reading, the use of print cues, and the handling and use of books. Observing what Anna and other children know about reading forces us to rethink current assumptions about beginning literacy at school. We can no longer believe that children come to school knowing nothing about written language. We need to observe to learn what they know and then build on the knowledge they bring to school. We must stop getting kindergartners and first graders "ready to read." Instead, we need to use techniques that continue to stimulate the processes of reading and writing that have already begun. Every teacher or interested parent can observe children's literacy learning by talking with children during reading and writing experiences. By probing after initial responses and asking, "How do you do that?" and "Why do you think so?" a glimpse is provided into the thinking and written language development of young children.

Observing Anna demonstrates that she, like other preschoolers, is forming generalizations about print in the unstructured naturalistic setting of her home and community. She is being read to and talked to about print in her home, in the supermarket, and in the parking lots of department stores. She is involved in reading and writing while playing school with her older sister and reading food labels at the breakfast table. She is learning to read and write by using print that is functional and meaningful to her. No one is intentionally *teaching* Anna to read.

In naturalistic settings, like at home and in the community, we can observe clues for organizing classrooms to expand on children's developing literacy. Teachers need to focus on meaningful ways to encourage children to continue developing their knowledge. School environments can be enriched with many story books to be read to children, for children to read to others, and for children to read to themselves. Play centers, such as a grocery store, provide opportunities for children to practice mathematical concepts, and to read grocery labels and writing bills and shopping lists, while enjoying themselves and interacting with other children. Functional print on calendars, weather charts, recipes, game instructions, song charts, classroom rule charts, and school lunch menus provide real-life reasons for reading. Writing in journals, answering pen pal letters, and authoring books are meaningful, even fun, activities with which children can succeed.

This case study of Anna was compiled by her mother, who is a teacher and researcher. Kidwatching is an important technique to pass along to parents who can be helped to realize that, even at a very young age, their children are interacting with print in the environment and in books and that these interactions are real reading events.

Parents also can be helped to see the importance of these events so they will continue to encourage their children's literacy development through nonstructured active interactions. This is possible because "seeing is believing." Parents who have been encouraged to be kidwatchers will see their children talking about print, reading their names or reading books to a baby brother, and will know their children can read. When kidwatching is cooperatively done by teachers and parents a team approach develops so that the child, the parents, and the teacher are all involved in extending the child's literacy development in a natural, functional manner.

References

Clay, M.M. *Reading: The Patterning of Complex Behavior.* London: Heinemann Educational Books, 1977.

Clay, M.M. *A Diagnostic Survey: Concepts about Print Test.* Auckland, New Zealand: Heinemann Educational Books, 1973.

Doake, D. "Book Experience and Emergent Reading in Preschool Children," doctoral dissertation, University of Alberta, 1981.

Ferreiro, E., & Teberosky, A. *Literacy before Schooling.* Translated by K. Goodman. Exeter, New Hampshire: Heinemann Educational Books, 1982.

Goodman, K.S., & Goodman, Y.M. "Learning to Read Is Natural," in L.B. Resnick & P.A. Weaver (Eds.), *Theory and Practice of Early Reading,* Volume 1. Hillsdale, New Jersey: Erlbaum, 1979.

Halliday, M.A.K. *Explorations in the Functions of Language.* New York: Elsevier North-Holland, 1977.

Harste, J.C., Burke, C.L., & Woodward, V.A. "Children's Language and World: Initial Encounters with Print," in J. Langer & M.T. Smith-Burke (Eds.), *Reader Meets Author: Bridging the Gap.* Newark, Delaware: International Reading Association, 1982.

Huey, E.B. *The Psychology and Pedagogy of Reading.* New York: Macmillan, 1908.

Smith, F. "Learning to Read by Reading," *Language Arts, 53* (March 1976), 297-299, 322.

Reading-Like Behavior: Its Role in Learning to Read

David B. Doake
Acadia University

Reading stories, nursery rhymes, and jingles to young children has always been regarded as a "good thing" to do. Studies of early readers have consistently recorded that one of the most important features of these children's experiences has been that they have been read to from very early in their lives and that they have grown up in book oriented homes (Teale, 1978). The specific contribution parents make to their children's reading development by reading to them on a regular basis has been described in some detail in an article by Teale (1981) and was the focus of an ethnographic study by Doake (1981).

A transcription of the interaction that occurs when children, books, and their parents come together, can never reveal the joy and enthusiasm that is present in the experience. The following one, however, does demonstrate what has come to be recognized (Doake, 1981; Holdaway, 1979) as a highly significant behavior that seems to emerge in children consistently, as a result of their being read and reread familiar stories by parents who encourage their participation in the reading. In this transcript, Adrienne, aged 18 months, is being read Bill Martin's *Brown Bear, Brown Bear* (1970) for the third time by her mother. Adrienne's contribution to the reading is underlined. The brackets indicate lines that were said simultaneously.

Text	*Adrienne and her mother*
Brown bear,	Brown (mother pauses) - bear,
Brown bear,	Brown bear,
What do you see?	What do you (pauses) - see?
I see a little bird	I see a liddle bird,
Looking at me.	Looking at (pauses) - me.
Redbird,	Redbird,

Redbird, What do you see?	Redbird, What - (A. pauses and reruns). Redbird, Redbird, O.K.! Wait, Wait. Let me - (mother laughs) Redbird, Redbird, What do you see?
I see a yellow duck	I see a (M. pauses) - I see a yellow duck - Wheeee!
Looking at me.	Looking at (M. pauses) - me.
Yellow duck, Yellow duck,	Red Yellow duck, Yellow Yellow duck Yellow - ck What (M. pauses) - do you seeee!

The story continued to be read in this shared manner, with Adrienne participating exuberantly and with supreme confidence. The pleasure that was being experienced by both mother and child was clearly evident in their voices.

This example reveals that even though the story has been read to Adrienne only twice before, she was already able to reproduce a considerable amount of it. Some of this reproduction was assisted by the mother pausing at certain points in the story where the language was highly predictable (e.g. What do you - see), but at times Adrienne was able to reproduce parts of the text unaided (e.g. I see a liddle bird; Redbird, Redbird,). She had no difficulty completing the lines with the appropriate words, demonstrating that she had already identified the rhyming patterns of the language and had developed control over its syntax. Perhaps even more significant, her fluent reconstruction of the "liddle bird" line showed she was prepared to experiment and approximate in her efforts to retrieve parts of the story for herself. Most important, her mother refrained from attempting to correct this high quality "miscue." Adrienne's enthusiasm for the task and her enjoyment of the rhyming nature of the language was apparent in her insertion of an extended "Wheeee!" and in her drawing out of "seeee!" at the end of the line.

The strategy that Adrienne was using to participate in the reading of her story was initially described by Clay (1972) as "talking like a book" (p. 28). More recently the term "reading-like behavior" (Doake, 1981; Holdaway, 1979) has come to be used, with Holdaway also referring to it as the process of "reenactment."

This article will examine reading-like behavior in some detail: why and how the behavior develops; its characteristics and its role in reading development; and, finally, the implications of reading-like behavior for classroom teachers in the teaching of reading. The examples come from audiotapes made over a seven month period in the book oriented homes of four preschool children as they "read" favorite books with their parents or the author.

Why Reading-Like Behavior Develops

One of the early references made to reading-like behavior can be found in Huey (1908) when he commented on the values of parents reading to their children and saw it as an outcome of children attempting to emulate the reading behavior of their parents as they read and reread familiar stories to them. It was Huey's view, that given plenty of books and someone who will read to them regularly, "...the child will keep it up [improvising the story] by the hour and the week and the month, and his natural learning [to read] is only a question of time" (p. 332).

More recently, researchers such as Gardner (1970), Bissex (1979), and Cohn (1981) have made references, as a result of their studies, to the apparent ease with which young children have been able to reproduce favorite stories after hearing them read repeatedly. It was not, however, until the publication of Holdaway's, *The Foundation of Literacy* (1979), that any detailed examination of its relationship and contribution to the processes involved in learning to read, became available. He correctly described it as a highly significant but "...neglected feature of early literacy" (p. 40) and saw it as a means by which children can begin to self-direct, self-monitor, and self-correct their own learning to read strategies.

By being read to regularly from very early in their lives, children soon begin to demonstrate their growing enjoyment of the experience. Their attention span increases, their repertoire of favorite stories expands, and they begin demanding that these be read over and over. Their avid listening to stories in the secure and close proximity of a loved parent becomes a deeply rewarding, warm, human experience for the children and their parents. Through the sounds and rhythms of the rich and inviting language, through the interesting and colorful illustrations, through the constant stimulation of their receptive imaginations, and through the reliving of these experiences in anticipatory ways, the children soon begin to develop very high expectations for books and reading.

Children begin to see books as sources of personal pleasure and derive from them a type of satisfaction they can secure in no other way. They quickly learn how to handle books in the physical sense and begin to use them in their independent play activities. The foundations have been laid for the continued development of a powerful inner drive for them to want to gain independent access to the experience they enjoy so much.

By being in the company of an adult who regularly provides an oral model of reading behavior and by constantly associating books and this behavior with pleasurable and desirable activity, young children are placed in a state of disequilibrium (Piaget, 1955) for they are sharing in an experience over which they have no control. According to Piaget, when children are placed in this situation, they will automatically strive to achieve a state of equilibrium by attempting to gain mastery over the experience, especially if it has been a pleasurable one for them.

At this stage of children's reading development, reading a story and telling a story are seen by them as identical processes. The way to achieve equilibration is to seek repetition of the experience through asking their parents to "Read it again." By following along as the story is read and reread they are able to learn to page and picture match its reproduction through reading-like behavior. When asked how she had learned to "read" one of her stories Gillian (5:4) pointed out, "Well, they [her parents] keep reading it to me and I keep following it." Of course the facility with which young children learn to retrieve their stories is aided considerably by their amazing ability to absorb great quantities of language with apparent ease (Stross, 1978). It is also assisted by their remarkable aptitude for internalizing control over a variety of story types through being read to (Applebee, 1979).

When a powerful inner drive to want to learn and a natural aptitude for learning are coupled with parents, who not only select highly predictable stories (Rhodes, 1981) to read to their children, but who read in a way that invites children to participate, then learning to reproduce stories through reading-like behavior becomes a relatively simple process. This learning becomes even easier when it is permitted to operate in a noncorrective, no-fail environment where the children are encouraged to experiment and approximate in their attempts to "read." When these conditions prevail, children have the opportunity to take the initiative and direct their own learning, a characteristic which Torrey (1979) found to be clearly evident in the behavior of early readers. They are also the conditions which govern the ease with which children master the intricacies of learning oral language.

Unfortunately, parents may see the reproducing of stories through reading-like behavior as a process of rote memorization and view it as harmful to their children's reading development. They may have become convinced by those who stridently proclaim the merits of an analytical approach to the task, that children have to begin to learn to read by "sounding out" the words. Since "sounding out" requires a careful, sequential inspection of each letter in each word being read, any method of learning which does not demand this is seen as harmful. As a result, parents may do what one mother in the Durkin (1966) study did when she found her son reproducing stories through reading-like behavior; simply stop reading to their children.

The appearance of reading-like behavior in children's activities can be facilitated or restricted by the nature of the experience they have with books. If children are being read to on a regular basis, are allowed to chose their favorite stories to be read over and over, and are invited to participate in the reading, using whatever strategies seem appropriate, reading-like behavior will almost certainly begin to appear in some form. Children's remarkable capacities to learn language and their abilities to absorb story structure make the process a relatively simple one. As Gillian (5.6) blithely explained, when asked how she had managed to learn so many of her stories in this way, "Well, I just do it!"

How Reading-Like Behavior Develops

From observations made of preschool children engaged in the activity of gaining independent access to their favorite stories (Bissex, 1979; Cohn, 1981; Doake, 1981; Holdaway, 1979), it is clear that meaning dominates their efforts to retrieve stories. From the very beginning, they do not seem to be concerned with reproducing the exact words. What they strive for is to have their version make sense. They simply "read" it, using their knowledge of its structure and of the patterns of written language to do so.

As stories are read and reread, children will frequently begin to participate in their reading in a variety of ways. If the story is a highly predictable one which has a rhyming, repetitive, and/or cumulative pattern to its language, they may begin to join in during the first reading. Usually, however, they will listen attentively during the first few readings, seemingly to engage in a silent rehearsal before attempting to overtly participate in the process of learning to reproduce the story themselves.

In my observations of children, four participatory strategies (Doake, 1981) seemed to emerge as children became increasingly familiar with certain stories. Sometimes they would use an indecipherable mumble in their attempts to read along with the reader. Gradually, their mumbling would become more intelligible as a story was reread, with certain key words (usually nouns and verbs) becoming recognizable first. "Mumble reading" would then emerge into "cooperative reading" where, as the label implies, the reading of the story became a shared activity. The participants' voices would be in unison, then one voice would be slightly ahead of the other, and sometimes one voice would be reproducing the story alone.

While reading with me, Gillian (5:7) used the strategy of "cooperative reading" to gain more control over the reproduction of *Bambi, Thumper, and Me* (1977). The relative positions of the words in the transcript reflect which voice was leading and when they were in unison (D = Doake, G = Gillian, T = Text):

D: "How would you like living alone in the forest
G: "How would you like living alone in the forest

D: with no one to talk to," she cried. (stops reading)
G: with no one to talk to," she cried. "Not only that,

G: June the 15th was my birthday and no one remembered.
T: but June 15 was my birthday and no one remembered.

G: So I'm just taking the gifts that she - that they
T: I was just taking the gifts that everyone

G: forgot to give me," she explained.
T: forgot to give me," explained the poor fairy.

Although Gillian departed from the specific words used in the text on four occasions (indicated by the underlined portions) her reconstructions did not depart from the meaning of the story and her "miscues" were all high quality ones. She commenced "reading" just behind me but soon caught up with my voice, took the lead, and then reproduced her version of the story independently. This was done with great fluency, using excellent intonation and appropriate phrasing. Throughout this cooperative reading of the 37 pages of the story her enthusiasm and involvement never flagged. She seemed quite determined to gain mastery over the reproduction of this story which had been "personalized" by the inclusion of her name, that of her brother, and those of their pets.

The most frequently observed strategy being used by the children was that of "completion reading." This occurred when the reader paused at various points in a story inviting the children to complete the sentence. The strategy was demonstrated by Adrienne in the example in the introduction to this chapter. Parents seem to know intuitively where to pause in their reading in order to invite their children to complete a sentence or a phrase. Sometimes, their pause might require a single word, but sometimes they might provide only the first word of a sentence or a phrase. When asked why they did this, the parents usually indicated that they enjoyed having the children participate in the reading in this way and that it seemed to make it more of a shared activity.

"Echo reading" is the fourth strategy. It occurs when children repeat a phrase or a sentence immediately after it is read to them. Sometimes it appears quite spontaneously. At other times the conditions for use of echo reading were deliberately organized by the child, as can be seen in the following transcript of Gillian (5:11) who, by this stage of her development as a reader, seemed to have worked out that the sooner she was able to reproduce a story through reading-like behavior, the sooner she would be able to read it, making use of the print on the page. The story, *Button Soup* (1975) was a recent arrival in the house from the Disney book club and she had asked me to read it to her. Rather than wait to be invited to participate in the reading, however, she immediately set up the rules for echo reading. She did the same thing with her mother when the story was read to her the third time.

G: But first you've got to read—Hmm—this, then I have to—and then when you've finished, I have to read after you.
D: I see. (Starts reading but reads too much for her to remember.) A long time ago a traveller named Daisy was riding a stage coach out west. Are you going to read after me?
G: Yes.
D: (Rereading) A long time ago a traveler named Daisy was riding a stage coach out west. Do you want to read that sentence or what?
G: Hmm. O.K. A long time ago—(her memory fails her)
D: a traveller named Daisy
G: a traveller named Daisy
D: was riding a stage coach out west.
G: was riding a stage coach out west.

The story continued to be read in this manner, although on many occasions, Gillian took the lead and reproduced sections without my reading them first. As soon as it was finished she requested that it be read again and continued to use the same procedure.

As books become an integral part of children's lives and their feelings for the sounds of language grow, the incentive to recreate this intensely pleasurable experience provides them with a powerful inner drive to participate in story reading in an increasing variety of ways.

The Characteristics of Reading-Like Behavior

Reading-like behavior as it occurs in young children, possesses two major characteristics. In its initial stage it is usually extremely fluent and expressive, and resembles the reading of a competent adult reader. As readers gain more experience and accuracy (at the word level) in retrieving their stories and become more aware of the role print plays in reading, their reading-like behavior begins to exhibit a more arhythmical quality. They commence trying to match what they are saying with what they are seeing on the page and start to point to the word with their voices and/or their fingers. Because of this, the reproduction of their stories becomes more deliberate and methodical, although the syntactic and semantic cohesion of the story are usually maintained.

Fluent reading-like behavior. Gillian's father, when asked for his observations concerning her use of reading-like behavior, remarked that:

> She'd listen. Then all of a sudden she would repeat the whole thing, or repeat large passages of it. She always paid very careful attention when you read it. I guess she is *absorbing the story*. (The writer's emphasis.)

This ability to "absorb the story," and then to recreate it making sophisticated use of written dialect "on the run," is the outstanding characteristic of fluent reading-like behavior.

Although transcripts cannot reveal children's confidence, energy, and sophisticated use of intonation, they do illustrate how meaning dominates their efforts. In the following examples, the parts of the texts that have been reconstructed differently by the children are underlined for the purposes of clarity.

Text	*Sean (2:11)*
<u>The next day was Sunday again.</u> <u>The caterpillar</u> ate through one <u>nice</u> green leaf, and then he <u>felt</u> <u>much</u> better. (Carle, 1969)	But Tuesday (self-corrects). On Tuesday he ate through one green leaf, and den he feeled better.

Text	*Jennifer (3:10)*
The three bears went into the bedroom.	And they went into their bedroom. And the Daddy said,
"Somebody has been lying in my bed!" said the Great Big Bear in his great big voice.	"Somebody was sleeping in my bed!" (Read in a very deep voice.)
"Somebody has been lying in my bed!" said the Middle-sized Bear in her middle-sized voice.	And the Mummy said, "Somebody was sleeping in my bed!" (Read in a "middle-sized" voice.)

Text	*Gillian (5:7)*
"My tail!" exclaimed Thumper. "What's wrong with my tail?" A look of surprise came over the little rabbit's face when he turned around and discovered it was gone.	"My tail!" exclaimed Thumper. "Why don't you like it?" A look of surprise came over the little rabbit's face. "My tail!" he said, "It's gone!"

These children have been able to absorb the meaning of their stories, engage in deep level processing, and generate meaningful written language "on the run." They were not simply imitating and remembering but creating and composing their version of the stories, using the written dialect and their knowledge of story structure to do so. Sean, for example, skillfully collapsed the two sentences into one, transforming "the caterpillar" into the pronoun "he." Since at this stage of his development, he had not learned to use the irregular form of the verb "felt," he simply applied the grammatical rule with which he was familiar, adding the past tense marker "ed" to the verb "feel" to maintain agreement. He even engaged in the process of self-correction, possibly anticipating that "But Tuesday" (every day of the week was Tuesday to Sean) would not fit with the remainder of the sentence.

Both Jennifer and Gillian brought their stories to life by the dramatic use of their voices. They demonstrated their ability to carry a story forward in terms of its plot and sequence and provided excellent examples of the kind of transformational activity young children engage in as they reconstruct their stories. Whereas Jennifer cleverly recomposed the way in which direct speech is used in her story, Gillian adroitly converted reported speech into direct speech. Her version

("My tail!" he said, "It's gone!") could even be considered to have improved the original ("...when he turned around and discovered it was gone") by providing more impact for the event.

By developing their ability to reproduce the meaning of stories at the automatic level of processing, using more complex patterns of written language to do so, young children are laying the foundations for becoming fluent readers. Their control over these nonvisual (Smith, 1978) sources of information serve them well as they engage in the process of predicting what is coming next on the page. Now, all that is left for them to do is to develop control over the visual information (Smith, 1978), the print on the pages of their story. The next stage of development of reading-like behavior provides them with the opportunity to do so.

Arhythmic reading-like behavior. The fluent, and eventually accurate reproduction of their stories, at times literally with their eyes closed, changes to a reproduction where the children begin to attend to cues in the print as well as those available from their language and meaning sources. In order for this to take place a number of things have to happen.

As parents read to children, they point to the print on occasions. They provide them with opportunities to experiment with learning to write. In addition, children are constantly exposed to written language being used in highly functional ways in the environment (Harste, Burke, & Woodward, 1981; also see Haussler's article in this volume). Through these experiences, children become increasingly aware of print, some of the conventions which regulate its production, and some of the purposes it serves. The principles of directionality, for example, become established and understandings concerning the concepts of a "word" and a "letter" start to emerge. Children begin to realize that the print on the pages of their books plays an important role in the process of reading. They may point to certain words and ask "What does this say?" or ask the reader where he or she is reading. With this increasing awareness of print and of its relationship to reading, their fluent reading-like behavior takes on a more arhythmical quality. They begin to voice and/or finger point as they reproduce their most favourite stories.

Once children try to match what they are saying with what they are seeing, the problem of achieving an exact match appears. Sometimes it occurs because they do not reproduce the story accurately at the word level, but usually it is the result of the line of print containing multisyllabic words. Because they are enunciating the words precisely, children treat each syllable as a separate word and consequently, run out of words to point to in a line of print.

In the following transcript, Gillian (5:7), who was just beginning to use arhymthmic reading-like behavior a great deal, ran into a multisyllabic word problem (T = Text, P = Pointing, G = Gillian).

T: I was sitting in a tankard one day
P: × × × ×
G: I-was -sit - ting - No! (Tries again)

T: I was sitting in a tankard one day
P: × × × ×× × ×
G: I-was-sitting-in-a - tan - kard-one-

T: tankard one day
P: × × × ×
G: (Tries again) tan - kard-one-day

T: Just biding my time.
P: (Stopped finger pointing and pointed with her voice)
G: Just-passing-my-time.

Gillian overcame the problem caused by her syllabicating "sitting" probably by realizing that it was one word or by actually seeing that "ting" could not be "in." By this stage, she had a repertoire of sound-to-symbol relationships, and was also able to recognize some words at sight, and "in" was one of them. She ran into more difficulty, however, with "tankard" which she syllabicated very carefully, pointing to "one" when she said "kard." At that stage, she realized that she had two more words to say but only one to point to. She took a rerun, but again treated "tankard" as two words. This time she continued to the end of the line and simply pointed to the word "day" twice to compensate for her error in matching. Gillian then abandoned finger pointing, later giving as her reason, "'Cos when I point, I get all mixed up." She did, however, continue to voice point but, after another line and a half, switched to fluent reading-like behavior, reconstructing her version of the story as usual. She seemed to set out to overcome the problem of exact matching over the next few months through engaging in a great deal of self-directed practice, on an almost daily basis, at retrieving familiar stories for herself.

Four months later, Gillian (5:11) indicated that she wished to try to continue reading a story on her own, with the comment, "I think I can read it now" and proceeded to do so:

Text	*Gillian*
"You won't find any food around her," he said.	(Reading fluently) "You won't find any good—No!—That's food." (Reruns, this time voice pointing) "You - won't - find - any - food - around - h - here," he said.
He tried to hide some dirty dishes.	He tried to hide some dirty dishes. (Reruns, this time voice pointing for part of the sentence) He - tried - to - hide - some dirty dishes.

It seems probable even though she read the first line fluently, Gillian was still looking at the print. In the process of doing this, her eyes moved ahead of her voice and she realized that what she was saying did not match what she was seeing (No—That's food). As a result, she reverted to arhythmic reading so that she could eye-ear-voice match more accurately. For the next sentence she returned to fluent reading but, in order to run a check on her accuracy at the word level, she reread, this time voice pointing until she was satisfied that she had been right the first time and finished up reading fluently again.

One of the final transcripts recorded with Gillian (5:11) was her attempt at reading Sendak's *Where the Wild Things Are* (1963) after it had been read to her only three times. The following brief excerpt demonstrates how far this little girl had come in her efforts to master the process of reading for herself:

Text	*Gillian*
So he was sent	So Max went—(self-corrects partly) So he went
to bed without eating anything.	to bed without eating anything.

That very night in Max's room a forest grew.	That night—(Points to "very" and asks "What does that say?" Before she can be told she rereads, self-corrects and begins voice pointing.) That - very - night - a - jungle - (self-corrects) a - forest - grew. (When asked how she knew that the word was not "jungle" she pointed to the "f" in "forest" and said, "That's not 'juh.' It's a 'fuh'.")

In a very real sense, Gillian was now using the strategies employed by competent adult readers, despite the fact that her graphophonic knowledge was still not fully developed. Her reading was intonationally alive. She read with great fluency, except when she reverted to arhythmic reading in order to run a visual check on her predictions. She was spontaneously providing herself with the opportunity to establish an understanding, at the intuitive level at least, that the easiest way to read is to combine the use of the nonvisual and the visual cueing systems available to her. She used each of these systems as much or as little as she needed to, in order to engage in the process of reading. Significantly, she was in control of her own learning, monitoring her own performance, and self-correcting when she felt that it was necessary. She was, in fact, using all the strategies that Smith (1978) believes children should use in order to learn to read.

> A child can only learn to read by reading. Only by reading can a child test his hypothesis about the nature of the reading process, establish distinctive feature sets for words, learn to identify words and meanings with a minimum of visual information, and discover how not to overload the brain's information-processing capacity and avoid bottlenecks of memory. (p. 185)

Implications for Teachers

Although all of the data presented and discussed in this chapter resulted from observing how preschool children can and do go about the task of learning to read as an outcome of their shared book experiences in their homes, there are some important implications which emerge for teachers.

First, children can begin to learn to read as soon as they are read to. The commonly held assumption that learning to read is a secondary or derived language learning process, dependent on some predetermined level of competence in the use of oral language, must be questioned. There is no such thing as a period of "reading readiness" for children. Learning to listen to stories, learning to participate in their reproduction, and learning to retrieve them through reading-like behavior, are all legitimate, entirely appropriate, and vitally important learning to read strategies. As children engage in using these strategies, they are not going through a period of readiness to learn to read. They are actively involved in the process of learning to read.

Second, teachers need to acknowledge fully the crucial importance of children's home experience with books. Not only should they continue to encourage parents to read to their children, but they need to explain why, how, and what they should be reading to them. The characteristics of reading-like behavior can be described and preferably demonstrated to the parents, and its potential contribution to their children's reading development made clear. Stress should be placed on parents' *inviting* their children's participation in shared reading activities but never *demanding* it, encouraging experimentation and approximation, but not requiring accuracy when the children attempt to reproduce their favourite stories for themselves.

Third, young children can begin to learn to read by being immersed in rich and memorable written language. Unfortunately, the language in the current crop of basal readers in widespread use in schools has been drained of all its life, colour, and predictability. The probability that children will want to reread these stories again and again would seem to be remote. There is an urgent need for all children to be surrounded with a plentiful supply of children's books of proven quality. Particularly, there should be available in every classroom, a library of predictable books (Rhodes, 1979), the language and story structure of which, children can rapidly gain control over because of their rhyming, repetitive, and cumulative patterns. Nowhere is this need greater than with those children who, throughout their preschool years, have never enjoyed the pleasures of being read to on a regular basis by their parents. To expect these children to form powerful inner drives to want to learn to read by doing aimless and confusing "reading readiness" workbook exercises, followed by trying to learn to read "stories" that are devoid of any interest or imaginative force in their use of language, is expecting the impossible.

Fourth, teachers in the kindergarten and primary grades can explore ways to bring the features of the shared book experiences of the home into their classrooms. Daily reading of a variety of "the best" picture books should occur in large and small group situations. If some children have come from non-book-oriented-homes, they almost certainly will need to be read to individually. This can be done by children from higher grades or by parents or other selected adults coming into the classroom for this purpose. Requests for the rereading of favourite stories should be complied with. Since it is not possible, when reading to groups, for all children to see the print in the books clearly, a selection of the most popular stories should be made into "big books" so that the print and the illustrations are easily visible for the children. It was Holdaway (1979) and a group of innovative teachers in New Zealand who first experimented very successfully with bringing the bedtime story concept into the classroom through using enlarged books in order that all children share both visually and vocally in their reading. That this success was achieved with innercity children, many of them learning English as a second language, and with whom many other methods of teaching reading had failed, makes that experiment all the more significant.

"Big Books" should be read with all the enthusiasm and expression that the teacher can muster. As they are read and reread, the active, unison participation of the children is encouraged. To assist the development of their attention to print and in the control of directional and matching skills in the children, the teacher points to the print as it is read, being careful not to destroy the cohesion of the story. In addition, at least one listening post should be available in the classroom. Here the children, with multiple small book copies of the "big book," can follow along and participate in the reading as a recording is played on an audiotape. Other opportunities also need to be given to them to reread their favourite stories independently or with their peers. The development of reading-like behavior and its use by children to take control of their own learning to read strategies is almost assured.

Fifth, shared book experiences of the type outlined should be associated with an active program of "learning to write by writing" where the same principles of experimentation and approximation prevail. Other activities might include chanting and singing in unison with the words always recorded in large print for all to see, dramatizing and illustrating favourite stories and occasionally putting stories to music. In such a program, teachers will find their role changing from that of an instructor who constantly assumes responsibility for children's learning by controlling it and correcting it, to that of a facilitator who provides children with the opportunity to take responsibility for their own learning in stimulating and enjoyable ways.

The specific details of such a whole language literacy learning program are described in Holdaway's (1979) book, *The Foundations of Literacy*. The program was also introduced successfully into a grade one classroom in Canada in 1978 (Doake, 1980; Hennigar-Shuh, 1980) and is now being used widely in schools across the country.

Learning to read by reading can become a reality in our classrooms, provided we supply the conditions for such learning to take place. We have to restore our faith in children as self-directed learners. As Holdaway (1979) suggests, our instruction should be

> emulative and invitational rather than prescriptive. It will support and not supplant the learning system of each learner, and will express itself in the respect and trust for the divergent ways in which children teach themselves the task they wish to master. (p. 202)

The basics that we should be returning to are the basics that children and parents have been using the world over in learning to communicate with each other.

References

Applebee, A.N. "Children and Stories: Learning the Rules of the Game," *Language Arts, 56* (September 1979), 641-646.

Bissex, G.L. "Learning to Write and Learning to Read: A Case Study," doctoral dissertation, Harvard University, 1979.

Carle, E. *The Very Hungry Caterpillar*. Cleveland, Ohio: Collins World, 1969.

Clay, M.M. *Reading: The Patterning of Complex Behavior*. Auckland: Heinemann Educational Books, 1972.

Cohn, M. "Observations of Learning to Read," *Language Arts, 58* (May 1981), 549-556.

Doake, D.B. "Report on the Shared Book Experience Approach to Learning to Read," unpublished paper, School of Education, Acadia University, 1980.

Doake, D.B. "Book Experience and Emergent Reading Behavior in Preschool Children," doctoral dissertation, University of Alberta, 1981.

Durkin, D. *Children Who Read Early: Two Longitudinal Studies*. New York: Teachers College Press, 1966.

Gardner, K. "Early Reading Skills," in K. Gardner (Ed.), *Reading Skills: Theory and Practice*. London: Ward Lock, 1970.

Harste, J.C., Burke, C.L., & Woodward, V.A. *Children, Their Language and World: Initial Encounters with Print*. Bloomington, Indiana: Language Education Department, Indiana University, 1981.

Hennigar-Shuh, J. "The Shared Book Experience," *Journal of Education, 6* (1980), 1-5.

Holdaway, D. *The Foundations of Literacy*. Sydney: Ashton Scholastic, 1979. (Distributed by Heinemann Educational Books.)

Huey, E.B. *The Psychology and Pedagogy of Reading*. New York: Macmillan, 1908.

Martin, B. *Brown Bear, Brown Bear*. New York: Holt, Rinehart & Winston, 1970.

Piaget, J. *The Language and Thought of the Child*. New York: Meridan Books, 1955.

Rhodes, L.K. "I Can Read! Predictable Books as Resources for Reading and Writing Instruction," *Reading Teacher, 34* (February 1981), 511-518.

Sendak, M. *Where the Wild Things Are*. New York: Harper & Row, 1963.

Smith, F. *Understanding Reading*, second edition. New York: Holt, Rinehart & Winston, 1978.

Stross, B. "Perspectives: Language Acquisition and Teaching," *Language Arts, 55* (September 1978), 749-755.

Teale, W.H. "Positive Environments for Learning to Read: What Studies of Early Readers Tell Us," *Language Arts, 55* (November/December 1978), 922-932.

Teale, W.H. "Parents Reading to Their Children: What We Know and What We Need to Know," *Language Arts, 58* (November/December 1981), 902-912.

Torrey, J.W. "Reading that Comes Naturally: The Early Reader," in G.T. Waller & G.E. MacKinnon (Eds.), *Reading Research: Advances in Theory and Practice.* New York: Academic Press, 1979.

Walt Disney Productions. *Bambi, Thumper, & Me.* Burbank, California: Me-Books Publishing Company, 1977.

Walt Disney Productions. *Button Soup.* New York: Random House, 1975.

Watching Young Writers

Glenda L. Bissex
Norwich University

When a child who is just beginning to talk refers to water as "wa-wa," parents are thrilled that the child has successfully identified the name with the thing and come close enough to adult pronunciation to be understood. When a child who is beginning to write puts down DRAKTHENS for "directions," adults see an error and may worry that the child will form a wrong habit if it is not corrected. The focus is on what the child does not yet know (the conventional spelling) rather than on the knowledge the child has demonstrated of the alphabetic principle of our writing system, of specific sound-letter relationships, and of letter forms and sequencing.

Adults seem to have faith that children will develop accuracy in speech without constant corrections—how many ten year olds do you know who still say "wa-wa"?—but we respond differently to beginning writers (and readers). Because an error is in writing, it may appear permanent and thus in need of immediate erasure and correction lest it become established. Yet the child who wrote DRAKTHENS did not regard that spelling as permanent, for a month later the child wrote DRAKSHINS, two years after that DIRECKSHONS, and in another year spelled the word conventionally. Although the child had correctly copied several *-tion* words two years before mastering "directions," the correct spelling had not made sense in terms of what the child understood about sound-spelling relationships and so he had not learned from this instruction.

Is learning to write such a different process from learning to speak that we must take a different approach to it, that we can have faith children will learn to speak correctly yet believe they need constant instruction and correction in order to learn to write? How much of the difference lies in the different conditions under which speaking and writing have generally been learned, that is, the home and school environments? At home, children hear speech, are spoken to and practice speaking frequently; they have adult models, functional as well as emotional motivation to learn, and a tutorial relationship with at least one accomplished speaker of the language. If we enlarge the notion of "instruction" to include not only explicit teaching but also the availability of information in the children's environment and the presence of reasons for them to engage with it, then we see that children are indeed "taught" to speak at home. We see also that children may learn to write in school through means other than formal instruction: by writing every day and for reasons that are real to the child, by being written to, by seeing writing and writers, by asking questions and receiving wanted information about print.

Studies of child language development show us that children do not learn merely by imitation since they use constructions and forms of words that are not spoken around them. For example, after children become aware of plural and past tense endings, they tend to regularize all plurals and past tenses: "mouses," "goed" or even "wented." Children certainly have not been taught to do this, but have overgeneralized rules learned from their observations of the speech around them and through their own reasoning. Children do not regard these learnings as permanent. Continuing to listen critically to the language around them, they find they have to revise such "rules," and these forms drop out of their speech. Like little scientists, they are constantly making and testing hypotheses about language, among other things.

Learning about Writing

Children in a literate society start learning about written language long before they enter school. They learn from television, they learn from cereal boxes and toothpaste tubes, they learn from road signs—they learn from the print in their environment and from the adults they see using print. Before they can write conventionally, they write in their own ways but with the knowledge that writing communicates meanings and words, as these early recollections from young adults suggest:

> I remember, before school years, doing a lot of scribbling. Although this scribbling meant nothing to my family, I can recall being able to read the whole thing. As the family giggled and thought how "cute" it was, I would sit in my chair and read my scribbles.

> Since I can remember, I wrote. I remember taking crayons and writing on the walls and my mother would yell at me because it was scribbling. But wouldn't it be funny if I wrote a word—she probably wouldn't have yelled at me then. I really remember wanting to express with my pencil, pen, or whatever, but I couldn't; no one understood.

From looking closely at scribbles and scribblers, Harste, Burke, and Woodward (1981) concluded that:

> Children as young as three, regardless of race or socioeconomic status, differentiated writing from drawing. . . .Generally the children's art was characterized as being global, centralized and connected. Children, prior to the product being particularly representational to the adult eye, usually drew a large figure in the center of the page having a unity or cohesiveness of lines converging about this point. Their writing, on the other hand, was typically linear, spaced, and located off center. (pp. 127-128)

When children first write, Ferreiro's studies (1982) of three to six year olds show us, they will represent an object by a single letter-like shape. Then, moving closer to our writing system, they will use a combination of several varied shapes to represent a name. For some time, the number of letter-like forms required for a word corresponds to the size or quantity of the object named: more letters for "horse" than "chicken" and more for "carrots" than "carrot." Only after trying out this theory do children discover the correspondence between writing and speech, first reasoning that letters represent syllables and, finally, sounds. Children puzzle over the relationship between print and meaning or speech before schooling compels them to do so, and their understanding evolves through a series of hypotheses about that relationship. Many of the theories they try out and the conventions they invent (such as syllabic writing, dots to separate words, and writing from left to right) are or were used in other written language systems (Bissex, 1980; Harste, Burke & Woodward, 1981). Children do not leap from illiteracy to an understanding that our writing system is alphabetic when they receive their first phonics lesson.

> Children go a long and complicated way before discovering that writing surrounding them is alphabetic in nature. They explore other hypotheses, some of them not being adequate for the alphabetical system, although they would be appropriate for other systems of writing.
>
> The writing that precedes the alphabetical period is far from unstructured: It provides evidence of children's efforts in the search for an understanding of the laws of the system. (Ferreiro, 1982, p. 56)

Once children have grasped the alphabetic principle (that our writing system is based on letters representing speech sounds) and know the names of at least some letters, they invent their own systematic spellings—a further stage in their active search for the laws of our writing system. Read (1971) has shown us how these young spellers reason. Consider how the spelling FEGR (finger) might have been invented. Without benefit of phonics lessons, this young writer could have abstracted the sounds *f* and *r* from the letter names "*F*" and "*R*": *F*EG*R*. The *G* whose sound cannot be derived from its letter name, was probably supplied by an adult in response to the child's question about it. The nasal (*n*) before a consonant is typically not represented by inventive spellers because the nasal sound cannot be heard or felt in the mouth as a separate segment. The jaw and tongue remain in one position for *-ng*. Since the *e* in "finger" cannot be heard or felt as separate from the *r*, it is not represented by children who are spelling by ear and by mouth, using everything they know about the spoken language they have already mastered in order to figure out written language. Many very young spellers, Read found, represent short *i* with the letter *E*, as in FEGR. Why? Either because the place of articulation in the mouth for "ih" and "ee" are closely related, or because the letter name "E," when pronounced slowly ("ih-ee"), starts with short *i*. As well as abstracting sounds from letter names, inventive spellers use letters to stand for letter names, as in D*A* (day) and AGR*E* (angry).

In sum, children use their knowledge of speech sounds and of the alphabet, combined with some information requested from adults, to devise a spelling system. Read stresses the systematic nature of invented spellings; children's judgments about how to represent sounds are consistent and rule-governed and, as subsequent research has confirmed, amazingly uniform across the different groups of children studied. Yet this immature system is not fixed but is in a constant state of reevaluation and change, moving increasingly toward more complete and conventional spellings.

Knowing that writing has meaning and functions, understanding the alphabetic principle of our writing system, and establishing rules for representing speech sounds are not all a child must have accomplished in order to write. Clay (1975) reveals the many graphic and spatial principles children master as they move into writing. They learn that writing is linear and that in our system it goes from left to right and top to bottom of a page. Before children represent speech sounds in their writing, they learn not only about directionality and the use of space but about patterns, for example, the "generating principle"—that letters recur in variable patterns—so that with knowledge of only a few letter shapes a child can produce strings of print that resemble conventional writing.

Observing What Children Have Learned about Writing

Children spend several years learning about print *before they enter first grade.* Since the start of schooling marks only the beginning of formal instruction in writing, not the beginning of children's learning about written language, what does this mean for first grade teachers? It means that teachers need to find out right away what children *already know* about written language in order to tell where effective instruction can start. By the end of the year, if writing folders are kept for each child with pieces accurately dated, his or her progress will be clearly visible.

This is how one first grade teacher, Mary Ellen Giacobbe (1981), found out what her children could do as writers. Each day during the first week of school she introduced five or six children to journals (books containing 40 pages of unlined 9″ x 12″ paper for them to write in). These children worked at the writing table while the others were assigned elsewhere in the classroom.

> I circulated around the classroom observing and talking with the children. "Tell me about your building."..."Why do you think the sand goes through this strainer faster than through that strainer?"..."How many cubes do you think it will take to fit across the top of the desk?"
>
> Someone tugged at my sleeve and I turned to see Mark standing by my side with his journal. "Tell me about your drawing, Mark," I said.
>
> He pointed to each part of the drawing and said, "This is the ocean and this is a sailboat and this is the anchor. These are clouds."
>
> He had written BD for boat and KLD for cloud. (p. 99)

If Giacobbe had not asked Mark about his drawing, she might not have understood his writing. She watched Ellen write: THE TRCE WAS TACAN A WEC (The turkey was taking a walk).

> She read it to herself, crossed out the *T* in *Tacan*, changed it to a *w* and on top of a *wec*, she wrote *D the hall*. Her message now read: THE TRCE WAS WACAN D THE HALL (The turkey was walking down the hill). Already Ellen knew that she could change her message so that it said exactly what she wanted it to say. She was rereading and revising.
>
> My attention was drawn to the tap, tap, tapping of the black marker on David's page as he was creating a snowstorm. He wrote: I SO SO (I saw

> snow). David said, "This is a big snowstorm. A real blizzard." As he touched each word, he read "I saw snow."
>
> I asked David, "What do you notice about the words *saw* and *snow*?" He replied, "They both begin with the same sound." (p. 100)

Giacobbe found out that David understood what a written word was and already knew some phonics.

> As the blank pages in their journals came alive with drawings and words telling of their experiences, I could see these children had entered school ready to engage in the active process of writing. They were writing their own workbooks. They were showing me what they knew as well as what they needed to know. There were no errors to be red penciled. Just information showing me what the next step of instruction should be. (pp. 100-101)

Other teachers ask the whole class to write at the same time, using single sheets of paper, while the teachers circulate around the room to observe how the children are writing: Are they sounding out spellings? Which children are not yet using letters to represent sounds but rather are showing a more visual knowledge of print by writing strings of letters or other symbols? Are children writing from left to right and from top to bottom of the paper? Are children asking for and giving one another information about spellings or letter formations? Are some children able to read back what they have written? (In the early phase of invented spelling it is not unusual for children to have difficulty reading their writing.) Do some writers make self-corrections and revisions as they work? Have children already memorized the spellings of some words? Did someone at home teach those spellings, the teacher might inquire, or were the spellings picked up from reading? The teachers need not instruct at the beginning; they are essentially finding out information about their children's learning by observation, listening, and questioning.

Teachers will learn much about their students' concerns and interests as they draw and write if children generally choose their own topics rather than respond to assigned topics. First graders usually have no trouble taking this initiative, especially if they start out by drawing. As they share their writings, in small groups or as a class, they gather more ideas. From observing children writing and from talking with them about what they write, teachers will come to know their students' lives as well as their skills. Teachers will find that ground, between their own knowledge and their students' knowledge, between their own lives and their students' lives, where they can meet those children and thus truly teach.

When teachers ask children to show what they know, teachers are faced with more diverse responses than are revealed through filling in worksheets or following assignments. Having evidence of how children are not the same at the beginning of school, teachers will not expect them to be at the same, standardized place in their writing development by the end of the year. They will expect children to grow and learn, and will see their essential role as being responsible for that *learning* rather than for *teaching*, in the sense of covering a curriculum and correcting errors.

Observing Development in Writing

In another first grade room, near the end of the year, we could see these two examples of writing:

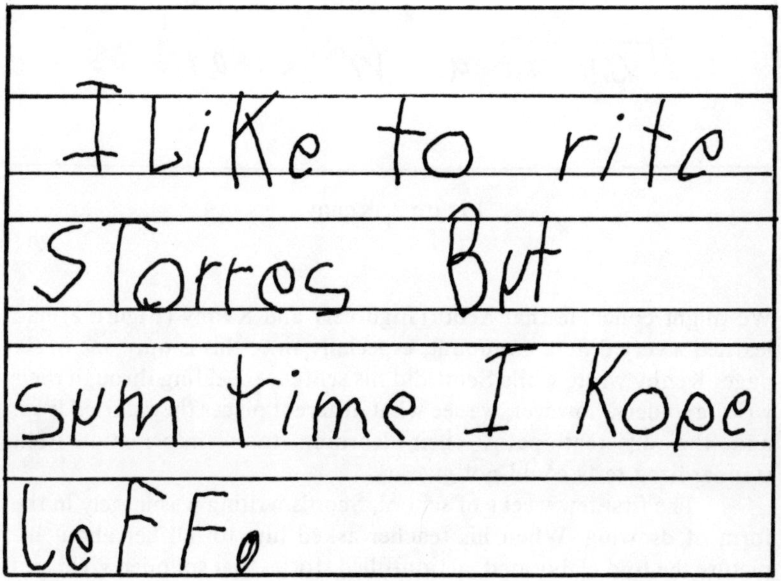

Figure 1. Scott.

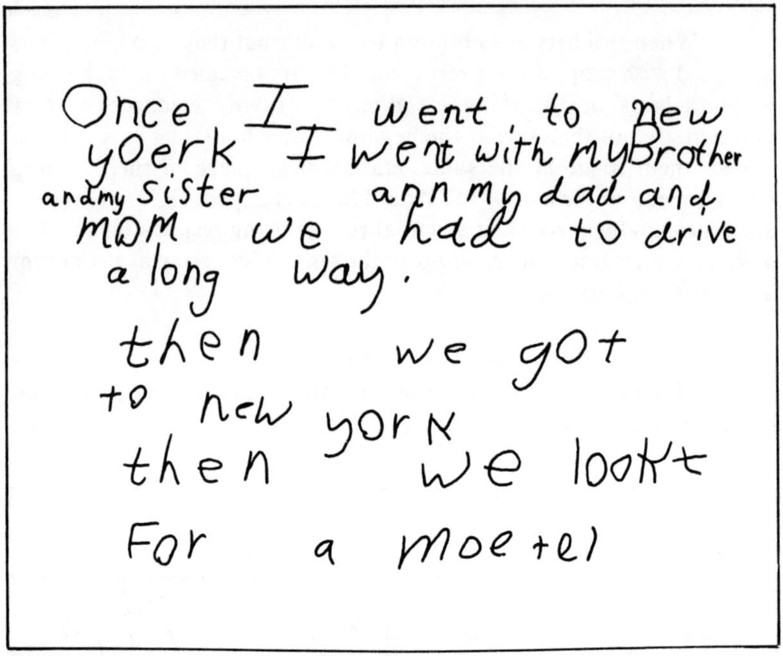

Figure 2. Kenny.

We might conclude that Scott (Figure 1) and Kenny (Figure 2) had learned a very different amount, especially since this is only one of six pages Kenny wrote while Scott did his sentence. Leafing through their writing folders, however, we see what different places they started from and the different paths their learning took—information that standardized tests could not give us.

The first few weeks of school, Scott's writing was largely in the form of drawing. When his teacher asked him to tell her about his picture, he told elaborated, action-filled stories that sounded vivid and exciting but appeared somewhat incoherent when written down, such as this one from the second day of school: "The rocket was starting to take off and the people got in. They saw treasure on the ground. The people jumped out. The rocket was starting to blow up." The only writing on his drawing of the rocket (see Figure 3) was his name, copied from a placard on his desk, and the date, copied from the blackboard.

Figure 3.

The first week of school, Kenny, drew a detailed picture of three pigs standing in front of three houses and the big bad wolf approaching. He wrote (not copied) his name and APBBW (*a p*ig, a *b*ig *b*ad *w*olf). "A pig made a house out of straw and then a big bad wolf came," was what he said about his writing. The influence of children's literature on both the content and form of Kenny's writing was clear from the start. Many of his pieces the first weeks of school began "Once upon a time. . . ."

Scott, two weeks after his rocket drawing, made a house with a door and a window and a face in the window—a sort of revised rocket (see Figure 4). Starting with the bottom line and working upward when he ran out of space, he wrote two strings of letters, many of them reversed. When asked about his piece, Scott told this story:

> It was getting sunny and he was thinking about his old friend named Puff the Magic Dragon. He wished he was here. He was watching if he would come. He writed a letter to him. He wanted to sail away with him. Finally he got there. Puff the Magic Dragon says go home because he had the sneezes. It was so sad that he comed back that boy because the big man poured some soup to make the sneezes go away.

Figure 4.

Although Scott's teacher worked with him on identifying and writing letters to represent a few of the sounds in his dictated stories, he did not move readily into invented spelling but rather seemed to need more practice with letter forms first. Two months later, he wrote a solid page of letter strings (Figure 5) and "read" what he had written: "This is Sheldon. He is a big dog and he jumps on the man. He goes to bed and he sleeps for one hour and a half and I got a pony with him. My dog hunts for rabbits." While his letters did not seem to correspond to sounds, the amount he had written was much more in proportion to the amount he told.

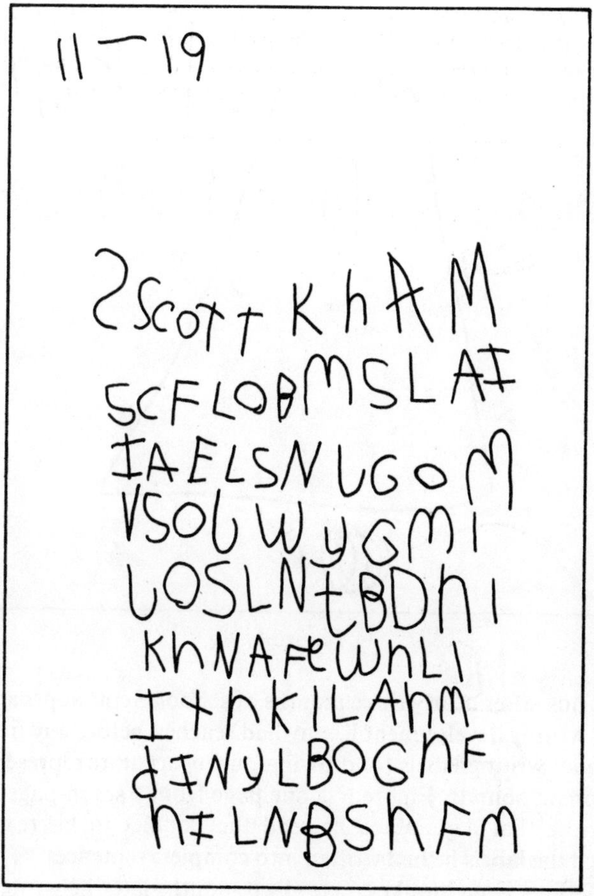

Figure 5.

Ten days later, he invented his own phonetic spellings, as for "rocket" in Figure 6, although he was still writing strings of letters that did not represent sounds.

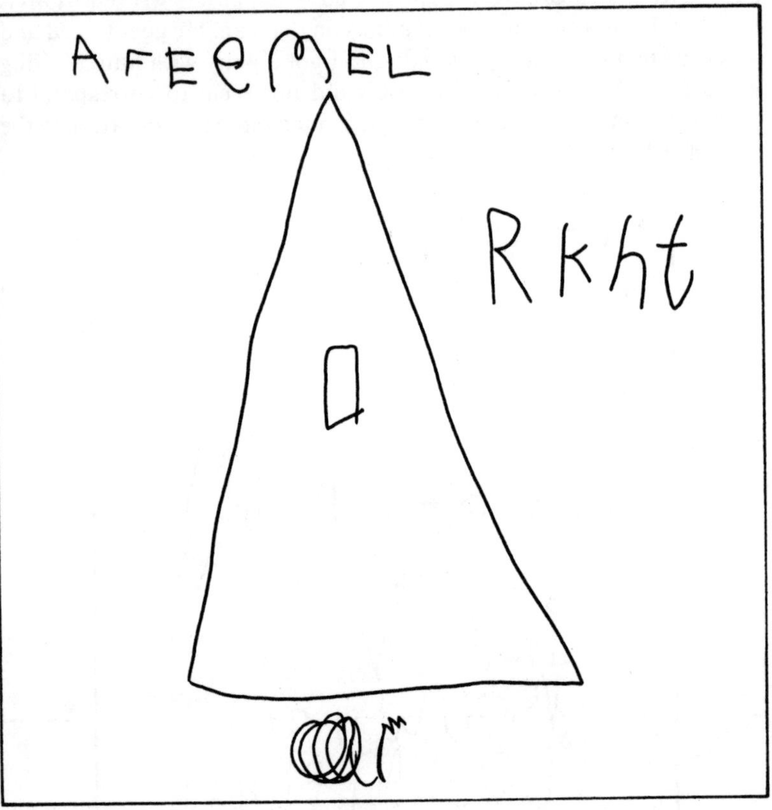

Figure 6.

Thus, after nearly three months of school, Scott approached the point of writing development Kenny had reached before any first grade instruction: writing labels for drawings, using accurate representations of consonant sounds. Figure 6 is one page from a seven-page booklet Scott wrote that day. When he read the booklet to his teacher, he expanded the labels he had written into complete sentences: "This is my rocket," "This is my donkey," etc. Two months later he wrote out the full statement behind the labels, as in Figure 7: "This is my little house."

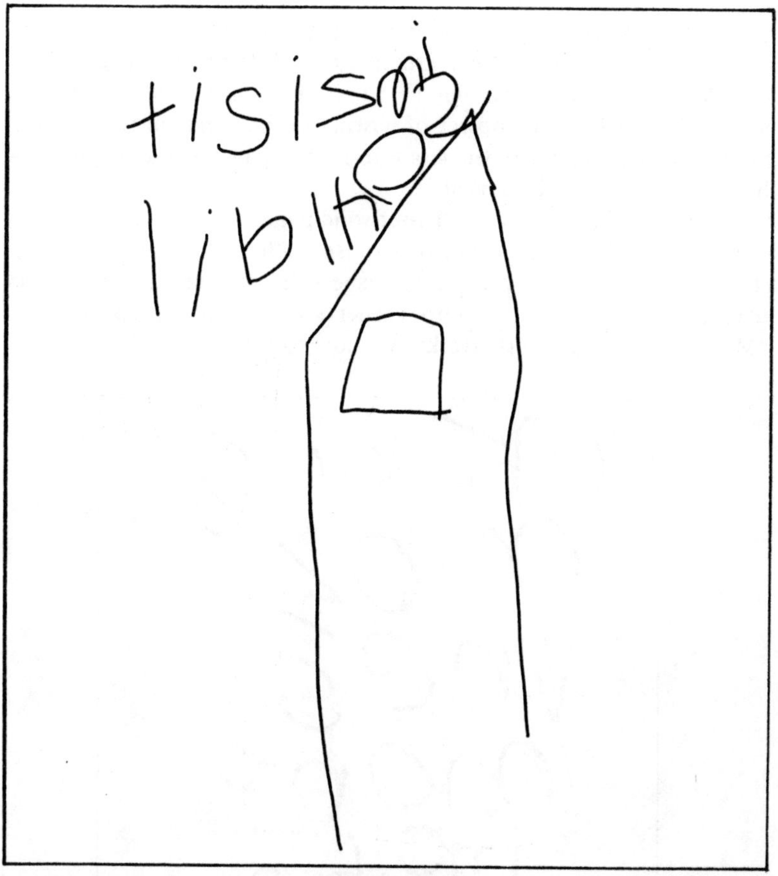

Figure 7.

What had happened to Scott's imaginative tales and vivid language? Scott, like some other storytellers in his classroom, had limited his language to what he could write. When they started spelling inventively, and even shortly before—as if in anticipation of the limits of their own ability to represent language in print—they reduced their stories to simple, repetitive sentence patterns, such as "This is. . ." and "I see. . . ." These formulas could be kept easily in mind while the children labored to sound out spellings and recall correct letter shapes. Scott's early action narratives tumbled out so fast even an adult writer could barely keep up transcribing them. Just as children start reading at a level far below the level of oral language they comprehend, children start writing at a level far below the language of their own speech. Transcriptions by the teacher preserve the vitality and zany charm of children's oral stories, and may help to develop basic reading concepts and skills, but keep the power of writing in the hands of the teacher. Scott's written language was less interesting than his oral language—but he had done it all himself!

In February Scott wrote four solid pages of print—no drawings at all. Looking at one page of this unusually long story about his dog (Figure 8), we can see what, in retrospect, he was rehearsing with his letter strings almost three months earlier (see Figure 5). This page reads: "My dog was very smart. He knows how to roll over."

Figure 8.

Scott's last first grade writings (see Figure 1) and one of his earliest (see Figure 3) show the full course of writing development. It no longer appears that he has learned little about writing during first grade.

Scott was not pushed to copy writing beyond what he could produce, nor was he removed from his writing classroom to do directionality and readiness exercises. His teacher gave him time and faith and encouragement to continue to learn from his own writing. And he did. "Children have shown to us that they need to reconstruct the written system in order to make it their own. Let us allow them the time and the opportunities for such a tremendous task" (Ferreiro, 1982, p. 56).

Conclusion

When we appreciate the depth of children's understanding—how they start from the most fundamental and difficult questions about literacy, when we understand how much they need to know and do manage to learn beyond what is in our textbooks and worksheets and lesson plans, we become more aware of the many ways in which children learn about writing. We are then led to appreciate the many ways in which we teach: For instance, by allowing children space to ask their own questions, to guide their own learning, and to inform us of what they need to be taught. We teach by surrounding children with a richly literate environment which evokes their questions about print and draws them toward using print. We teach by confirming what children know—the knowledge they can grow on—as well as by supplying new information.

Children come to see themselves as they are seen by others. Do we see our students as learners or as mistake-makers? Do we see ourselves as nurturers of growth or as collectors of errors—as gardeners or as animated red pencils? We teach by what we see as well as by what we say.

References

Bissex, G. *GNYS AT WRK: A Child Learns to Write and Read.* Cambridge, Massachusetts: Harvard University Press, 1980.

Clay, M. *What Did I Write?* Auckland, New Zealand: Heinemann Educational Books, 1975.

Ferreiro, E. "The Relationship between Oral and Written Language: The Children's Viewpoints," in Y. Goodman, M. Haussler, & D. Strickland (Eds.), *Oral and Written Language Development Research: Impact on the Schools.* Urbana, Illinois: National Council of Teachers of English, 1982.

Giacobbe, M.E. "Who Says that Children Can't Write the First Week?" in R.D. Walshe (Ed.), *Donald Graves in Australia: "Children Want to Write. . . ."* Rozelle,

Australia: Primary English Teaching Association, 1981. (Distributed by Heinemann Educational Books, Exeter, New Hampshire.)

Harste, J., Burke, C., & Woodward, V. *Children, Their Language and World: Initial Encounters with Print.* NIE Final Report. Bloomington, Indiana: Indiana University School of Education, 1981.

Read, C. "Preschool Children's Knowledge of English Phonology," *Harvard Educational Review, 41* (February 1971), 1-34.

Watching and Listening to Children Read

Dorothy Watson
University of Missouri at Columbia

In late September, a nine year old friend dropped by for a chat. Our conversation drifted to school work and, predictably, I asked Janey what she was reading. After telling me about the books she was reading at home, including ones she had written herself, she volunteered, "but I guess you want to know what I'm reading at school. You know," she continued with all the assurance gained from four years and four weeks of schooling, "we can't really read until we finish our tests. After that we can get into our groups; we can go to the library then, too. After the tests."

Janey explained that all this made perfectly good sense because "the teacher doesn't know how we read until the scores come back."

I stifled a rebuttal and pinned Janey's two page story on my bulletin board.

The purpose of this article is to help teachers use observations rather than formal testing to find out (from the first day of school to the last) how their students handle text in a variety of forms and in a variety of situations. By using information gained from these observations, teachers not only have reliable data for assessment, but have a realistic base on which to plan curriculum and instructional procedures. But before turning to the what, when, and how of observing students, teachers need to consider what they believe about language and how children learn language; that is, they need to be aware of their own theoretical position concerning the reading process. When beliefs are clear, teachers have a better understanding about their expectations of readers, as well as a guide for making instructional decisions.

A View of Reading

The suggestions in this article are consistent with a view of reading that holds to the idea that readers construct meaning as they bring information that is already in their heads to the messages authors have encoded in text. The information readers use has many dimensions, including background experiences, knowledge of language, expectations about the text, perceptions of themselves as readers, and information gained from everyone and everything in the context of the situation in which they are reading. The works of Goodman (Gollasch, 1982), Smith (1978), and Rosenblatt (1978) support the view that reading is a transactive process that involves both the potential of the reader and the potential of the text. For example, when proficient readers are presented with interesting, well-written text they look like what they are—good readers reading good discourse. If these same readers are presented text that is unpredictable, lacks cohesion, is conceptually inappropriate, and holds no interest, the students will appear to be poor readers—their potential diminished by poor text. Readers who do not have requisite background knowledge or appropriate linguistic experiences may cause a well-written text to appear poorly composed. When we observe changes in students' behavior as they meet different texts, we must be aware of both text and reader potential and look for the dimensions of influence each has on the other. A transactional view of reading forces us to become textwatchers as well as kidwatchers.

Watching the Reader: When to Observe

This text-contributing/child-contributing view of reading demands that we observe the reader before reading, while reading, and after reading (Robinson, 1980). Let's consider how each phase is important.

Before the book is opened students have experienced life and language, and they have formed opinions of themselves as learners and readers. They have also formed opinions about the content and the format of the text they are to read. Proficient readers use appropriate information from their own background knowledge, as well as signals from the context of situation (setting, participants, purpose) to anticipate meaning (Halliday, 1978). Proficient readers expect to find certain kinds of messages couched in certain forms depending on the circumstances. Math books, Judy Blume stories, cereal boxes, and public bathroom walls signal specific concepts, language, and conventions. Good readers know this and use such knowledge to construct meaning, even before their eyes are on the print.

Teachers can get an idea about children's willingness to bring their own off-the-page information to the reading act by asking students what they expect to find in different texts: a warranty for a toy, instructions for a video game, a gum wrapper, *Time* magazine, the science book. The specific information children have in their heads (before reading a particular text) can be tapped by the teacher's invitation: "Tell me everything you know about the subject." For example, before inviting her students to read a biography of Benjamin Franklin (Fritz, 1976), one fifth grade teacher asked her students to tell everything they knew about Franklin. The children offered information in many forms (words, phrases, titles, even a picture of a kite). The teacher listed all contributions, accurate and inaccurate, on the board. She asked the students to look for patterns, ways to categorize the information. Labels emerged for some categories, and questions arose about the accuracy of some of the information. The teacher used the students' responses to assess how much background information they had or were willing to present to the class that would aid in reading the text. More personal comments about the activity were revealing: "If it's like the story of Samuel Adams, it will be great!" "I have trouble reading anything in that book. Can I work with Ned?" This before-the-book-is-opened activity provides information on which to make decisions about classroom organization, and reveals students' judgments of their own abilities to handle the assignment. By listening to children the teacher can immediately encourage some students to begin reading with no further delay; can invite other children to read a conceptually related but far "friendlier" text; can suggest that reading partners join efforts or that a child pursue another activity that is of equal or perhaps more worth.

While reading, proficient readers use both off-the-page information (prior experiences and situational circumstances) and on-the-page information to direct their strategies—sampling print, predicting emerging structures and meanings, confirming or rejecting their predictions, correcting if necessary, and constructing meaning. By observing Jonathan and Leroy as they were reading silently, a second grade teacher learned a great deal about their strategies for comprehending text. When Jonathan didn't know a word, he interrupted his friend to ask the pronunciation. Leroy, on the other hand, made pencil marks in the margin of his book when he came to something he didn't know, but always continued to read. Leroy knew he would probably be able to figure out meanings on his own as he gathered more information from the author. Observing these two boys, the teacher made a point of helping Jonathan find more productive and self-reliant strategies in order to construct meaning, and she made a point of asking Leroy if his strategy was paying off and of encouraging him to continue its use if it proved helpful.

Following reading, students have options. They can share their new information and feelings with others; they can use the new experience as a basis for further readings; they can store the experience for later use; or they can never consciously consider the information again. After Donald, a third grader, read a story from *The Magic Listening Cap* (Uchida, 1955), he combined an episode in "Three Tests for a Prince" with his abiding interest in the movie, *Raiders of the Lost Ark,* and wrote the following in his journal (see Figure 1). By watching Donald's after-the-book-is-closed activity it was not difficult to see that this reader/writer enjoyed and understood "Three Tests for a Prince"; no need for a quiz or book report. By comparing his new journal story with earlier attempts both Donald and his teacher agreed that he was developing a real knack for writing very good beginnings and endings of stories—they caught the reader's interest. They also saw that Donald was taking more risks with spelling; his attempts always made sense, and his spelling was moving slowly but surely toward more and more standard forms. But most important of all, they found that Donald wanted to continue working on this piece, possibly comparing the prince's other tests with more of Indiana Jones' adventures. Donald's next book was in the making!

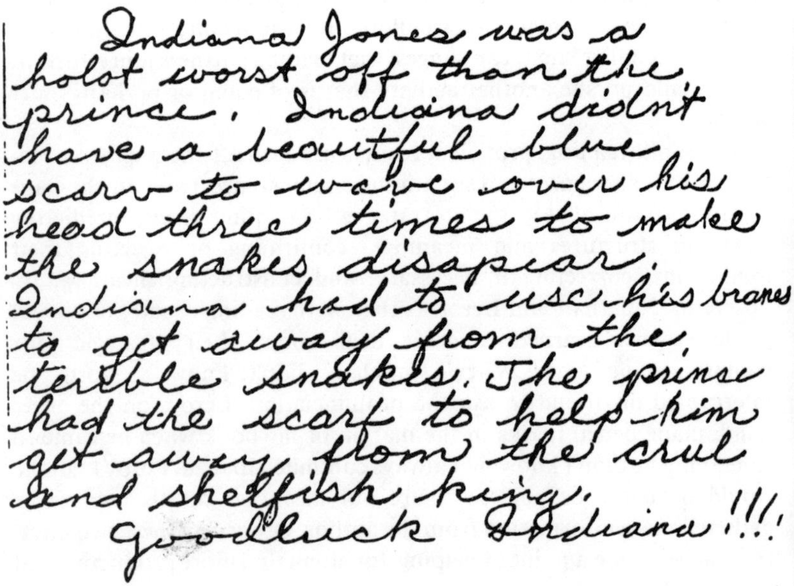
Indiana Jones was a holot worst off than the prince. Indiana didn't have a beautiful blue scarv to wave over his head three times to make the snakes disapear. Indiana had to use his branes to get away from the terble snakes. The prinse had the scarf to help him get away from the crul and shelfish king. Goodluck Indiana!!!

Indiana Jones was a
whole lot worse off than the
prince. Indiana didn't
have a beautiful blue
scarf to wave over his
head three times to make
the snakes disappear.
Indiana had to use his brains
to get away from the
terrible snakes. The Prince
had a scarf to help him
get away from the cruel
and selfish king.
Goodluck, Indiana!!!

Figure 1. Donald's journal entry.

Watching Readers: What to Look For

The transactional view of reading helps us know what to look for as we observe children interacting with texts. We must focus our attention on certain aspects of readers' behaviors and texts, but at the same time we should be flexible about what we observe. Here are some possible questions to consider when watching readers.

Concepts about Print and Print Settings

1. To what extent does the student attend to print? For example, does the student focus on the print as someone else is reading?
2. How does the student handle books? For example, does the student hold the book right side up, turn pages one at a time, and point to the place where one should begin reading?
3. Does the student expect the print to make sense and have personal meaning? For example, does the student seek out text that will satisfy his/her need for information about feeding hamsters?
4. How does the student use information from the print setting, i.e. where the print is found, its format, who asked that it be read, why it is being read?

Use of Background Knowledge

1. How does the reader bring background knowledge and linguistic information to the reading situation?
2. How does the reader approach text? Is there an effort made to appreciate and live the written experiences by relating the text to his/her own life?
3. How does the reader use memory as a reading aid? For example, when asked to read a familiar song, riddle, or self-authored story, does the reader use memory (i.e. familiarity with the material) as a basis for predicting and making inferences?

Use of Strategies

1. How does the student handle the information giving systems of language? Does the reader use a flexible strategy which encompasses all language cues (e.g. semantic, grammatical, sound/symbol) to construct meaning or does the reader rely on a single cueing system (e.g. symbol/sound)?
2. Does the reader proficiently sample, predict, and construct meaning from text?
3. Does the student monitor his/her reading by asking, "Am I making sense of what I am reading?"
4. Does the reader self-correct when the flow of language and meaning are interrupted?
5. Is there a dialect or first language influence on the student's reading and how does the student handle this influence?
6. What strategies does the reader use to approach suitable but unfamiliar text?

View of Self as Reader

1. What does the student think of himself/herself as a reader?
2. In what circumstances and how often does the student make the decision to read?
3. What risks are taken by the student as he/she reads?

4. How realistic is the student's judgment of his/her knowledge of concepts and discourse forms needed to read various texts (e.g. science or history materials, poems or drama)?

The answers to these questions will provide information that is immediately applicable in building a reading program. However, if long lists bore you, perhaps Smith's advice (1973) will give you ample guidance, "Find out what a child is trying to do and then help him do it" (p. 195). Good kidwatchers make it a point to see the student's strengths first. This does not mean that problems are ignored. It simply indicates that teachers need to build their reading programs on what students are doing right, not on what they are doing wrong.

Informal Kidwatching: Observing Spontaneous Activities

Kidwatching is an ongoing process that begins the minute children enter the classroom and continues throughout the day. It involves informal assessment of student use of language in real situations.

Let's look at what happened in a first grade on the first day of school.

> The teacher welcomes the children as they enter the room and invites them to sit with her to chat and get better acquainted. On the board there is a nametag for every child. Within three minutes, Robin notices his nametag and points it out to the group. The teacher asks if anyone else can find his/her name. Almost immediately Mary, Jimmy, and Rose find their tags. As the names are removed from the board Mike, Peggy, and Marty feel more confident and find their tags. Ricky chooses Robert's tag and the teacher praises Ricky for making a good guess and urges him to try again. Ricky is hesitant and the teacher asks the class to read aloud with her the remaining names. As the children read their names they get their tags. The teacher talks with the children about why they have nametags and then she asks each child to stand and read his or her tag to the other children. She asks every child to read one other nametag of someone they know, and then she asks if anyone wants to read the nametag of someone they don't know. Robin, Jimmy, Mary, and Marty read two names each. Steve reads his name and the two other Steves in class.
>
> The teacher tells the children that she has written each of them a letter; they discuss their experiences with receiving letters and what might be in their teacher's letter to them. Clara and Jimmy tell about the letters and cards they get from their grandmother. Bill, Joe, and Ricky say they have never gotten a letter, but their parents have.

The children go by twos to the mailboxes and locate their letters by finding their names under their boxes. Most of the children find their names immediately, a few get help from their partners. Six children, including Joe, Nancy, and Bill, read the remaining names with the teacher in order to find their letters.

Again the children discuss what they might find in their teacher's letter to them. Several children say that the letter will begin with, "Dear -----," and end with "I love you." The children open their letters, all of them hold the paper right side up and read, "Dear -----." Rose slowly reads aloud the entire letter with support from Marty and Gwen. As Rose reads, Clara and Carol begin to mumble along, pointing to the print. Delbert announces that he can't read and his teacher recommends that he pretend to read. Joe makes a telescope of his paper and peeps at Nancy who discovers that letters make dandy fans. However, both Nancy and Joe tell what was in their teacher's letter after it is read aloud. The teacher and the children read the letter that has been copied on a large piece of chart paper. Children wearing blue read it, and volunteers read it. Rose, Mike, and Robin read the letter as a trio with Robin looking at the print and Mike and Rose looking at their audiences.

The teacher then invites the children to write a letter to her. They discuss what they might write about, discuss not being able to write (pretending is okay), choose either lined or unlined "stationary," and begin to write their letters by using scribbles, pictures, letters, words, sentences, and always—meaning. The teacher becomes a "talking secretary" for Nancy, Robert, Janis, Becky, and Delbert. More than half the children read their letters to either their partner or their teacher.

The teacher watched, listened and learned that three of her students could read unfamiliar predictable print (Rhodes, 1981). She found out that her students knew a great deal about the functions of a letter (e.g., It tells you something about what's happening and asks questions.), and the form of a letter (e.g. It begins with "Dear -----," and ends with "I love you."). She discovered that all the students could reply to a letter. Some wanted to dictate their messages and have her write, while others scribbled, drew, and used some standard lettering to create their messages. She learned that Janice, Becky, and Delbert needed a great deal of encouragement, support, and confidence building. As the teacher was learning about her students on this first morning, the twenty-five first graders were finding out something about themselves—they could read and write, and "that," in the words of one six year old, "is what I came to school to do."

Within the first few days of school, teachers can learn about their students' reading behavior by inviting them to 1) listen to stories and predict next ideas, sentences, and words; 2) read the repetitive phrases or last lines of stories (e.g. "...and Drummer Hoff fired it off") written on the board or read from an oversized "Big Book" (Holdaway, 1979); 3) read silently something of their own choosing; 4) read notes that arrive from the nurse or principal and compose a reply; 5) read their own and group compositions; and 6) read signs and notices around the school and neighborhood.

More Formal Observational Techniques

In most cases, informal observation and listening results in solid information on which to build a reading program. More formal techniques, however, help us confirm hypotheses.

The Burke Reading Interview (1980) provides data for understanding how students perceive reading and themselves as readers. This straightforward interview takes about five minutes to administer and consists of the following questions that can be modified depending on the students:

1. When you are reading and you come to something you don't know, what do you do? Do you ever do anything else?
2. Who is a good reader?
3. Why is ______ a good reader?
4. Do you think ______ ever comes to something s/he doesn't know when s/he is reading?
5. If ______ did come to something s/he didn't know, what would s/he do?
6. If you knew that someone was having trouble reading, how would you help that person?
7. How would a teacher help that person?
8. How did you learn to read?
9. What would you like to do better as a reader?
10. Do you think you are a good reader?

From the answers to these few questions a teacher can determine a student's personal model of reading. Students reveal in their answers what they believe reading is all about ("sounding out syllables," "knowing the words," "getting meaning") and how they think reading should be taught ("learn the sounds of the letters," "learn every word and get them right," "understand what you know and what the author knows"). Such information lets the teacher know if the child's personal model of reading is consistent with the teacher's and provides a realistic basis on which to develop appropriate reading strategies.

Another technique which can help the teacher is miscue analysis (Goodman & Burke, 1972), an investigation of the reader's digressions from the text. It provides teachers with information about how students handle the information cueing systems of language (semantic, syntactic, graphic, and phonemic) as well as how they use information in their heads and in the text to construct meaning. For example, Mike's miscues are marked on the story below. Substitutions are written above the text, omissions circled, insertions marked with ^, repetitions underlined and marked Ⓡ, corrections underlined and marked Ⓒ, and pauses longer than five seconds marked P.

Andre's Secret

Splash!

Before Andre knew what was happening, his boat had turned

upside down. The big load of wood he had worked so hard to cut

had spilled into the water all around him. Frightened, Andre

cried out for help. At the same time he wondered if anyone

could hear him.

It might appear that Mike is a poor reader who needs more word attack skills. However, from a transactional perspective Mike is using the cueing systems of language to sample, predict, correct, and construct meaning. His miscues are high level ones which help him maintain consistent meaning. Let's consider Mike's reading.

1. Substitution of *Arnie* and *Andy* for Andre.

   Mike is unfamiliar with the name Andre and attempts to make a reasonable substitution. When he decides on Andy he stays with it for the remainder of the story. This is a high level miscue.

2. Omission of *Splash!*

   Mike is not willing to take a risk without more redundancy in the text. He might be urged to fill in the omission after reading further. This omission did not detract from the story. Also, in Mike's retelling (below) he says, "Andy splashed into the water. . . ."

3. The omission of *had*, the substitution of *slipped* for *spilled*, and the substitution of *worried about anyone hearing* for *wondered if anyone could hear*.

   These miscues show Mike's attention to grammatical, semantic, and graphic cues. These are high level miscues.

4. The correction of *when* for *what, ov-* (over) for *upside down*, *out of* for *into*.

   These miscues show Mike's ability to correct in order to gain grammatical acceptability, again high level miscues.

After reading the entire story Mike was asked to tell everything he could remember. He began with:

> Well, that was a good story because Andy found his granddad's ax. But it started out bad when Arnie put too much wood in a little boat and. . .well, it turned over and Andy splashed into the water and he was scared that no one would hear him yellin'. He was also froze when they pulled him out. . . .

Even from this small portion of Mike's retelling it is apparent that he was monitoring for meaning. Although he made many miscues, they did not disrupt the reading process. Mike constructed meaning, and he expressed that meaning in the retelling—using his own preferred language.

Miscue analysis may be carried out in a formal manner by tape recording a student's reading, marking the miscues as above, and coding the information (see Goodman & Burke, 1972). It can also be done informally as teachers listen to children read different materials. Children can be instructed to make note of their own miscues and discuss them later with the teacher or the class (Watson, 1978). Once teachers add miscue analysis to their assessment procedures they never again listen to children read in the same way. Miscue analysis helps teachers look at what children are doing "right," while becoming aware of their problems in reading.

Another more formal technique for gathering information in a natural setting is ERRQ (Estimate, Read, Respond, and Question). ERRQ combines the retelling procedure of miscue analysis with the questioning procedure of ReQuest developed by Manzo (1968, 1969). The technique can be used with student and teacher, student partners, and in small and large groups. The basic procedure follows:

Estimate: The student quickly looks over the text and estimates the amount of text, s/he can read with understanding. This estimate should be based on the student's background experience with the concepts involved, the author's organizing structure and style, as well as the student's past successes or failures with similar discourse. After the student estimates how far s/he can read with understanding, s/he pencils in a (✓) in the margin.

Read: The student reads aloud or silently. In rare instances the teacher and the student may read together. Usually the teacher decides how the reading is to be done, but the student might make this decision.

Respond: The student responds by giving both his/her reaction to the message and by retelling the text.

Question: The student asks the teacher a question(s) followed by the teacher asking the student a question(s) about the selection read.

The ERRQ procedure can be followed step by step, or it may be modified by the teacher or the readers. For example, readers may estimate a "reading distance," discover that they are monitoring for meaning and decide to read farther before responding. On the other hand, readers may overestimate and decide to respond before the full distance is reached. In either case students have the opportunity to gain control, to have a say about their own reading. Once readers make an estimation, they seldom ignore their commitment. Another modification involves the questioning procedure. Although students always are encouraged to ask a question, it may not always be productive for the teacher to ask a question.

The Estimate, Read, Respond, and Question (ERRQ) procedure provides a format for students to reveal their ability to size up a passage, judge their own proficiency, talk about themselves as readers of a particular passage, read silently and aloud, explore their own minds and the mind of the author in order to respond to the text, and, finally, to develop their own ideas and seek further information through questioning.

Summary

No two snowflakes, popcorn kernels, or children are exactly alike. Therefore, to watch, enjoy, and describe snowflakes, popcorn kernels, and kids, a variety of devices is needed that can be used flexibly and, in the case of snowflakes and kids, fast!

Standardized measurements for nonstandardized kids fall short of helping teachers watch, enjoy, and describe. Scores don't sharpen our vision or insight. They don't bring a smile or knowing nod. A score of 3.2 doesn't begin to describe a child's ability to use language.

Classroom observation offers a natural, positive and professional way of gathering information about the reading process. Kidwatching teachers believe that curriculum must be based on the strengths of children; that making a mistake is not the end, but rather an indication of what readers are trying to do. These teachers continue to broaden their own knowledge about language, about learning, and about the reading process. They do this because they realize it will help them know better what to look for when they observe children. The techniques suggested in this article are only a few methods that allow teachers to discover their students' proficiencies and problems while encouraging the natural process of learning to read.

References

Burke, C.L. "The Reading Interview: 1977," in B.P. Farr & D.J. Strickler (Eds.), *Reading Comprehension: Resource Guide.* Bloomington: School of Education, Indiana University, 1980.

Fritz, J. *What's the Big Idea, Ben Franklin.* New York: Coward, McCann & Geoghegan, 1976.

Gollasch, F.V. (Ed.). *Language and Literacy: The Selected Writings of Kenneth S. Goodman,* volume 1. Boston: Routledge & Kegan Paul, 1982.

Goodman, Y.M., & Burke, C.L. *The Reading Miscue Inventory Manual.* New York: Richard C. Owen Publishers, 1972.

Halliday, M.A.K. *Language as Social Semiotic.* Baltimore, Maryland: University Park Press, 1978.

Holdaway, D. *The Foundations of Literacy.* Sydney, Australia: Ashton Scholastic, 1979. (Distributed by Heinemann Educational Books, Exeter, New Hampshire.)

Manzo, A.V. "The ReQuest Procedure," *Journal of Reading, 13* (November 1969), 123-126, 163-164.

Manzo, A.V. "Improving Reading Comprehension through Reciprocal Questioning," doctoral dissertation, Syracuse University, 1968.

Robinson, H.A. "Reading and Writing Strategies throughout the Curriculum," paper presented at the 14th Annual Conference on Reading, University of Missouri at Columbia, 1980.

Rhodes, L.K. "I Can Read! Predictable Books as Resources for Reading and Writing Instruction," *Reading Teacher, 34* (February 1981), 511-518.

Rosenblatt, L. *The Reader, the Text, and the Poem.* Carbondale, Illinois: Southern Illinois University Press, 1978.

Smith, F. "Twelve Easy Ways to Make Reading Hard," in F. Smith (Ed.), *Psycholinguistics and Reading.* New York: Holt, Rinehart & Winston, 1973.

Smith, F. *Understanding Reading,* second edition. New York: Holt, Rinehart & Winston, 1978.

Uchida, Y. *In the Magic Listening Cap: More Folktales from Japan.* New York: Harcourt Brace Jovanovich, 1955.

Watson, D. "Reader Selected Miscues: Getting More from Sustained Silent Reading," *English Education, 10* (December 1978), 75-85.

Part Three
Children Using Language and Learning through Language

Introduction

Language is functional; it is a tool for learning as well as communication. In Part Three the writers focus on how and what we can learn from observing children using language in different contexts and for different purposes. Some look at children using language to communicate with peers and their teacher. Others probe the ways they use language to explore and to understand the world they live in, that is, to learn.

In the first section, the articles focus on observing oral language use. Genishi explains that communicative performance, the use of language in social contexts, requires that children know both the linguistic and social rules that will enable them to interact effectively with listeners. She explains how children acquire this knowledge and then describes two ways to observe and document changes in oral language as young children use it in communicating with others in the classroom.

Then, combining observation with analysis of tape recorded talk in an ethnically mixed classroom, Michaels and Foster examine what happens when first and second grade students run the sharing time activity by themselves. We "listen" as children, using very different discourse styles, communicate their ideas and learn from classmates who serve as a sympathetic but discriminating audience. The writers indicate that traditional criteria do not distinguish successful sharers from less successful ones, and suggest that mismatches between teacher expectations and the students' discourse styles may result in misassessment of their abilities. Kiefer and DeStefano focus on helping teachers understand cultural variation in language. After looking briefly at structural differences, they explore some of the less understood but more significant social differences in style and use which teachers may encounter, including verbal and nonverbal patterns that may cause misunderstandings. They close with suggestions about ways to observe and adapt curriculum to the styles and needs of language users from different cultural backgrounds.

Milz, a teacher and keen observer, opens the section on written language use. Milz believes that children learn to write by writing. She describes how she sets up a supportive environment and then, by means of examples, illustrates the many ways and different purposes for which her first graders use writing. Calkins observes children learning to think through writing. She describes how, in classrooms where teacher-child conferences became models for child-child conferences, she saw that children began to interact with their emerging texts, asking themselves questions about content and process which had been asked of them. Calkins discusses the impact of these conferences on children's learning.

Smith-Burke stresses that language is at the heart of the teaching-learning process; through talking, writing, and reading children acquire new knowledge and reshape their understanding of the world. In her examples, we see children learning from each other in contexts where they are encouraged to talk about their reading and experiences, and where they control the direction their discussions take. The teacher watches and listens, intervening when necessary to help children extend their learning. Hickman concludes this part of the book by describing ways to observe children's responses to literature. She uses primary and middle grade examples to illustrate how children reveal information about their progress toward mature understanding and critical appreciation of literature as a form of written language.

ORAL LANGUAGE USE

Observing Communicative Performance in Young Children

Celia Genishi
The University of Texas at Austin

Hand in glove, yin and yang, horse and carriage, body and soul, Jekyll and Hyde, mind and matter are all couplings that come to mind when I try to capture the interrelationship between form and function in language. You can't have one without the other whenever you speak. All speakers know the bits and pieces, the forms, that make up a language; and they know how to put those pieces together to say meaningful things. They know the uses, or the functions, of the bits and pieces. They know both forms and functions without needing to be aware of how much they know or of how they blend form and function every time they speak. This article begins with a brief summary of what forms and functions children acquire and how they are acquired. The second section is a presentation of how we can tap that knowledge in classrooms. The purpose of our "language-tapping" is to discover how children's language changes and develops and, consequently, how to improve our teaching. When language is used freely in settings that encourage it, we have opportunities to listen to and notice both the forms and functions children constantly draw upon, combine, and express. Two ways to observe what they do with language, anecdotes and audiotape recording, are included, along with examples of talk from preschoolers.

Becoming Competent Communicators

Research in the past twenty years has changed the way we look at children's language development and learning. Insights from psychology (Piaget & Inhelder, 1969) and linguistics (Chomsky, 1965) have led to the conception of the child as a hypothesis tester, a thinker who over time can unconsciously formulate the rules of language. Studies begun in the 1960s of children's early utterances (Brown & Bellugi, 1964; Ervin & Miller, 1964) led us to seek descriptions of what children said, in terms of developing grammars, not a single grammar that we would judge as incomplete from an adult perspective. We no longer see the child as a passive responder who imitates whatever s/he hears. Instead, the child is able actively to discover how language works.

We refer to children's knowledge about sounds, meanings, and syntax as *linguistic competence.* Part of this knowledge consists of syntactic rules for combining forms to create grammatical utterances, for example, the general rule for placing a subject before the verb in an English sentence, or the rule for adding *-ed* to most verbs to indicate past action. (For a fuller discussion of linguistic development, see Lindfors' article in this volume.) We best understand the way these forms are acquired in light of their uses or functions for children and the people around them. Using linguistic forms in social contexts requires children to know both formal or grammatical and social rules that enable them to communicate effectively with their listeners.

The knowledge of social and linguistic rules that enable us to speak and interact appropriately in different situations is called *communicative competence.* As Hymes (1974) broadly defined it, it is the child's "ability to participate in its society as not only a speaking, but also a communicating member" (p. 75). When speakers activate their rules in varied situations and convert their knowledge or competence into behavior, we can refer to that behavior as speech or *performance.* What we observe in classrooms, then, as children listen, speak, or write are aspects of their *communicative performance.* Sociolinguists, those who study the social aspects of language, have demonstrated that individuals' performances consist not of a single style of communicating, but a variety of *styles.* These reflect the features of the situations that one experiences, whether the speaker is an adult or a child (Cazden, 1970; Labov, 1970). We speak differently with a stranger in a position of authority, a close friend or family member, or a casual acquaintance. The child in the classroom or day care center may communicate quite differently in an individual testing situation with a resource person, at lunchtime, in conversation with the teacher, and with the school nurse.

How do children acquire linguistic and communicative competence? Child language researchers generally respond that children acquire both through *interaction* with people and objects (Brown, 1973;

Wells, 1981). According to a developmental perspective, communicative interactions begin at birth, so that the first year or two of life are now considered crucial for understanding the processes of acquisition. The study of this prelinguistic period yields detailed records of infant-caregiver interactions (Trevarthen & Hubley, 1978). Behaviors such as turn-taking, smiling, and bubble formation all contribute to communication, even when the infant's "conversational" turn is saying "Baa." Before the first words are uttered, the infant is learning about what is socially expected and appropriate as those around him/her are producing examples of what is linguistically appropriate. Means or forms for communicating initially seem global; for example, the infant's cry. As days and weeks go by, the forms become differentiated so that the crying baby becomes a cooing, then babbling infant, able to utter consonant-plus-vowel syllables, such as "bababa" or "mama." Early words are eventually combined according to the syntactic rules of the language children hear and use.

At the same time, children differentiate in other ways. Newborn babies initially appear to communicate a single meaning; crying functions to indicate unhappiness or dissatisfaction, often because of hunger. In a short time, caregivers recognize that cries are differentiated. There may be a cry for hunger, one for loneliness, one for pain. According to Halliday (1975), children's early communications are full of meaning. There are functions and a range of possible meanings well before there are linguistic forms to specify those meanings. Prelinguistic children may use nonverbal means to express biological needs, regulate others' behavior, and assert their own importance. By the time the first words are uttered, children have a good understanding of what language is for, in other words, how it functions in human interaction. (For an application of Halliday's functions to children's speech in school settings, see Pinnell's chapter in this volume.)

As children acquire language functions, they also begin to learn rules for differentiating among social situations. As infants, children respond nonverbally in different ways to family and strangers. Later as speakers, they demonstrate social rules for talking—or not talking—to varied categories of people. Bilingual children who have learned two languages in their preschool years acquire additional rules about when they speak one language or the other (Lindholm, 1980). The acquisition of rules for language choice appears to be well grounded by the time children are three or four years old. Like monolingual speakers, bilinguals make inferences about social and linguistic appropriateness, based on continued interaction in diverse social settings. For all children, knowledge of the forms of language develops simultaneously with knowledge of uses and functions.

The blending of language function and form in children is natural and has a long history by the time they join nonfamily groups, such as a play group, day care, or public school. When we look at young children in school settings, however, we often see the separation of function from form. We eventually expect children to *decontextualize*, to learn how to use language independent of familiar contexts as when we ask them to tell a story about a past event, or read or write about experiences that are not their own. We also expect them to learn terms that enable them to talk about language; terms like *verb, sentence*, and *syllable*. When being able to talk about and analyze language becomes a goal in itself, form has become primary, and the place of function recedes. Although a major goal of education in our society is to teach children to use language in an analytic and decontextualized way, it is also our goal to encourage natural uses of language, especially in the first years of schooling. In the next section, I describe basic ways of observing oral language as young children use it, as they combine form and function in order to communicate with those around them.

Ways of Observing

The term *observing* has a variety of connotations relevant to a teacher's work. First, there is the sense that one who observes notices significant things that others miss. Second, we may attribute fairness to observers; they stand apart from the action and may, therefore, be cooler and more objective than participants involved in the activity. Third, in the classroom context it may connote the luxury of time. Teachers usually need to be in the center of things, so that observation is an additional task that may not get done. Teachers most often observe on the run; they notice things as they occur but may or may not remember details of children's performances. Making observations more systematic helps teachers to remember some details and also to use what they observe to improve their teaching or to promote children's development and learning. Two basic ways of recording observations of children's language are anecdotal records and audiotape recording. (For others see Almy & Genishi, 1979; Boehm & Weinberg, 1977; Irwin & Busnell, 1980.)

Anecdotal Records

Of the two techniques, the anecdotal record is simpler since it is a direct means of recording what you observe and requires no special equipment. All that is needed is paper and pencil (or index card and pen) and an incident or impression you have had. In a preschool where I taught, we used index cards and filed them in a small metal box. The content of the cards will vary depending on the amount of time you have and the amount of detail needed to reconstruct what you observed. Some teachers might observe communication between two children and document it in this way

2/12/82: Tray and Elisa talk about poker chips.

Tray: Hey, you got too many.
Elisa: No, I don't. You got all the red ones.
Tray: But you can't even count.

Tray asks me to count with him. Elisa leaves.

This brief anecdote is full of potential lessons for teachers. With respect to communication, teachers can learn something about the children's forms and the uses to which Tray and Elisa put language. Their forms are colloquial (*Hey, got*); both use standard English negative structures (*don't, can't*). What strikes the teacher, however, is the function of their talk. They are having a short argument about possession of the poker chips. Tray calls on the teacher to help settle it by counting even after Elisa appears to lose interest and starts another activity. The teacher has some evidence that Tray is beginning to understand counting and may plan to focus on Elisa the next time they have math. The teacher also decides that these five year olds use colloquial forms appropriately and sees no need to correct a form like *got*.

Another teacher, or the same teacher sometime later, may expand this anecdote so that more details are preserved. This is the expanded version

2/12/82: Tray and Elisa are in the puzzle and manipulative area, playing with the poker chips. (Elisa looks a little irritated.) They have been there for about five minutes, sorting them (I think by color). The conversation that I caught was

Tray: Hey, you got too many.
Elisa: No, I don't. You got all the red ones.
Tray: But you can't even count.

Tray soon asks me to help count. I do that with him even though Elisa leaves before I get there. Tray is satisfied because he did have fewer chips than Elisa. (I should remember to see how he counts on his own and to see how Elisa does in math the next time.)

This filled-in anecdote contains enough detail so that teachers reading it weeks later will remember much of what was communicated. They separate with parentheses their interpretations, plans, and guesses from observations of behavior. The anecdote demonstrates that children communicate about activities, often self-selected, that interest and engage them. The content may not resemble that of a language arts lesson; it may be related to math, cooking, social studies, art. Talk about any activity reflects children's communicative performance and may or may not be directly related to language or books.

This teacher has used her anecdote to informally assess two children's language use and their counting ability. To be meaningful for the teacher, it should be supplemented by other anecdotes. These will provide further information about Tray's and Elisa's development and will help the teacher document changes that may not be captured by checklists or test scores. Parents, too, might be interested in the content of anecdotes when they confer with teachers. If teachers are fortunate enough to have aides or team-teaching colleagues, they may read each other's anecdotes when reviewing individual children's progress or when planning for the future. Teachers who want children to take part in as many activities as possible will see if a child is always in the housekeeping corner or in the book area. They can then plan a small group activity with that child and others in different areas. As the activity changes, the child's use of language will probably also change.

Tape Recordings

Teachers whose schools provide cassette tape recorders or who have their own may supplement or replace anecdotes with records based on audiotapes. Since taping preserves actual speech, the audiotape holds several advantages. First, if a teacher has no time to take handwritten notes, s/he can tape an activity or lesson for review later. Second, to document the growth of language over time, tapes can be saved and compared to each other. This might be especially informative for teachers with children acquiring a second language. Third, because memories are imperfect, records based on tapes may lead to more accurate judgments of children's language abilities than handwritten anecdotes. Careful transcriptions of talk can guard against overestimating or underestimating the quality of communicative performance.

If you are a novice at using audiotape recorders, these practical guidelines may help:

1. Locate a portable cassette tape recorder. (If you are planning to purchase a basic model, they range in price from about $20 to $150.) One that can be battery operated might be the most practical. Since you probably won't record long interactions, a 60 minute audiotape cassette (30 minutes on each side) is suitable and sturdy.

2. Choose the activity or setting that interests you. Depending on the age of the children you teach, you may want to be present throughout the taping. You might choose the part of your classroom that is most free of background noise.

3. Do a trial recording with children present as soon as possible. If the equipment is a novelty to them, you may need a few desensitization sessions so that children have a chance to ask questions, perform, and learn what the tape recorder does. Before you record, test to see that the equipment is working. Also, check occasionally while recording to make sure that the microphone is working or that you have not run out of tape. Generally, the sound quality is better with an attached microphone than with the built-in microphone that most recorders have.

4. Listen to your recording as soon as possible. If at first you get unintelligible samples of speech, try again, next time perhaps with the tape recorder, or microphone, in a different place.

5. Once you have recorded some talk that is clear and that will tell you about an aspect of the children's communication, you might choose typical segments to transcribe verbatim. Selecting what is typical or valuable for your purposes can be time consuming; doing the transcription is more so. Both selecting and transcribing involve listening many times to the tape. The written record, however, may provide you with the richest documentation of your children's communicative performance.

6. For the ambitious or for those of you with aides or student trainees, there are additional bits of data that might be useful when a group of children are talking. A coding sheet could help make your observation more complete and systematic (see Figure 1). A coding sheet of this type may help with later transcription or interpretation by identifying speakers and concurrent behaviors.

Figure 1. Classroom observation.

Date ________________

Observer's Name ____________________________

Children Participating	Who Speaks to	Whom	Speech Fragment	Nonverbal Behaviors
Tina, Carl, Lyn, Ellen	Ellen	Carl	Don't you wanna...	Picks up legos; shows to Carl.
	Carl	Ellen	Yeah, I'm gonna put...	Starts building with legos.

The essence of communicative competence and performance is variation of language form and function from setting to setting. Recording, even for brief periods of time, in different settings or activities can contribute to a fuller and fairer assessment of children's performance in the classroom. The following are four examples of talk from a nursery school classroom. They reflect the ways five year old Will communicated in a variety of contexts.

Example 1

Teacher: Does anyone remember what we talked about? What's inside of us, under our skin?

Jenny: Bones.

Teacher: Bones. Right. And we have places where our bones come together, and they bend. Those are called joints. Can everybody say *joints*?

Children: Joints!

Teacher: Right. Well, today I brought some paper and I want you to try to use it like your bones are used. Like your backbone can bend like that, can't it? And your arm bone...your elbow bends like that. And I brought papers for you to *bend* all different ways. And you glue on. And when we get through, we'll have pictures that will move around on the paper.

Child: That's okay.

Teacher: You can put them on top of each other or however you wanna do it. Just, we can bend them and just glue. I'll do a couple of glues here to show you how to do it. And then when we get all through with them, and they get dry, they will wiggle. And they'll be bent, which is just like our bodies will bend.

Will: Look what I can do. I can bend.

Teacher: You sure can. Look at his back bend just like that skeleton.

Will: I can bend!

Teacher: Right. Let me see your legs bend. How do your legs bend?

Will: This way.

Teacher: Wow. They bend up and down and back and forth, too.

Will: (giggle)

Will has been participating in a teacher-directed group lesson on bones and, although his contribution is not extensive, he uses language for what Halliday would call a "personal" function, to assert his own presence and importance. A contrasting conversation is one that Will initiates.

Example 2

Will: Teacher, guess what time I got up this morning?

Teacher: What time did you get up this morning?

Will: Six thirty-three.

Teacher: My goodness, you got up early.

Will: What time did you get up?

Teacher: I got up at seven o'clock.

Will: I got up earlier than you, didn't I?

Teacher: Yes, you did. Well, the first time I got up at 4:30, but then I went back to bed.

Will: Why did you get up at 4:30?

Teacher: Because my little boy delivers papers *early* in the morning. And when it's raining, he can't ride his bicycle. Do you get a paper real early in the morning?

Will: No. We get ours about 7 o'clock.

Teacher: Well, it comes before then. Did you know that?

Will: When?

Teacher: It comes about 5:00 o'clock.

Child: And that's true!

Will: I know it is.

Teacher: And the boy that throws it has to get up *real* early.

At this point Will's language forms are developed enough so that we pay little attention to them; there is nothing irregular about them that attracts notice. His conversational abilities impress us as he initiates a topic and keeps it going by asking questions. Later in the exchange, the teacher in turn asks a question to extend the conversation further.

Yet another setting shows Will engaged in dramatic play, using language playfully and imaginatively. The repetition and sing-song quality of his intonation show that he can be as involved in pretending as he was in exchanging information with the teacher.

Example 3

Will: I took your money! I'm the police, and I got all your money, 'cuz you're a robber, Jenny.

Jenny: You are.

Will: *You* are. I had it first, but I let her play with it (not clear whom he speaks to here). I'm a robber! I'm a robber! I'm a robber! I'm a robber! (sing-song intonation) I'm playing robbers, I'm gonna be robbers, too. Take the babies away! (screams) I got babies. Teacher I'm playing robbers. Teacher, teacher, I'm playing robbers.

Teacher: You are.

Will: Yes. Gimme, gimme, gimme. I'm a robber.

A look at Example 3 would suggest that Will is enthusiastically getting into a role. But this is a far different slice of language from Examples 1 and 2. Will's talk is repetitious and, therefore, reflects his playfulness rather than his abilities to inform or sequence conversation.

A final example shows Will with three year old John:

Example 4

Will: I need to see what size your jogging shorts are.

John: They're not jogging shorts.

Teacher: Will, we're having a story now—leave John alone.

John: They're not jogging shorts.

Will: What are they?

John: They're big-boy pants.

Teacher: OK.

Will: Jogging shorts *are* big-boy pants.

Teacher: That's what some people call them. John. Let's try again. Will, Will. John, I don't want you bothering him.

John: Teacher, teacher.

Teacher: Would you please leave him alone? Tell him (to John).

John: Leave me alone. (pause) Leave me alone. Leave me alone. (Will ignores these requests.)

Teacher: Will. Will. Either leave John alone or move over here.

Will: I'll move over here.

Teacher: OK, thank you.

(Genishi & Di Paolo, 1982, pp. 64-65)

Will is a talkative, assertive preschooler, and these four examples are not intended to be typical of all five year olds. The examples, however, do show what we can learn from audiotaped recordings of children. Without the recordings it's unlikely that an appraisal of Will's language would be as varied, complete, and rich as it is. Our portrait of his communicative performance is constructed through talk from a whole group lesson on bones, a Will-initiated conversation with the teacher about getting up in the morning and newspaper deliveries, a playful and repetitious monologue, and an argument about whose definition of *jogging shorts* is correct. He shows himself to be often cooperative and sometimes resistant, as in Example 4. The functions and forms of Will's talk vary from one setting to another, and no one setting could aptly or accurately capture his communicative performance.

Conclusions

In this article I have reviewed briefly how linguistic and communicative competence are acquired and have suggested two basic techniques for observing and documenting children's oral language in educational settings. Anecdotal records and audiotaped recordings help us supplement results of formal tests that children might take as preschoolers or primary grade pupils. By nature language is both unitary (form-tied-to-function) and multifaceted; observing children using it in a variety of settings gives a fairer estimate of the many facets than a single test can.

As teachers and teacher educators we make choices about the aspects of language to encourage in children. We can take an integrative, developmental view, based on the inseparability of listening, speaking, and literacy; we can seek connections among a range of expressive media, between oral and written language, between form and function. We can assume that talk will happen during sharing time, art, social studies, science, lunch. . .or, in contrast, we can focus on the presentation of discrete skills that are broken down into components, such as shapes, sounds, and letters; we can plan activities that require children to sit quietly and complete form oriented worksheets. They may eventually do more talking *about* language than *with* language. In keeping with recent interactionist research and theory about child language acquisition, I choose to support the integrative and developmental view. Applying that perspective in classrooms and centers will not exclude attention to forms of language, but will help incorporate and use forms-with-functions. That use of language in many different activities will provide us with settings for eavesdropping, conversing, and observing.

References

Almy, M., & Genishi, C. *Ways of Studying Children.* New York: Teachers College Press, 1979.

Boehm, A.E., & Weinberg, R.A. *The Classroom Observer: A Guide for Developing Observation Skills.* New York: Teachers College Press, 1977.

Brown, R. *A First Language: The Early Stages.* Cambridge, Massachusetts: Harvard University Press, 1973.

Brown, R., & Bellugi, U. "Three Processes in the Acquisition of Syntax," *Harvard Educational Review, 34* (Spring 1964), 133-151.

Cazden, C.B. "The Situation: A Neglected Source of Social Class Differences in Language Use," *Journal of Social Issues, 26* (1970), 35-60.

Chomsky, N. *Aspects of the Theory of Syntax.* Cambridge, Massachusetts: MIT Press, 1965.

Ervin, S.M., & Miller, W. "The Development of Grammar in Child Language," in U. Bellugi & R. Brown (Eds.), *The Acquisition of Language. Monographs of the Society for Research in Child Development, 29* (1964), Serial No. 92.

Genishi, C., & Di Paolo, M. "Learning through Argument in a Preschool," in L.C. Wilkinson (Ed.), *Communicating in the Classroom.* New York: Academic Press, 1982.

Halliday, M.A.K. *Learning How to Mean.* London: Edward Arnold, 1975.

Hymes, D. *Foundations in Sociolinguistics: An Ethnographic Approach.* Philadelphia: University of Pennsylvania Press, 1974.

Irwin, D.M., & Bushnell, M.M. *Observational Strategies for Child Study.* New York: Holt, Rinehart & Winston, 1980.

Labov, W. "The Logic of Nonstandard English," in F. Williams (Ed.), *Language and Poverty.* Chicago: Markham, 1970.

Lindholm, K.J. "Bilingual Children: Some Interpretations of Cognitive and Linguistic Development," in K.E. Nelson (Ed.), *Children's Language,* volume 2. New York: Gardner Press, 1980.

Piaget, J., & Inhelder, B. *The Psychology of the Child.* New York: Basic Books, 1969.

Trevarthen, C., & Hubley, P. "Secondary Intersubjectivity: Confidence, Confiding, and Acts of Meaning in the First Year," in A.J. Lock (Ed.), *Action, Gesture, and Symbol: The Emergence of Language.* London: Academic Press, 1978.

Wells, G. *Learning through Interaction: The Study of Language Development.* New York: Cambridge University Press, 1981.

Peer-Peer Learning: Evidence from a Student-Run Sharing Time

Sarah Michaels
Michele Foster
Harvard University

Sharing Time in Elementary School Classrooms

Two striking characteristics of elementary school classrooms are the amount of talk that goes on within them and the fact that, on average, teachers do significantly more of this talking than the children (Barnes, 1976; Flanders, 1967). In most classroom activities, teachers elicit information, and then evaluate the child's contribution (Mehan, 1979). Through these instructional sequences, children are called upon to use language to demonstrate learning; seldom are they allowed to use language to entertain, inform, or to interest others. This is because the child's audience is ordinarily the teacher and much of the child's classroom talk is limited to filling in teacher created slots.

An exception to this general pattern is "sharing time" (also called "show and tell" in some classrooms), one of the few activities in which children are expected to talk at length to the entire class on a topic of their own choice. Recently several ethnographic researchers have looked at sharing time as a recurring speech event, and have documented the kind of talk and participation that occurs (Michaels, 1981; Lazarus, 1981; Wilcox, 1982; Dorr-Bremme, 1982; New, 1982). Each of these studies has described a teacher-led activity in which children are called upon to give a narrative account about some past event or describe an object brought from home. Teachers generally play pivotal roles, responding to each child in turn, and have the final word on what counts as an appropriate topic.[1] Because of the teachers' evaluative roles as well as their asymmetrical relationships with the students, sharing time turns come to be heard from the teachers' perspective. Thus, while teacher-led sharing time activities do allow for more extended talk, the teachers' expectations and evaluative criteria for what counts as good sharing time talk usually prevail. In order to be considered competent, children must conform to the teachers' expectations as to how information should be organized and presented. Competence then becomes narrowly defined.

A Student-Run Model of Sharing Time

There are other models of sharing time that deserve attention. We have observed a first-second grade ethnically mixed classroom of 20 children in which the children run sharing time by themselves, collaborating with and evaluating each other's sharing time turns without benefit of teacher.

The data on this sharing time activity were collected over an entire school year using audiotapes and fieldnotes, supplemented by interviews with children as well as the teacher, regarding their perceptions of the activity and knowledge of the norms for "good" sharing time talk. By combining observation with analysis of tape recorded talk, we are able to provide an account of the activity as a recurring speech event, as well as to document the strategies different children use in organizing information and holding the floor. These same methods can be used by practicing teachers in their own classrooms.

Sharing time in this classroom takes place in a rectangular shaped group meeting area. The area is bordered on two sides by bookcases. The children sit on the floor, partially obscured from view, and are thereby afforded some privacy. This group meeting area is also used by the teacher and students for other large group activities. Sharing time occurs daily, immediately following lunch and a brief recess period. At this time the children are called to the activity by the teacher, Mrs. James, who announces, "O.K., Jeannie's the group leader." The group leader (a different child each day) sits on a chair which is placed in the entrance to the area and calls on children to share from among those who bid for a turn by raising their hands. In addition to selecting children to share, the child leader is responsible for monitoring individual behavior and maintaining group order.

There are clearly defined rules for participation at sharing time and, occasionally, before turning sharing time over to the leader, the teacher reviews the rules. These include that only one person can share at a time, that the leader gets to choose the person who will share, that children have to raise their hands if they want to talk, that children who misbehave will get a first warning and that if children misbehave a second time they get a second warning and go back to their seats. While the teacher reviewed the rules infrequently, we noted that this coincided with the presence of a weak group leader. It may be that the teacher's purpose in these interactions was not primarily to reinforce the children's knowledge of the rules, but rather to indirectly establish the authority of the group leader.

Although everyone agrees on the rules, all infractions which violate the "first and second warning" rule are not clearly spelled out and the child leaders interpret violations of this rule differently. For example, with some leaders lying down on the floor was treated as an infraction while with others lying down on the floor was acceptable behavior. Nonetheless, the first warning allowed children to figure out which violations were in effect each day before being sent back to their seats. In spite of this ambiguity and the young age of the children, the turn taking, sanctioning, and isolation from the group worked smoothly. The children acceded to the child leader's decision and only once during our observations was there a disagreement over the invocation of the "warning rule" and the teacher, who is always within earshot, stepped in to help negotiate the problem.

The important point here is that while there are clearly defined rules about appropriate ways of behaving which are probably necessary for the speech event to proceed in an orderly fashion, there are *no teacher rules governing topic, style, or amount of time that each person can talk.* The children themselves evaluate sharing time turns, and determine what counts as appropriate or "good" talk. And it is the children who respond with questions and comments, which often serve to clarify or expand on a child's topic. Thus, left to their own devices, sharer and audience together control what gets talked about and how a given topic is developed.

Children's Sharing Time Styles

In this classroom two distinct but equally successful and valued sharing time styles have emerged. For purposes of discussion, we will call these styles "the lecture demonstration" and "the performed narrative." What distinguishes these two styles is both topic and stylistic features of presentation. The lecture demonstration tends to be about an object or event, a presentation of factual information. Children using this style often rely on external supports—objects—to bolster their presentations and hold the audience's attention.

The performed narrative, on the other hand, tends to be a personal narrative account, emphasizing interaction between two or more people (usually close friends or relatives). This style is characterized by the use of stylistic features similar to those used in a dramatic stage performance (Wolfson, 1978).

Dialogue:	My mother said, "That's it. You're going to bed" and I thought she was talking to me and so I said, "No, I don't wanna go," crying and crying. And she said, "Renee, why're you crying?" and I said, "Cuz I don't wanna go to bed."
Gestures:	I'm gonna smack you and I go (slap, slap, slap on face) and then I went (slap, slap, slap) again.
Sound Effects:	And then it snowball went *PHSSS...PHSSS* and then she was gonna throw it this way but I went up and it went through right here and I went like this and went *PHSSS*. It went *PHSSS*.
Asides:	They kept going like this and they weren't hitting each other till the ten rounds, till they went like this, both of 'em fell down like this. *It was really funny*, and then...
Repetitions:	I said, "look up there. Sure ain't Superman" and he said, "Sure ain't Superman" and I said, "That's what I just said, sure ain't Superman."
Shifting to Present Tense for Emphasis:	I *said*, "mama, I won't, I won't tell you what you what you look like this time cuz it's too funny" and she *goes*, "watch it" and I *go* "why not, please say it" and then she *goes*, "I'll help you up anyway" anyways she, then she *helped* me up.

Each child has a predominant style, but all are free to experiment with both. And while the children as a group appreciate both styles at sharing time, some children are considered better storytellers than others. Over time, we have noted the emergence of "star sharers" in this classroom. These children are called on to share frequently (often more than once in a given sharing session), and hold the floor for extended periods. It is not unusual for star sharers to continue uninterrupted for three to four minutes. The longest single narrative recorded is eight minutes long. Additionally, when these children share, there is evidence of heightened audience attention, signalled through active listenership (laughter, nodding, eye gaze, comments such as "uh huh," "mmmm," "uh oh!"). Moreover, the children we identified as star sharers were consistently selected by other children in interviews when asked, "Who do you really like to listen to at sharing time?"

It is by examining the performances of two star sharers who are masters of their respective styles that the features of the lecture demonstration and the performed narrative can be most clearly seen. These two turns occurred during the same sharing time episode.

Lecture Demonstration Style

In this turn, Paul, a second grader, talks about some rocks he has brought from home.

Paul: This is what I found.
This is called, um, um, salt rocks.

Child: Salt rocks!

Paul: They're um they're a kind of rock that's white and they have a little salt in 'em. . . .They're are lots in here, 'cuz I picked 'em up and my friend said I could have some. And they're salt rocks. . .O.K.? They're going around.

Paul passes the rocks to the child sitting next to him and the children pass the rocks around the circle. Immediately following Paul's talk about the rocks there is a series of questions and comments from the children.

Child: There are some dirty ones.

Paul: Those look much better with the white, dirty and white, like that, put together.

Child: Why are they called salt rocks?

Paul: Because they have salt in 'em.

By elaborating on each of the questions and comments, Paul is able to hold the floor. As the children examine the rocks that are being passed around they comment to each other about them. At this point a child raises his hand and is recognized by the child leader.

Child: Yesterday, me and Nancy went ice skating.

This remark is ignored by the other children, and it appears that Paul still has the floor. In fact, another child immediately says,

Child: I have a question to ask Paul.

Matt: (Child leader) O.K.

Child: Do salt rocks taste like salt?

Paul: No. . .(inaudible) I thought for a minute these were um ice, and then I thought they were like, crystal things. . . .I'm going to go around here because those people didn't get to see 'em.

There are several rounds of questions or comments followed by Paul's elaboration. At one point Paul who continues in this teaching mode, stops to chastise a child for putting the rocks in her mouth.

Paul: Don't eat them! Look at it! They're dirty. I found 'em in a place where it's dirt.

Finally there is a lull in the verbal exchanges and the child leader asks if Paul has finished.

Matt: (Child leader) All finished?

Paul: Oh no, yeah, yeah, but people can ask me questions.

Only one child has a question.

Child: Why are those, um those um, spots in 'em? Are they dirt caught in 'em?

Paul: Yeah.

Twice more Paul solicits questions.

Paul: Anybody else have questions?
Anybody else have questions?

His request yields additional questions and a comment.

Child: Know what? If you had a round thing and then two of them, a black one and a white one,. . .and then you could glue it and then, then you could make a ring.

Paul: Yeah.

Another child raises her hand but before the group leader can recognize her, Paul anticipates still another question.

Paul: What's the question Jackie?

Paul is mistaken. The child doesn't want to ask a question; she only wants to share. Finally the child leader closes out Paul's turn telling everyone that "It's over guys, it's over."

In this turn, Paul uses a marked school register in describing and passing around his rocks. He speaks slower than he normally does in casual conversation, enunciates clearly, and solicits questions from the audience, much as a teacher would in a science demonstration. But while his style is formal and instructional in tone, his performance depends crucially on audience questions and comments upon which he can elaborate, and thereby hold the floor. His initial lecture before questions, comments, and elaboration lasted 20 seconds; his entire turn, however, lasted seven and one-half minutes. Paul expects children to ask questions and capitalizes on audience participation. The children in this class see Paul's style, and others like it, as informative. During an interview a child said that Paul "tells about things that you can learn from. He told one thing in sharing but it was hard to understand. All I know is that you can learn from it." It is also worth noting that when children were asked, "Who do you think your teacher would pick as the best sharers in the class if she came to sharing time?" they unanimously selected children who used the lecture demonstration style, having pegged this kind of talk as "instructional." This suggests that these first and second grade children are well aware of differing styles and see some as more school like than others.

The Performed Narrative Style

In the following turn, Rene, also a second grader, gives a highly complex narrative about a sequence of events that took place during a Thanksgiving holiday visit to her paternal grandparents. The entire narrative lasted six and one-half minutes, during which time Rene held the floor uninterrupted.

Our analysis of the narrative suggests that it consists of five related segments, each marked off by a subtle shift in time, location, and activity, but each bearing a clear thematic relationship to the other segments. The different segments are marked off through changes in tempo and intonation, and each segment is a fully formed unit, with an introduction and logical sequence of events. There is thus cohesion within a segment and thematic ties across segments.

In the first segment, Rene provides a general orientation to the narrative, setting the scene with respect to time (Thanksgiving), place (her grandparents' house), people on the scene (grandparents, father), and activity (eating dinner). In this segment, Rene characterizes family relationships through a series of performed dialogues, giving examples of her father's outlandish childhood behavior as seen through her grandfather's eyes.

> Rene: Um, ... at Thanksgiving when I went to my grandma and grandpa um, .. we were, ... we had all-all this FOOD. ... and I was at the table, right? And I, and I was saying, and I said, ... and I ss.. it was the day before Thanksgiving, and I said to my, I was REALLY, REALLY, stuffed because we were .. um, cuz we just had finished eating, and I said, I'm so so full I could eat a Thanksgiving turkey. And she said, well you could eat the stuffing too. And I said, I said, why don't you and daddy put the stuffing in bed, ... and, and ...

and daddy – my father looked at me and he said, HUH!?, HUH!?. That's what, that's what he always does when um I say something like ... he should be CHICKEN or something, he goes, ... HUH, HUH (laughs) he goes like that. ...And um my grandfather always makes um .. jokes about him being so dumb when he was little, like he said one time, he said, ... um, ... he said, ... he's at the kitchen table he said, when your father was about ... ten he didn't know his feet from his head, and he would put his shoe:s on his head and his feet .. on top. (laughs) And um, then he goes, well you're BA:LD da:d. (laughs) And um, then he goes, well guess what? You didn't have any hair when you were .. five ... an .. and he said, .. and he said, now I bet that was a JOKE. And he said, no .. I don't (...), I only have eight plus seven, and everyone laughed.[2]

In this segment, Rene uses a variety of stylistic devices: extra loudness, gestures, shifts to present tense, and dialogue. It appears that each anecdotal dialogue is intended to provoke audience laughter. Rene, herself, laughs after each dialogue but the only response she gets from the audience is a muffled snicker.

Rene then moves into the second phase of her narrative. In this segment, she introduces animals—a raccoon family and a pair of rabbits—who come knocking at the door later that same evening. She establishes cohesion between the first and second segment of the narrative by providing the explicit temporal shifter, "when we were um, sleeping," while maintaining the Thanksgiving theme, and focal characters (grandparents and father). Moreover, she skillfully weaves together apparent fact and fiction—feeding make believe visiting animals real leftover Thanksgiving turkey.

Rene: And um we heard um .. wh – when we were um, sleeping, ... I heard a scratching noise ... And I snuck out ... to the um door and there was a, um, ... there was ... a mama racoon scratching at the thing with um .. five babies. And I um, and I called n – nana, my grandmother, and my .. grandfather and my daddy, to come and they, we, and they, we let 'em in for a minute, ... and they gave 'em some milk and stuff, ... and we gave 'em some milk and a little bit of, of left over turkey, .. and um ... we let 'em out.

The audience by this point is evidencing all the outward signs of involvement—nodding, leaning forward toward the speaker. Rene then recounts a similar animal anecdote.

Rene: Then uh, and in midnight, ... ac – actually it was like two o'clock in the morning I heard a scratch again, and I went to the same room and it was just a little, little baby rabbit with his mo—with one mother, and he was so:cute and, ... I fed THEM some milk, ... and some left over turkey, and um then I an um, ... then I let THEM out.

This second anecdote serves as a kind of "variation on a theme." Rene repeats key phrases (some milk and leftover turkey, let them out) and elicits the same appreciative responses from the audience as she got the first time around. By the time there is a *third* knock at the door, the children in the audience are making anticipatory noises. Rene introduces her grandfather instead of an animal and begins to round out this segment.

Rene: ... A minute LATER, I heard another [knocking
Child: [Ooooh
Rene: at the door. I opened it up, and it was my GRANDFATHER (laughs) saying, what's all the noise (chuckles) out there, oh ha (laughs), and, and um, after that day, I never let anything, a living thing in ... except um ... except uh, .. I forget.

At this point, a child in the audience suggests a continuation of the animal theme by uttering with pronounced rising intonation

Child: Animals

followed by another child's suggested

Child: Bears

Rene picks up on this lead and immediately launches into the third segment of the narrative introducing another animal episode which shifts setting but is nonetheless still linked spatially to the previous narrative events. In this segment, Rene appears to build on the topic suggested by the child who said "Bears" by telling a "scary animal" episode.

Rene: I almost got, I almost got really scared. Because it, of it. There's three, um, ... HAWKS near their house that live there, ... they try to swoop around and get all the birds, 'cuz they put out bird feeders and stuff. They, um my grandma and grandpa, they look down on the bird feeders and they try to catch all their birds. And the hawk was flying around, I could see it, I walked out. And I saw this big flying shadow outside. Now it couldn't be Superman. It just couldn't be. I looked up and I went, AH. For real. I was terrified 'cuz I thought he was gonna like, come down and tear me apart or something, and I was screaming. I screamed, and I ran back up, yeah, I was really scared, I even spilled the water that I was supposed to um, be watering the garden of my grandfather. I was SCREAMING and um, I went in um my father said, Rene what's the matter. I said, look up there sure ain't Superman, (audience laughter) and he said sure AIN'T superman and I said that's what I just said, sure ain't Superman, and he said, yes it is, and I go, it is not, it's a vulture, I mean, … a [HAWK

Child: [HAWK

Rene: and um, he said, oh my God, we'd better, we better close the windows, 'cuz we had all the windows open, 'cuz it was pretty cold.

In this segment, Rene uses a variety of expressive stylistic devices: increased loudness, dialogue, and repetition of key phrases such as "sure ain't Superman" (repeated four times).

In the fourth segment of the narrative, Rene again shifts temporally but establishes cohesion between parts three and four by using the explicit connector "and the next day," and by continuing the hawk theme. She makes use of expressive devices: sound effects of various sorts, ranging from hawk noises to the sounds of drums and musical instruments, as well as dialogue, warning of the hawk menace.

Rene: and the next day I went out an, I rode my bike. Right before um, I opened the door and stuck my head out, to make sure there was no hawk, and there weren't. And then um, I was ridin' my bike, up and down, up and down, and all of a sudden I hear this, AH AH AH AHA BL-BL-BL (noises) I wonder if Rene's home (more noises), and it was Sean, I went I went ah, I hope it's not him again. And instead then um, over came Sean by me, a five year old and a sev--, six year old, and um they were both going, bl-bl, toot chch ch ch toot (noises), and they were going toot chch ch ch toot (laughs), and wah wah, they were making all these weird noises, and I started saying, PHEW, I'm glad it's you, and they said we wanted to warn you about the, the HAWK going by, and I said OH MY GOD, and I took my bike into the garage and I said G'BYE, (laughs) and I went inside again.

She begins the final segment after a pause, relating the events with a temporal connector, "and that night … ." She continues the hawk theme with more expressive sound effects (hawk noises), gestures, and dramatic replays of holding her breath from fright, and listening for the hawk (with her hand at her ear, turning her head from side to side).

Rene: … And that night I was SCARED half to death, I couldn't go to SLEEP. And I kept remembering my, in my mind I kept um thinking I heard ARK ARK (hawk noises), and I kept on, listening going, (hand to ear turning head from side to side) I even stopped breathing for a moment. . . . (holds breath) and I thought I heard a, I thought I heard something, I thought I heard someone going ARK ARK (hawk noises), but I didn't, I was just hearing things, cuz I was so sca:rd.

Child: I have a question.

Rene: And we had some pumpkin pie for dessert.

C's: MMMMMMM

Rene appears to be about to round out her entire narrative by returning to the original scene, saying "and we had some pumpkin pie for dessert." At this point, however, she is interrupted by a child in the audience requesting clarification of something she had said earlier:

Child: Why did your dad say, um, we'd better close the windows because, um and then you said and um 'cuz you said, 'cuz we opened the windows because it was *cold*. You said that, instead of hot.

Rene denies this challenge:

Rene: No I didn't, I didn't say cold or hot, I just said, I said, ... I said we opened the window because ... I said we opened the windows because um we needed to uh cool off the turkey.

As it turns out, Rene was indeed guilty of being unclear at this very point in her narrative. She had actually said

Rene: and um he [father] said oh my God, we'd better, better close the windows, cuz we had all the windows open, cuz it was pretty cold.

If we look closely at the way Rene uses 'cuz' here and at other points in this narrative, it appears that cuz can function in two distinct ways: 1) as a causal indicator (its more conventional use) and, 2) as a signal of interjected background information. In this passage, it appears that the first instance of cuz (cuz we had all the windows open) serves as a marker of background information, telling us that the windows were already open and the second instance of cuz serves as a causal explanation of why the windows had to be closed (cuz it was pretty cold). On the basis of this analysis, the other child's confusion is certainly justified, as is Rene's denial of any actual mistating of the facts.

The point here is that while these children tolerate and appreciate the introduction of fiction or embellished facts, if it advances the story line, they are an attentive, critical audience, expecting that what they hear will make sense. It often happens that to satisfy the audience, the sharer must clarify temporal relationships ("When did this happen?"), location ("Where were you?"), referents ("Which sister?"), or provide clearer descriptions of objects that the child is telling about but not able to show.

What follows Rene's narrative is a two and one-half minute discussion led entirely by the children in which the children contribute all they know about hawks.

Rene: (in response to a question about the power of hawks) They're strong birds, they can catch mice real good.

Paul: Their claws look like a screech owl, their claws, they can go (sound—krch) like that and cage the mouse and then they go (makes eating motion with hand to mouth), they eat it.

Sean: Um do you know how big a hawk is? How big?

Rene: There's different sizes but the one we saw is as big as this (makes motion with hands) as big as this (makes motion with hands) as big as um my hands are out and strong too. (laughter)

Sean: My dad said um a grownup um what did you say, hawk?

Rene: Yeah.

Sean: Grownup hawk could from .. from .. from wing tip to wing tip um they could grow about ten feet.

C: What's ten feet?

C: (motions with hand approximately 3 feet)

Sean: No, bigger than that.

C: Bigger than my mom.

Mrs. James: (who had just approached the group) I'm about five feet.

C: Bigger than her.

Rene: Yi! Yi! Yi!

Sean: Two times as big as my mom.

The discussion continues and children offer examples of abilities that hawks possess, and animals that they prey on. What began as a narrative account about a child's personal experiences developed into an informative discussion that generated generalizations and analytic thinking applying math concepts. Similar to Paul's sharing time turn, audience input was a major factor in developing the child's original narrative intentions.

Audience Involvement

These examples illustrate two very different sharing time styles used commonly by the children. While Paul and Rene's turns differ widely in terms of topic and stylistic features used, they have an important element in common. Both children attend to and capitalize on audience involvement.

There is evidence in other successful sharing time turns of skillful monitoring and incorporation of audience input, on occasion leading to the development of new strategies and new sharing time genres. For example, in December, a child introduced a genre which later became known as the "dream sequence." Each day this child told one chapter of a dream, closing with a "to be continued" ending. New characters were introduced daily and the dream characters were invariably children from the class. Children looked forward to these sequences and always held a slot open for them. We have also noted a strategy that we call "topping," that is, challenging or embellishing upon a previous speaker's story. In one such "topping" instance, a child gave a performed narrative about visiting relatives (cousins) and playing on a water bed. Another child, an arch enemy and best friend of the previous speaker, immediately followed with a performed narrative about a relative, an uncle, who happened to live in the New York Greyhound Bus Station. But when he visited his niece in Boston, he stayed at the YMCA where he had a water bed as well. *His* water bed, however, was filled with goldfish! In both of these cases, as in Paul's and Rene's turns, children show themselves to be adept at making their contributions relevant to audience concerns.

"Good" Sharing Time Talk

In studies of teacher-led sharing time activities, researchers have noted a "literate bias" on the part of teachers in responding to or evaluating a child's discourse (Michaels, 1981; New, 1982; Wilcox, 1982). In her study of an ethnically mixed Berkeley first grade, Michaels suggested that the teacher's criterion for "good" sharing time talk was focused discourse on a single topic evidencing clarity of topic statement and explication, as in simple descriptive prose. She found that children whose discourse style was at variance with the teacher's own literate style and expectations received less practice than children whose discourse more closely matched that of the teacher. This mismatch frequently resulted in interruptions, misunderstandings, and what is worse, misassessment of children's abilities. New (1982), in a study of a Cambridge second grade classroom, discussed the teacher's preference for stories with a beginning, middle, and end. Such an expectation mirrors a *literate story model* in which there is a "sequential presentation of events or actions, such that the connection between one or more of the events is evident within the story" (Cook-Gumperz & Green, in press).

In analyzing sharing time turns from the classroom with child-run sharing time, we have found that these "literate" criteria fail to differentiate the successful from the less successful sharing time turns. We find, for example, both successful and unsuccessful turns (as indicated by audience response) that have a clear beginning, middle, and end. At the same time, we find highly successful turns like Rene's which are characterized by a series of complex, thematically related anecdotes, rather than a simple sequential progression of actions.

What does appear to differentiate sharers in this classroom is their attention to audience. Throughout these sharing time episodes the audience reacts and signals excitement, interest, confusion, impatience, and boredom. The successful sharers pay close attention to and capitalize on the immediate reactions of their audience in selecting an appropriate topic and style of presentation. Moreover, the successful sharers continually monitor audience cues and feedback. When their talk is not appreciated or understood, these children shift or modify their topic and style to meet the demands of the audience.

It has been suggested that through discourse activities such as sharing time, teachers help children develop valued language skills and literature discourse strategies that are required in written communication (Scollon & Scollon, in press; Michaels, 1981; Wilcox, 1982). It must be noted, however, that the development of a literate style consists of more than mastering a set of discourse strategies concerned with topic development. Effective writing must equally be concerned with other factors relating to genre, style or register, and audience expectations. There are, for example, professionals whose writing fails miserably, not because they have inadequate topic development nor because they have failed to establish cohesion within the text, but because they have written in a style inappropriate to the audience they had hoped to reach.

So much attention has been directed at dichotomizing and explaining the differences between written and spoken language that it is impossible for some to consider any similarities between the two forms. Like spoken language, written language has a sociolinguistic dimension and writers, like speakers, must be aware of and know how to speak to their audience. Knowing how to communicate effectively to different audiences for a variety of purposes—controlling several styles—can only enhance one's speaking and writing ability by allowing for flexibility in meeting shifting communicative demands. However, one can practice different styles and judge their effectiveness only if one has many different opportunities to try them out on a sympathetic but discriminating audience.

What is important about the classroom speech event described here is that it allows children to fully demonstrate the narrative and descriptive discourse skills they bring with them from home, and build upon this competence and sophistication in the classroom. The children serve as a critical audience for one another who, while appreciating multiple modes of discourse, expect sharing time turns to be worth listening to. Children will without reluctance tell a sharer, "That's boring." And with no teacher to hold the floor open for them, these children try various strategies, including style shifts and the development of novel genres, to hold the audience's attention. Through peer/peer imitation, topping, and evaluation, over time, these children are becoming more skillful in their use of language.

The teacher's stated goals for this activity are limited to giving the children an opportunity to talk to each other, leading a group of peers, and learning to ask and answer questions. It seems that these goals are more than being met. In this child-run sharing time activity, where implicit notions about correctness are absent and with an audience that is interested, *children learn from one another*. They are free to explore ideas by reliving the past, describing the present, or creating a new world, to entertain, amuse, or inform. In Halliday's terms (1982), these children are learning *through language*, facts about each other and the world, while at the same time becoming more *skilled users of language*, by attending to a sympathetic but discriminating audience of peers.

Acknowledgement: Work on this chapter was supported by a grant from the Spencer Foundation. Thanks also to Courtney Cazden for comments on an earlier draft.

Notes

1. See Lazarus' study (1981) in which the teacher consciously modified the role she played, changing the activity from a teacher moderated discussion to a conversation.
2. Transcription conventions are as follows. Clauses are marked off by commas, indicating rising intonations. Periods indicate falling intonation, signalling the completion of the intonational phrase. Pauses are marked as "..." indicating a measurable pause, or ".." indicating a short break in timing. Extra emphasis or loudness is indicated by capitalizing letters. Vowel elongation is indicated with a ":" after the elongated syllable. Brackets indicate simultaneous speech.

References

Barnes, D. *From Communication to Curriculum.* New York: Penguin Books, 1976.

Cook-Gumperz, J. & Green, J. "Sense of Story: Influences on Children's Storytelling," in D. Tannen (Ed.), *Coherence in Spoken and Written Language.* Norwood, New Jersey: Ablex, in press.

Dorr-Bremme, D. "Behaving and Making Sense: Creating Social Organization in the Classroom," doctoral dissertation, Harvard University, 1982.

Flanders, N. "Teacher Influence in the Classroom," in E. Amidon & J. Hough (Eds.), *Interaction Analysis: Theory, Research, and Application.* Reading, Massachusetts: Addison-Wesley, 1967.

Halliday, M.A.K. "Three Aspects of Children's Language Development: Language Learning, Learning through Language, Learning about Language," in Y. Goodman, M. Haussler, & D. Strickland (Eds.), *Oral and Written Language Development Research: Impact on the Schools.* Urbana, Illinois: National Council of Teachers of English, 1982.

Lazarus, P. "Kindergarten Children's Communicative Competence: An Ethnographic Study," doctoral dissertation, University of New Mexico, 1981.

Mehan, H. *Learning Lessons: Social Organization in the Classroom.* Cambridge, Massachusetts: Harvard University Press, 1979.

Michaels, S. "Sharing Time: Children's Narrative Style and Differential Access to Literacy," *Language in Society, 10* (December 1981), 423-442.

New, C. "Sharing Time as a Teacher Led Speech Event," paper presented at University of Pennsylvania Ethnography in Education Research Forum, March 1982, Philadelphia.

Scollon, R., & Scollon, S.B.K. "Cooking It Up and Boiling It Down: Athabaskan Children's Story Retellings," in D. Tannen (Ed.), *Coherence in Spoken and Written Discourse.* Norwood, New Jersey: Ablex, in press.

Wilcox, K. "Differential Socialization in the Classroom: Implications for Equal Opportunity," in G. Spindler (Ed.), *Doing the Ethnography of Schooling: Educational Anthropology in Action.* New York: Holt, Rinehart & Winston, 1982.

Wolfson, N. "A Feature of Performed Narrative: The Conversational Historical Present," *Language in Society, 7* (August 1978), 215-237.

Cultures Together in the Classroom: "What You Sayin?"[1]

Barbara Z. Kiefer
University of Houston
Johanna S. DeStefano
The Ohio State University

A large sign over the entrance to a municipal hall proclaims a "United Nations Festival." Inside, the flags and costumes of many countries assault the eye with color. A folk dance troupe whirls gaily on a central stage to the tune of native instruments. Visitors wander from booth to booth sampling each tasty ethnic treat or fingering samples of artisans' wares. This event serves to illustrate how we Americans are becoming more aware of the pluralistic nature of our society. The Civil Rights movement in the late fifties and sixties, the influx of Indo-Chinese boat people in the late seventies, and more recently the Cuban and Haitian flotillas, raised the consciousness of many of us concerning the diversity of ethnic, religious, and racial groups which characterize our society. In communities across the country, festivals celebrate our cultural ties. While such celebrations may call our attention to the diversity present among cultures, they do little to deepen our understanding of the extent to which cultural differences may affect the ways in which we communicate with one another—in our neighborhoods, at our jobs, and in our schools.

Teachers, perhaps more than any other group, are being confronted with a variety of cultural differences as they *use* language to educate children *about* language. Often as the year progresses, the task of educating disintegrates into a struggle to impose "correct" or mainstream forms upon children who may be confused by and uncomfortable with such forms. For example, one of the authors (Kiefer) recalls her experience with a second grade composed of middleclass white children and several Amish youngsters. She understood that differences in experiential background among the Amish children might lead to problems in reading comprehension—for example, when stories dealt with aspects of the technological age with which the children were not familiar. She felt a sense of frustration, however, as she tried to talk with the Amish children in the course of daily lessons. They seldom volunteered to talk, and when questioned directly either refused to answer or answered with a single word in voices too soft to be heard more than several inches away. When she expressed concern to other members of the school staff she was told that Amish children were often sent to speech therapists upon entering school in order to correct this "problem." Because the principal had forbidden them to speak anything but English in school, it was not until halfway through the year that she discovered the Amish children's primary language was a form of German and that it was the custom in Amish homes for children to be seen and not heard—they were *expected* to remain silent in the presence of an adult. She still regrets the humiliation she may have caused these children by expecting them to conform to her view of middleclass norms of behavior.

Unfortunately, her experience may be all too familiar to other teachers who care deeply about their students but who receive little instruction in the types of language behaviors to expect from diverse cultures, or little help in how to effect growth in language competencies. The task of sorting out the subtleties of language use as it varies from culture to culture is not an easy one and the fact that almost as many differences exist within groups as across groups compounds the problem. Because research has only begun to identify the diversity present in various speech communities, teachers have an important role to play in identifying patterns of variation among their own students and, thus, adding to this body of information. By kidwatching—that is, by developing techniques for effective observation, and by becoming aware of the dimensions of differences which may occur among cultures and of ways to apply this knowledge to actual classroom situations—teachers are in a unique position to build bridges rather than walls between cultures.

In order to become effective childwatchers, teachers first need to understand the dimensions of language use and how different cultural patterns may result in culture clash rather than in "cultures together" in the classroom. Teachers, because of training and experience, are most likely to be familiar with aspects of language form which may vary. These include pronunciation and enunciation, sentence structure, and vocabulary—aspects of language that are often the focus of language arts or reading lessons. Teachers may not be as cognizant, however, of more subtle aspects of language variation which occur in the social use system—the rules which govern our interactions with each other. This system involves participants' knowledge of when to speak and when to remain silent, appropriate forms for different language situations, and cues with which participants glue their conversations together. Nonverbal cues which sustain interactions are also a part of the social use system.

Differences in Form

Teachers involved in spelling and writing instruction are likely to notice differences in the phonological or syntactic system among cultural groups although they may not always recognize that these differences are as rule governed in minority groups as they are in the mainstream culture. For example, speakers of Black English may reduce final consonant clusters to a single consonant (*test* may become *tes'*) or apply the negative form throughout a sentence ("Can't nobody write no poetry") as do French or Spanish speakers. Chinese children may use a form like "Janet blouse" (Janet's blouse) because their native language has almost no final consonants and no final consonant clusters (Matluck, 1979). The pronunciation of the consonant groups "ts" and "bl" would be as difficult for these children as many Chinese forms would be for native English speakers.

Educators, though aware these structural differences exist, may still not be willing to accept them. For example, Miller (1977) describes an English teacher in rural Kentucky who constructed a miniature cemetery in the back of her room. Whenever her students used their Appalachian dialect, they were asked to write the offending word on a cardboard tombstone and place it in the cemetery. And a colleague from New England relates her own embarrassment and consternation when the faculty at her midwestern teacher's college asked her to attend speech therapy sessions in order to "cure" her dialect. It is not difficult to imagine what this "pathological" approach to structural variation might do to the self-assuredness of younger children.

Syntactic forms can also vary among cultures. Teachers may be familiar with such forms as "I warm" or "It warm" as well as "I am warm" or "It's warm." But they may not realize that such expressions follow rules appropriate to the speaker's cultural background. The nonuse of the copula (*to be*) in the type of structure "I warm" is common in all Asian languages (Matluck, 1979). Speakers of Black English, on the other hand, may delete the copula only in constructions which standard English speakers contract, yielding "I warm" from "I'm warm." It would be well to remember what Hymes (1972) stated apropos to these forms: "The vernacular speech of every society or social group, when studied, has been found to be based on complex, profound structures..." (p. xx).

Differences in Social Use

Structural aspects of language such as dialect differences represent only the surface of cultural variation, however. Less well-known but perhaps more deep-seated differences exist in the rules which govern our interactions with each other—the social use system. Just as children learn the forms of language in the context of their home communities, they learn how to use language with adults and peers in the same context. Like the Amish children mentioned earlier, the children of many cultures are expected to remain silent in the presence of adults—unlike many middleclass children who are encouraged to be verbal from a very early age. Ward (1971) observed that to rural black mothers in Rosepoint, Louisiana, "speaking is often equated with the quality 'bad'. . . . When babies learn to talk they are bad children" (p. 29). Learning *when* to use language in cultures such as these may come more from interaction within the peer group or with siblings than with adults in the community.

Philips (1982) found that native American Indian children in Warm Springs, Oregon, also are expected to remain silent when with adults and are expected to learn through observation rather than interaction. In learning household tasks such as curing hides or hunting game, children spend long periods observing adults instead of listening to elaborate verbal instructions. The children then test their skills unsupervised by adults. Philips states:

> The use of speech in the process is notably minimal. Verbal directions or instructions are few, being confined to corrections and question-answering. Nor does the final demonstration of skill particularly involve verbal performance, since the validation of skill so often involves display of some material evidence or nonverbal physical expression. (p. 387)

Children in Chinese and Vietnamese cultures have similar patterns of interaction with adults, most often learning by listening, watching, and observing an adult authority figure. In addition, many feel strong pressure to maintain the honor of the family and to live up to parental expectations. Thus, they may be reluctant to ask for help or to answer questions in order not to exhibit ignorance or lose face (Kang-Ning, 1981).

This reluctance of children of some minority groups to engage in conversation with adults can be misinterpreted by members of the mainstream culture. For many years black innercity children were thought to be verbally "deprived" when in fact they may have been reacting correctly to interactional patterns appropriate in their own culture.

One author recalls an incident during her own research (DeStefano, Pepinsky & Sanders, 1982) where the teacher tried to engage a black first grader in conversation about his art work.

> "That's lovely Dick. What a nice job—look how you've done the bird," she said. Dick (in accordance with his cultural pattern for showing respect to adults), kept his head down and continued to draw. Later, the teacher confided that Dick was a "sneaky child"—he talked a great deal on the playground but wouldn't talk to her.

Dick's response was perfectly acceptable and even "required" for a formal "adult to child" situation in his culture. His verbalizations on the playground showed his ability to perform competently in a different set of social circumstances. Yet they were both taken to mean something quite the opposite by his teacher.

This incident suggests that culture clash can result not only when children do *not* engage in talk with mainstream culture adults, but also when they use inappropriate language or talk at the *wrong* time. Matluck (1979) reports Hispanic children may be typed as sacrilegious for their use of "My God" or "By God" or for their given names such as Jesus. Another case in point is

> the Chinese child who learned to use "God Damn!" when he lost a point on the playground and shocks the teacher by using the same expletive upon losing a point in a classroom game. He has not yet learned the context appropriateness of certain kinds of language. (Matluck, p. 190)

In many black cultures the use of verbal responses during conversation—"Yes, yes" or "Right on" are signals that the listener is following the conversation and that the speaker is effectively making a point. Yet teachers who are used to nonverbal responses such as head nodding often consider this behavior unacceptable. Kochman (1969) recalls a black fourth grade student whose responses became cause for friction with his mainstream teacher.

> During the first month of my weekly observations, I watched the teacher's frustration with D____ steadily increase: "D____ I didn't call on you. I called on ____. Is your name ____? How many times do I have to tell you to raise your hand? D____ is that your voice I hear again? If I want your opinions I'll ask for them." By the second month D____ spent as much time alone for disciplinary reasons (in the hall, in the office, missing recess) as he spent with other children. (p. 383)

On other occasions, misunderstandings between teacher and students may occur when *patterns for group interaction* differ. Boggs (1972) reported that native Hawaiian children do not like to be singled out for individual attention and, when called upon to answer a question, a child might answer minimally if at all. Yet this same child might interrupt or call out answers when questions are addressed to another child or to the group. In contrast, Boggs found that when these children are invited to narrate, rather than being questioned directly, they wait until called upon and their responses are often lengthy. Boggs hypothesized that it is "basically unpleasant for a Hawaiian child to have a question directed to him by an adult. . ." (p. 307), a result perhaps of the child's cultural background where adults address individual questions to children primarily in disciplinary situations.

Other causes of misunderstandings between cultures can grow out of the use of nonverbal cues which are also an important part of the social use system. Teachers who are used to maintaining eye contact during conversation may feel uncomfortable when children keep their gaze lowered and misinterpret the behavior. Yet in many cultural groups the lowered gaze is a sign of respect. Byers and Byers (1972) report that Puerto Rican children lower their eyes when being chastised or reprimanded—to do otherwise would seem arrogant or rebellious—yet they are thought disrespectful in many mainland schools.

At other times facial expressions or gestures acceptable in one culture may be highly insulting in another. Matluck (1979) explains that

> the crooked finger gesture accompanying the spoken-or-unspoken phrase "Come here, Bobby," is considered obscene by the Chinese, as is the raised thumb for Hispanic speakers, the innocuous gesture used by hitchhikers on the road. . . .(p. 190-191)

"Body language" or positioning is another form of nonverbal behavior which may carry different meanings for different cultures. Members of the mainstream culture tend to maintain a certain distance between speakers and feel uncomfortable when someone violates their "space." Wolfgang (1979) reports

> that people from contact oriented cultures such as those from Latin America, Mexico, Italy, Portugal and Spain, would tend to touch each other more often, gesture more and space themselves closer than Anglo-Saxon British, Americans, or Canadians. This behavior might lead to Anglo-Saxons being stereotyped as "cold" and "unemotional." (p. 147)

Learning through Observation

We have attempted to provide a very broad survey of differences which may exist in language use among cultures. As teachers become aware of the dimensions of language use—in the structural system, in the social use system, and in nonverbal behaviors as well—they can begin to look more closely at their own classrooms, using personal observation to confirm or reject what previous research has suggested. Kidwatching can provide teachers with more specific information about language behaviors so that they may structure learning experiences which take into account the cultural background of their children and move them toward competence in many language situations.

Teachers might approach their own kidwatching the way an anthropologist would; keeping a notebook of anecdotal records (see Spradley, 1980) and making audio or videotapes of classroom activities. Such records allow teachers to more objectively examine language behaviors over time and to see patterns of interaction emerge which might not be evident on any one occasion. Boggs (1972) describes how observers were at first unaware of how their own actions either "turned off" or invited verbalizations from the Hawaiian children with whom they worked. As field notes accumulated and were examined, Boggs and his colleagues began to note that children felt threatened by direct attempts to engage them in speech, yet became quite voluble when adults' interest was expressed through a smile or simple eye contact.

As these observers reviewed their accumulated notes, they began to understand the kinds of situations which put children at ease and elicited more language—in this case informal, small group situations. Boggs' example (1972) illustrates the importance of listening to children as well as observing them.

> Obvious cues of the adult's receptivity occurred in other cases: consoling another child or holding a child in his lap. When these things happened, the child being held, and one or more looking on, would volunteer news and remarks and would open conversations. The tape recorder also came to symbolize the observer's receptivity. When it was set up children would come over to report news and ask to record. When in use, bystanders would often walk up, grab the microphone, and speak. (p. 306)

Actions, questions, or statements which indicate the listener's genuine interest may elicit a wealth of oral language. Lindfors (1980) presents the following transcript of a conversation between a black fourth grader and her reading tutor. Here, unlike more formal classroom situations, the setting was relaxed and informal, and the tutor's role was more likely that of a trusted adult rather than an examiner.

> C: Now I liked two hairy worms, dat makes six altogether. My sister say, "Ahhh." And den he, and den he got crawlin', I went. . .I was walkin' over dere and he go POW, and I stepped on it.
>
> A: Oh, wow, was he. . .?
>
> C: He was a-ah, honey we yelled and that juice went sliiiiiidin' all out.
>
> A: Yuk!! Oooh!
>
> C: It was a green caterpillah but he look like a hairy worm but he didn't have no hair up on him. And den I, I put it in a cup and I kep' it. It was on a flower at firs' and I got it off, my cousin picked it up and we kep' on playin' wid it and den I wan I wanted ta bring it ta schoo' but it die and we went ashes ta ashes an' dus' ta dus'. (p. 390)

The tutor's responses were almost minimal—a simple question ("Oh, wow, was he. . .?") and verbal expressions which showed the tutor had entered into the spirit of the child's story ("Yuk!! Oooh!"). Questions such as "*How* did you feel about that?" or "*Why* do you think so?" may draw out rather than dry up a child's responses. A statement like "Tell me what you are thinking" or even a hug or a smile can indicate genuine desire to listen to children.

As Lindfors says of "C":

> This "woman of words" performs with extreme skill—persuasive, descriptive, expressive, entertaining, and with a real flair for literary closure. Using language is a well-developed art for this child. (p. 390)

It will be up to the teacher to discover the situations and circumstances which might elicit such examples from their own students.

To do so it may sometimes be necessary for teachers to extend their observations from the classroom to the playground or the street corner. Knapp and Knapp (1976), collectors of childhood folklore, suggest that "in the unsupervised nooks and crannies of their lives, where they perpetuate centuries old folk traditions, children learn what no one can teach them" (p. 9). Teachers will be surprised and delighted to find that the "silent" children of the classroom are not only adept conversationalists with their own peers but that these children are skilled poets or verbal stylists. H. Rap Brown (1972) explains:

> The street is where young bloods get their education. I learned how to talk in the street, not from reading about Dick and Jane going to the zoo. . . .The teacher would test our vocabulary each week but we knew the vocabulary we needed. They'd give us arithmetic to exercise our minds. Hell, we exercised our minds by playing the dozens. (p. 205)

Indeed, the language of the street is often a triumph of verbal virtuosity, full of metaphor and rhyme, which grows out of an oral heritage that is universal in nature.

In addition to watching children at play, teachers may want to make home visits, for in many cultures the family unit represents a powerful force in the child's life. A visit to the child's home (when welcomed by the parents) can reveal not only patterns of language use which may not be apparent in a school situation but also help to establish a feeling of trust and cooperation between parents and teacher.

By observing children using language at school, at play, and at home, teachers can accumulate the kind of information which will allow them to take the next step in bringing cultures together in the classroom—making practical use of their observations.

Classroom Applications—Building Bridges between Cultures

We have discussed some of the dimensions of language variation which may exist in today's multicultural classrooms. At the same time we have warned that it is often difficult to sort out subtleties of language use and that variation can be idiosyncratic as well as cultural. We believe, however, that through careful "kidwatching" teachers are in a position to contribute to the growing body of knowledge in this area and to make meaningful changes in their own classrooms—both in the structure of lessons and in the content of the curriculum.

The argument that teachers can make a difference is supported by findings from several of the studies mentioned above. Boggs (1972) found that teachers who took advantage of Hawaiian children's preference for relating to adults in groups met with greater success when they addressed questions to the group rather than to individuals or when they allowed voluntary responses to flow freely.

Philips (1972) describes how one teacher made accommodations to tribal learning with her Warm Springs Indian children:

> As one sixth grade teacher put it, "I spend as little time in front of the room as possible." In comparison with non-Indian classes, Indian classes have a relatively greater number of group "projects." Thus, while non-Indian students are learning about South American history through reading texts and answering the teacher's questions, Indian students are doing group-planned and -executed murals depicting a particular stage in Latin American history; while non-Indian students are reading science texts and answering questions about how electricity is generated, Indian students are doing group-run experiments with batteries and motors. (p. 382)

Teachers do not single out children to give reports or to answer questions. "Rather the teacher of Indians allows more periods in which she is available for individual students to approach her alone and ask their questions where no one else can hear them" (p. 383). In fact, this teacher's approach resembles the kind of experiences we'd like to see in all classrooms—experiences which allow teachers to respond to the child's direction for building language competencies.

Other teachers have successfully used peer tutors or children from the upper grades to work with younger children in order to free them to work with individual students. Teachers in the Columbus, Ohio, area have instituted daily "buddy" reading time in which each child takes his turn reading from a favorite book and discussing it with a classmate. The children also work in pairs or in small groups on projects connected with books and they often initiate special projects among themselves. While these techniques can work well with all children, they may be especially successful when peers or siblings serve as teachers in the home culture as well.

As we learn to accommodate in the classroom the types of interactional structures with which our students are familiar, we can begin to broaden the language situations in which students communicate comfortably. It is important to remember that we are preparing children to live in a multicultural world and that these children will have to function efficiently in a variety of situations. Philips (1972) recommended that teachers not only be sensitive to the Warm Springs children's preferences for working in group situations, but that they also put a conscious emphasis on encouraging children to perform individually in front of peers in order to prepare the children to interact with people from other cultures.

A good way to expand children's situational competence is with the "literature" of the home and the playground. In many minority cultures great emphasis is placed on the art of storytelling. The Appalachian "Jack" tales such as *Jack and the Wonder Beans* (Still,

1977), tales from West Africa which feature Anasi the spider man (Dorliae, 1970), or the Iroquois legend, *The Dancing Stars* (Rockwell, 1972) which represents the pourquoi tales found in the lore of many American Indian tribes, are part of the same oral tradition that created the *Odyssey* and *Beowulf.* By asking children to 1) collect such tales from family members; 2) retell them in small groups, perhaps with flannel boards of puppets; or 3) write them down for a class collection, teachers are asking them to share part of their own cultural treasure and perhaps to recognize similar human themes in the folk literature of other groups. In more subtle ways they are also moving children toward individual performance and helping them to polish verbal skills so necessary to the accomplished storyteller.

The poetry and music of the playground also provides a rich source of classroom material. Rhymes and elaborate forms of verbal humor are common to many cultures. The "rappin" or "signifying" found in black innercity cultures requires a high degree of verbal skill. Brown (1972) explains that signifying was a way for young blacks to express their feelings most eloquently:

> But things bound to get better 'cause they can't get no worse.
> I'm just like the blind man, standing by a broken window.
> I don't feel no pain.
> But it's your world.
> You the man I pay rent to.
> If I had your hands I'd give 'way both my arms.
> Cause I could do without them.
> I'm the man but you the main man.
> I read the books you write.
> You set the pace in the race I run. (p. 207)

Brown argues, "And the teacher expected me to sit up in class and study poetry after I could run down shit like that. If anybody needed to study poetry she needed to study mine" (p. 205).

One of the authors (DeStefano) successfully used the poetry of the streets with her black fourth grade students in innercity Philadelphia. She would take the children for a walk in the neighborhood, asking them to be aware of sights, sounds, smells, and textures. When they returned to the classroom they broke into groups to discuss the walk in terms of one of the four senses. She then took the items and wove them into free verse, using the words of one of the youngsters (remembered from the walk) as a refrain:

> Ooowee it's hot
> Let's cross over to the *cool* side of the street.

The poem was typed for each child and used for choral reading—a wildly popular event. Similar success was had with other materials that the children composed themselves or which were a familiar part of their culture—popular song lyrics, folksongs or hymns. By using such materials, the teacher not only builds bridges between cultures but also makes connections to works of other fine literature which present sensitive and moving portrayals of many cultural experiences. These include picture books like Lucille Clifton's *Some of the Days of Everett Anderson* (1975), or Miska Miles' *Annie and the Old One* (1971), or novels such as *Roll of Thunder Hear My Cry* (1976) by Mildred Taylor, Laurence Yep's *Child of the Owl* (1977), and Jamake Highwater's *Anpao* (1977). And these experiences may also lay paths to fine poets like Langston Hughes and Maya Angelou.

Finally, to extend children's repertoire of spoken registers (DeStefano, 1978) or roles, the teacher may want to give children opportunities to "try on" other voices through creative dramatics. This role and subsequent language (register) switching can occur as children present the local news in the manner of Walter Cronkite or describe a school sports event a la Howard Cosell. Teachers can also use *improvisations* as a means for children to respond to favorite stories or as a way to highlight key portions of a literary work. Way (1967) suggests that such improvisations help the minority youngster to develop fluency across cultural lines by mastering his own speech in a wholly uncritical atmosphere. Then "out of this deep root of confidence comes the opportunity to realize quite dispassionately and fearlessly the many other ways of speaking..." (p. 122).

In Paterson's *Bridge to Terabithia* (1977), Jess, an Appalachian youngster, is uncomfortable with city-bred Leslie's literary talk:[2]

> Leslie named their secret land "Terabithia" and she loaned Jess all her books about Narnia, so he would know how things went in a magic kingdom—how the animals and the trees must be protected and how a ruler must behave. That was the hard part. When Leslie spoke, the words rolling out so regally, you knew she was a proper queen. He could hardly manage English, much less the poetic language of a king. (pp. 39-40)

Yet as his friendship with Leslie grows, and as they spend more time in Terabithia, Jess does manage to sound like a king. As the two battle an imaginary foe who has invaded their realm, Leslie cries out:

> "They have sounded the retreat!" the brave queen cried.
>
> "Yey!"
>
> "Drive them out utterly, so they may never return and prey upon our people."

> "Out you go! Out! Out!" All the way back to the creek bed, they forced the enemy back, sweating under their winter jackets.
>
> "At last. Terabithia is free once more."
>
> The king sat down on a log and wiped his face, but the queen did not let him rest long. "Sire, we must go at once to the grove of pines and give thanks for our victory."
>
> Jess followed her into the grove, where they stood silently in the dim light.
>
> "Who do we thank?" he whispered.
>
> The question flickered across her face. "Oh God," she began. She was more at home with magic than religion. "Oh spirits of the Grove."
>
> "Thy right arm hast given us the victory." He couldn't remember where he'd heard that one but it seemed to fit. Leslie gave him a look of approval. (p. 71)

This scene represents a moving episode in a sensitive story and is an example of how naturally children acquire a repertoire of roles when they play with language. As teachers encourage children to assume such roles from this and other literature, they provide a bridge to other worlds, just as Leslie took Jess "from the cow pasture into Terabithia and turned him into a king" (p. 126).

When we take time to watch and listen to children in a variety of language situations, and when we value the cultural traditions which the child brings to the classroom, at the same time that we seek to enlarge that child's language repertoire, we may discover unexpected "kingdoms" as well. At the Twenty-Sixth Annual Convention of the International Reading Association, Jamake Highwater challenged teachers to give children windows through which to see *many* worlds rather than mirrors of their own cultures. By kidwatching we can learn to look through these windows also, immeasurably enriching and enlarging our own world in the process.

Notes

1. We would like to acknowledge Deboral L. Thompson's aid in the preparation of this article.
2. From *Bridge to Terabithia* by Katherine Paterson (Thomas Y. Crowell). Copyright © 1977 by Katherine Paterson. Reprinted by permission of Harper & Row, Publishers, Inc.

References

Boggs, S.T. "The Meaning of Questions and Narratives to Hawaiian Children," in C. Cazden, V. John & D. Hymes (Eds.), *Functions of Language in the Classroom.* New York: Teachers College Press, 1972.

Brown, H.R. "Street Talk," in T. Kochman (Ed.), *Rappin' and Stylin' Out: Communications in Black America.* Urbana, Illinois: University of Illinois Press, 1972.

Byers, P., & Byers, H. "Nonverbal Communication and the Education of Children," in C. Cazden, V. John & D. Hymes (Eds.), *Functions of Language in the Classroom.* New York: Teachers College Press, 1972.

DeStefano, J.S. *Language, the Learner and the School.* New York: John Wiley & Sons, 1978.

DeStefano, J., Pepinsky, H. & Sanders, T. "Discourse Rules for Literacy Learning in a Classroom," in L.C. Wilkinson (Ed.), *Communicating in the Classroom.* New York: Academic Press, 1982.

Hymes, D. "Introduction," in C. Cazden, V. John & D. Hymes (Eds.), *Functions of Language in the Classroom.* New York: Teacher College Press, 1972.

Kang-Ning, C. "Education for Chinese and Indochinese," *Theory into Practice, 20* (Winter 1981), 35-44.

Knapp, H., & Knapp, M. *One Potato, Two Potato: The Folklore of American Childhood.* New York: W.W. Norton, 1976.

Kochman, T. "Culture and Communication: Implications for Black English in the Classroom," in A. Aarons, B. Gordon & W. Stewart (Eds.), *Linguistic-Cultural Differences and American Education. Florida Language Reporter, 7* (Spring/Summer 1969), 89-92, 172-174.

Lindfors, J.W. *Children's Language and Learning.* Englewood Cliffs, New Jersey: Prentice-Hall, 1980.

Matluck, J.H. "Cultural Norms and Classroom Discourses: Communication Problems in the Multiethnic School Setting." *Modern Language Journal, 63* (1979), 187-192.

Miller, J.W. "Appalachian Education: A Critique and Suggestions for Reform," *Appalachian Journal, 5* (Autumn 1977), 15.

Philips, S. *The Invisible Culture: Communication in the Classroom on the Warm Springs Indian Reservation.* New York: Longman, 1982.

Philips, S. "Participant Structures and Communicative Competence: Warm Springs Children in Community and Classroom," in C. Cazden, V. John & D. Hymes (Eds.), *Functions of Language in the Classroom.* New York: Teachers College Press, 1972.

Spradley, J.P. *Participant Observation.* New York: Holt, Rinehart & Winston, 1980.

Ward, M.C. *Them Children: A Study in Language Learning.* New York: Holt, Rinehart & Winston, 1971.

Way, B. *Development through Drama.* Atlantic Highlands, New Jersey: Humanities Press, 1967.

Wolfgang, A. "The Silent Language in the Multicultural Classroom," *Theory Into Practice, 16* (June 1977), 145-157.

Children's Books

Clifton, L. *Some of the Days of Everett Anderson.* New York: Holt, Rinehart & Winston, 1975.

Dorliae, P.G. *Animals Mourn for Da Leopard and Other West African Tales.* Illustrated by S.I. Wangboje. Indianapolis, Indiana: Bobbs Merrill, 1970.

Highwater, J. *Anpao.* New York: J.B. Lippincott, 1977.

Miles, M. *Annie and the Old One*. Illustrated by P. Parnell. Boston: Little, Brown, 1971.

Paterson, K. *Bridge to Terabithia.* New York: Thomas Y. Crowell, 1977.

Rockwell, A.F. *The Dancing Stars: An Iroquois Legend.* New York: Thomas Y. Crowell, 1972.

Still, J. *Jack and the Wonder Beans.* New York: G.P. Putnam's Sons, 1977.

Taylor, M. *Roll of Thunder Hear My Cry.* New York: Dial Press, 1976.

Yep, L. *Child of the Owl.* New York: Harper & Row, 1977.

WRITTEN LANGUAGE USE

First Graders' Uses for Writing

Vera Milz
Bloomfield Hills School District, Michigan

Each year a group of children and I learn together within the walls of Room 14 at the Way Elementary School in the Bloomfield Hills School District. Rosen and Rosen (1973), in considering the beginnings of writing, say "It is easy to think of many reasons why a young child should not want to write, and very difficult to think of reasons why he should" (p. 84). My first graders write daily both in school and in their nonschool environments beginning with the first day of school and continuing throughout the school year. Observing young children who are frequent writers can offer valuable insights into what children write to suit their needs and purposes. Although the focus of this article will be on writing, it is well to keep in mind that listening, speaking, and reading are all closely related language processes which permeate every classroom activity and usually surround each of the children's writing experiences.

A Supportive Classroom

The children and I live in an environment designed to encourage whole language development—not just writing. Reading, listening, and speaking are equally important, and provide a supportive, integrated framework as children learn to write. In constrast to classrooms where basal programs with manuals and elaborate checklists of sequential skills are used, the materials and activities in this classroom are selected to support children's interests and provide the content to be studied.

It has been my experience that children learn best when personal meaning and satisfaction are part of the learning activities. A classroom library of over two thousand tradebooks is available for children to read or listen to. Reading all of the books written by one author; following a favorite character, such as Ramona, through the books by Beverly Cleary (1977); or reading a selection of books on subjects like dinosaurs or crystals are some of the ways books are used by the class. If a story from a basal text is read, it is chosen to fit the current interests and ability of the child—not a publisher's sequence. Daily the children in Room 14 hear books read aloud, both for listening pleasure and to become familiar with written language so they can begin to build a frame of reference about how stories develop. As the children work in the classroom they are allowed to talk. Frank Smith (1978, p. v) maintains that children largely learn to read by reading, and that children will understand *how* to read by being involved in its use—a statement which I believe. However, I would extend this concept to apply as well to the learning of listening, speaking, and writing.

The children are expected to use writing from the first day of school. Writing supplies such as assorted paper, blank books, staplers, scotch tape, markers, and scissors are readily available. As each child finds a note from the teacher in a personal mailbox, a mailbox for the teacher is ready if a child wishes to respond. Letter writing is gradually extended to parents, pen pals, government officials, and favorite children's authors. An authors' corner displays seven framed letters from professional authors who have responded to booklets of letters sent by class members. Two photo albums hold letters received over the past five years after they are removed from the picture frames in the authors' corner. The children are encouraged to write individually to an author or, if enough interest is observed, to put their letters into a class book.

Within days after the school year begins, each child receives an 8½ x 11 spiral notebook to be used as a personal journal. This journal may include anything the child wishes to write about and each day I promise to read it and respond in writing if appropriate. No corrections are made, and the response is to the message the child writes. Copies of stories written by children from previous classes are displayed, and former students are invited to stop by to read their own creations of past years. Many of these students encourage the current residents of Room 14 to try writing their own new stories. Charts are often made by the children and teacher to keep the classroom running smoothly. Examples include a listing of how each child will return home when the school day is over, as well as a schedule of important activities which will happen during the day. If problems arise, such as a broken water faucet, a note tells children to use the sinks in other areas, as well as one to the custodian asking for repair help.

Sharing the belief of Britton (1975) that children "learn to write largely by writing and it is misguided to expect them 'to practice' in one lesson what they will actively employ in another" (p. 3), workbooks and ditto skill lessons are not used in the classroom. Instead, children write their own texts in a variety of forms such as notes, journal entries, and stories to suit their individual needs and purposes. They do not write to please the teacher but to a range of people in the world within and far beyond the classroom. Each letter written is actually mailed, journals go home with the writer when completed, and published stories are enjoyed in the classroom, but ultimately become part of the author's personal library at home.

Meet the Children

The population of Room 14 changes each year, but some things remain the same. The children are like kids everywhere in that they represent diverse ethnic and experiential backgrounds as well as varying interests and abilities. In each of the recent years, at least one child has entered the classroom directly from another country and has had minimal or no knowledge of English. Yet these children have lived in environments that have bombarded them with print and sound since birth, and they share a desire to interact and communicate with one another and nearby adults.

Teacher's Role

As I look back at my beginning years as a teacher, I can remember teaching children how to write. My classroom was directed by the teacher; yet, as a teacher concerned with producing writers, I had little insight into the learner's role.

As the school year began, correct letter formation was the first job to be accomplished. Gradually the children moved to copying words, sentences, and stories suggested by students in the classroom. Unfortunately, little time was left for putting one's own thoughts and feelings down on paper. A few children took the initiative of writing notes or a story on their own—usually complete with their own creative spellings and printing. Dictation allowed children to orally tell a story which could be transcribed into booklet form. However, I did not allow time for the flexibility needed for children to create writing to meet their own needs and purposes.

In the following statement, Clay (1977) raises the doubts I began to have in my early classroom experiences:

> I doubt whether there is any fixed sequence of learning through which all children must pass in early writing and this raises doubts in my mind

about any sequenced program that proceeds from the adult's logical analysis of the task and not from observation of what children are doing. (p. 336)

Today my classroom has changed. The children are learning to write before they are taught much about handwriting, spelling, or story formation. As the school year begins, I place a note from me in each child's mailbox (Milz, 1981). These notes serve to introduce me to my class, and I usually help the children read the message:

Dear Shauna,
I am Miss Milz. I will be your teacher.
Please tell me about you. I want to get
to know you.
Love,
Miss Milz

Within days, I am receiving notes back from my class. These first notes help me to get to know them. Most important they allow me to share in the child's construction of writing. As I receive a note, I observe what the child is writing, and respond from an adult perspective. For example, a child might write ILKU using all capitals and no word boundaries. As a response, I would use a conventional form, "I like you, too!" Gradually, children move to more conventional forms though they are not corrected or instructed to use them. As the children engage in other writing activities and choose the writing materials they wish to use, I respond with any requested information and spellings but they are encouraged to show what they can do themselves first.

As a classroom teacher I daily share my students' world and it places me in a position similar to parent researchers such as Halliday (1975) and Bissex (1980). Each described the language development of their own children within a social context they shared daily with the child. Halliday (1982) notes that significant others play an important part in the child's life as "they know what he means...what he understands. They are creating the system along with him" (p. 8). As Nigel's father, Halliday (1975) was the first to observe a particular sound his child had to describe an airplane flying overhead. When this sound dropped away, it was replaced months later by another word for airplane which was an imitation of the adult word, though still not the conventional form. Bissex (1980), in describing her son's early writing, tells of many notes and letters he wrote to his family as well as labels and captions for items in his immediate environment. When she found the following on his bedroom door she could read the message by "being there" with Paul.

DO.NAT KM.IN.ANE.MOR.JST.LETL.KES
[Do not come in anymore. Just little kids]

(p. 23)

Within the classroom, I am often the first person to gain meaning from a young writer's message, just as these parents were able to share and, thus, understand their children's meaning. My first readings of Ted's writing came as I realized he was recording an expression he said whenever he brought me a piece of writing, "So how do you like that?" (see Figure 1).

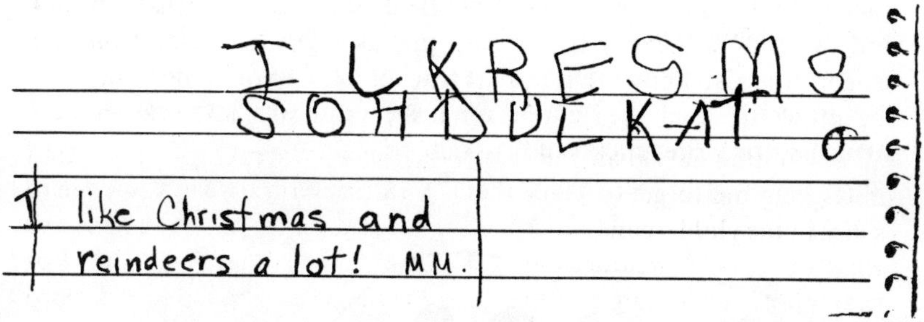

Figure 1. I like Christmas. So how do you like that?

Once I began to read Ted's messages, he felt success and began to write more each day. He knew his messages were important—not just the form. Yet, by using writing, he began to grow as a writer, and as his teacher I could help him to reflect on and extend his early attempts through my responses.

Uses for Writing

The first graders in my classroom use writing purposefully and always with a good reason. They have a meaning to communicate to a reader and quite clear ideas about the message they wish to convey. Through observation and the collection of samples of writing done in the classroom and at home, it is possible to identify specific uses these young children have for writing.

Establishing ownership or identity. Writing one's name happens on the first day of school. Labeling a possession is important when you share a classroom with 25-30 other children. Names are written on coathook labels or across a notebook cover. Later, names identify the writer of a note or the author of a story.

At Christmas time, Maleeaka and her mom stopped to visit Santa at the local shopping mall. As Santa handed her a book about himself, Maleeaka requested that he autograph it for her. When Maleeaka related the incident to me several things were evident. Maleeaka knows the names of many people that write books, and that authors are often asked to autograph their books. Since that time, Maleeaka has written two stories herself and identifies herself as a young author.

During December, Bridget was busy making Christmas gifts for her teachers. She hand decorated each wrapping and labeled the gifts to the appropriate teacher (see Figure 2). The art teacher received this package FROM BRIDGET BY BRIDGET. Bridget has learned that authors and illustrators identify themselves, just as a gift is labeled from the sender. She also knows that our art teacher has a hard name to say and the gift would reach the right person if she wrote MRS. KART rather than struggling to write, MRS. KURETH-ART.

Figure 2. Bridget's gift bag.

Building relationships. When newcomers enter our classroom after the school year has started, they are greeted with verbal "hellos" as well as with notes which help them to learn about their new classmates. When Marybeth arrived from China, she found notes in her mailbox such as the one in Figure 3 from Lisa. Though she spoke only a few words of English, she was shown her mailbox and given the notes. Two months later, she has learned to write a note as well as how to use writing to socially interact with her classmates (see Figure 4).

Dear Mary beth
I Hope you like
To Bein Room 14
I Hope you Make
lots of frind's

from
Lisa

Figure 3. Marybeth's note from Lisa.

Figure 4. Marybeth's note to Christina.

Just as children write notes to each other, they frequently write to me as their teacher. Through writing they begin to see me as a person with interests away from the classroom. Journal entries often call for a teacher response as does Jenny's question to me:

Yesterday	Yesterday
I WiS	I was
In a ChristMas	In a Christmas
Palie. I like	play. I like
Ben in	being in
Palis.	plays.
Do you	Do you,
Miss Milz	Miss Milz?

I don't know. I have
never been in a play.
M.M.

Another way that children can interact with others is through a written conversation, as first suggested by Carolyn Burke (1978) of Indiana University. Two children pass a note back and forth until a conversation is ended. Pamela and Tara had such a conversation on February 19 as they decided what they would do after school when Tara came to visit Pamela and her twin Mathew (see Figure 5). It is interesting to note that both girls control different words in writing, but both are able to gain meaning from reading the other's message. Through interactions, such as these, both children eventually will use the conventional forms of WANT and PLAY, as well as the other needed words.

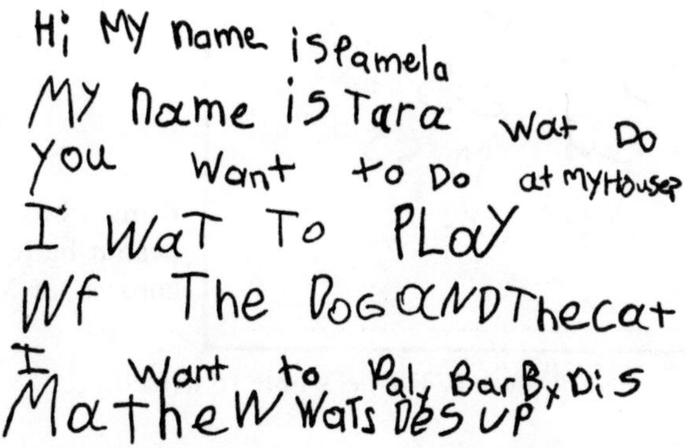

P: My name is Pamela.
T: My name is Tara. . . .
P: What do you want to do at my house?
T: I want to play with the dog and the cat.
P: I want to play Barbie dolls.
T: Mathew wants dress up.

Figure 5. Written conversation.

Remembering or recalling. As the children write daily in the classroom, they are learning that writing is a powerful aid to remembering. Journal entries help recall exciting events, special trips, or the day-to-day happenings in the child's life. A note to the office soon afterward brings the custodian with a paper towel replacement. An oral message might mean a long wait if he is busy with another job and then forgets our request. The 13 brownie scouts in our classroom learned this same lesson. They were given permission to order me one box each of my favorites—peanut butter cookies. Six of the children wrote themselves notes (see Figure 6) and then entered the information on their sales form when they returned home. They were the only ones who remembered to bring me my cookies.

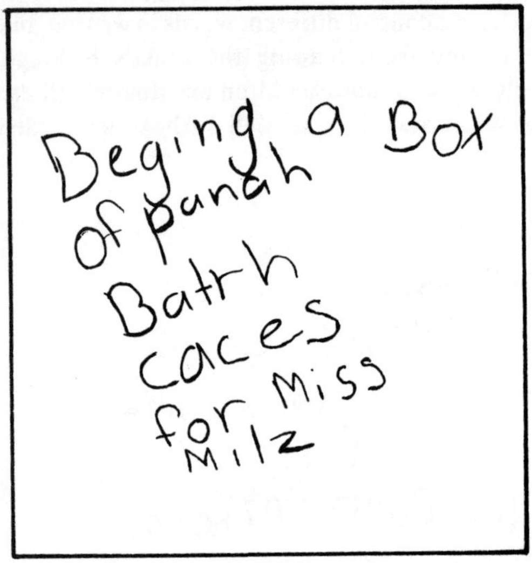

Bring a box of
peanut butter
cookies for Miss Milz

Figure 6. Rachel's note to herself.

When a meeting was changed from Monday to Tuesday, Jenny wrote a note to remind herself of the change and to help her mom remember, too:

for Mom and Jenny
Brownie Meeting (25)
Nett Tuesday May
right after school
in the gym Dont for
get
Love Jenny

Requesting information/items. Writing helps the young child gain information to solve the practical problems of everyday life, as well as to meet personal needs. Whenever I am sick I usually return to many get-well notes. The children have missed me and are concerned about why I am absent. Nicholas placed the note in Figure 7 in my mailbox as he sought information as to the cause of my illness, as well as to give me a wish for my recovery.

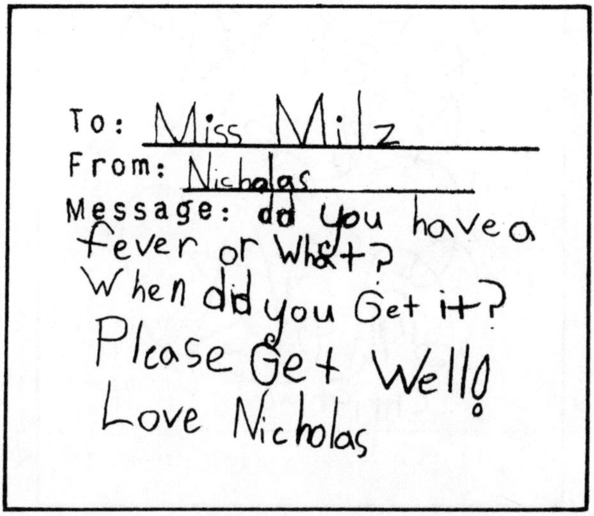

Figure 7. To Miss Milz from Nicholas.

Christina needed a menu and using a note was her way of getting it (see Figure 8). Writing not only informed her teacher of the need, but helped her to remember to ask for the item.

Figure 8. Christina's note for menu.

Recording information. Journal entries often explain what is happening in the classroom or at home. They note feelings and discoveries that affect the young writer. Words label a picture to represent in writing what has been drawn. As children share their journals, or reread them even years later, they begin to remember information about past and pleasurable events (see the entry from Tara's journal in Figure 9).

Writing also serves to record a change in routine. Our school keeps a record of where children are going after school if they are not

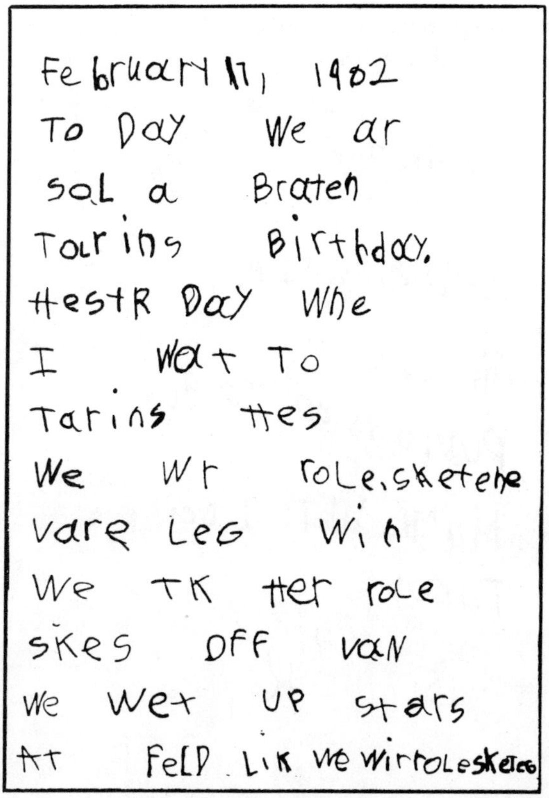
FebrUarY 11, 1902
To Day We ar
soL a Braten
Tarins Birthday.
HestR Day Whe
I Wat To
Tarins Hes
We Wr roLe.sketene
vare LeG Win
We TK Her roLe
sKes off vaN
We Wet UP stars
At FeLP. LiK We wirroLesketeG

Today we are celebrating Tarin's birthday. Yesterday when I went to Tarin's house, we were rollerskating very long. When we took our roller skates off. Then we went upstairs. It felt we were rollerskating.

Figure 9. Tara's journal.

returning directly home. As children bring these notes, I find they are taking over the task of writing the note except for a parent's signature. They are assuming the responsibility for regulating their own affairs although they realize that their whereabouts are the concern of adults. Michele brought a note which allowed her to visit a friend after school (see Figure 10), while Tagg used writing to inform me of his mother's inability to come to school on her regularly scheduled helping day (see Figure 11). Michele wrote as if her mother was composing the note. She realized her note required adult authorization. Tagg, however, was able to record his mother's message in his own words, so that he could bring the necessary information to his teacher.

Figure 10. Michele's permission note.

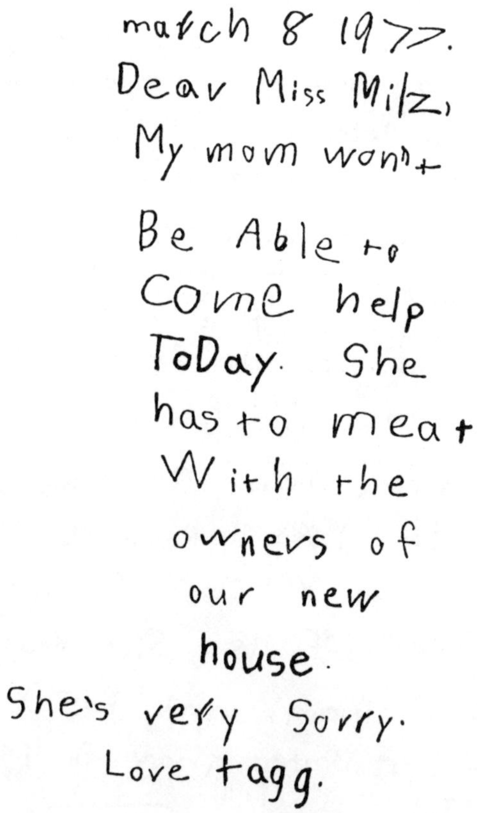

march 8 1977.
Dear Miss Milz,
My mom won't
Be Able to
come help
ToDay. She
has to meat
With the
owners of
our new
house.
She's very Sorry.
Love tagg.

Figure 11. Tagg's letter.

Fantasizing or pretending. Writing stories is an important use for writing by children in Room 14. As they hear stories written by professional authors or children who were previously students in this classroom, they begin to want to write themselves. Children draw from real events and personal experiences in their lives as they create imaginary stories. Storytelling conventions such as "Once upon a time" or "The end" are used, and children begin to experiment and gain control of the many aspects of writing a story. Lisa wrote the "If I Were" story in Figure 12 which illustrates the close relationship between writing and Lisa's own enjoyment of her favorite book, *Miss Nelson is Missing* (Allard & Marshal, 1977). She is able to maintain the pretense that she is the book as she names it.

If I Were a Book I Mite Be in a laibare
or I Mite Be With a girl or a boy
and The name Of Me Wuid Be My favirt
Book Miss Nelson is Missing. Cids like to
Read me. a girl brings me to School.
She Reds me to the clas. after School
She Brings Me Bake Home. She puts me
Bake in her Book Kase With All her
ater Books. All the Books are Scrosht.
Wine She hase frns over Thay
like To Read Me. Iam her favrit
Book. She loves To Read Me.
She Keeps Me Clen. She Taks
good Caer of Me. She Reads Me
To her Mom and her Dad
And her Brater. Thay All likeMe.
The END

Lisa

If I were a book, I might be in a library
or I might be with a girl or a boy
and the name of me would be my favorite
book, *Miss Nelson is Missing.* Kids like to
read me. A girl brings me to school.
She reads me to the class. After school
she brings me back home. She puts me
back in her book case with all her
other books. All the books are squashed.
When she has friends over they
like to read me. I am her favorite
book. She loves to read me.
She keeps me clean. She takes
good care of me. She reads me

to her Mom and her Dad
and her brother. They all like me.
The end.

Figure 12. Lisa's story.

A Charge for Teachers

Teachers are faced with a variety of school settings, room space, equipment, and scheduling as they live in a classroom with 25-30 children. It becomes a personal challenge to each of us to use whatever we have to make that area a place where children can think and learn to write as they create meaning. They need many opportunities where they can experience writing to suit their specific purposes. Shuy (1981) explains:

> Good language learners begin with a function, a need to get something done with language, and move gradually toward acquiring the forms which reveal that function. They learn holistically, not by isolated skills. Such learners worry more about getting things done with language than with the surface correctness of it. . . . They experiment freely and try things out unashamedly. (p. 107)

Teachers must remember that writing is a language process whose purpose is to convey a message to a reader. When this happens, first graders have become writers.

References

Allard, H. & Marshal, J. *Miss Nelson is Missing!* Boston: Houghton Mifflin, 1977.

Bissex, G.L. *GYNS AT WRK: A Child Learns to Write and Read.* Cambridge, Massachusetts: Harvard University Press, 1980.

Britton, J. & others. *The Development of Writing Abilities (11-18).* London: Macmillan Education, 1975.

Burke, C. "Written Conversation," unpublished manuscript, 1978.

Clay, M. "Exploring with a Pencil," *Theory Into Practice, 16* (December 1977), 334-341.

Cleary, B. *Ramona and Her Father.* New York: Morrow, 1977.

Halliday, M.A.K. "Three Aspects of Children's Language Development: Learning Language, Learning through Language, Learning about Language," in Y. Goodman, M. Haussler, & D. Strickland (Eds.), *Oral and Written Language Development Research: Impact on the Schools.* Urbana, Illinois: National Council of Teachers of English, 1982.

Halliday, M.A.K. *Learning How to Mean.* New York: Elsevier North Holland, 1975.

Milz, V. "A Whole Language Approach Writing Program," in S. Haley-James (Ed.), *Perspectives on Writing in Grades 1-8.* Urbana, Illinois: National Council of Teachers of English, 1981.

Rosen, H., & Rosen, C. *The Language of Primary School Children.* London: Penguin Education, 1973.

Shuy, R. "A Holistic View of Language," *Research in the Teaching of English, 15* (May 1981), 101-111.

Smith, F. *Understanding Reading*, second edition. New York: Holt, Rinehart & Winston, 1978.

Learning to Think through Writing

Lucy McCormick Calkins
Teachers College, Columbia University

"You can conference with yourself," nine year old Diane said to me one morning. "You just read the writing over to yourself and it's like there is another person there. You think thoughts to yourself. . . . You say things others might ask you." The brown eyed youngster paused, her glance shifting to my clipboard. "I talk it over with myself. I ask myself questions."

In his recent article, "Teaching the Other Self: The Writer's First Reader," Donald M. Murray (1982) describes writing as a conversation between two workers muttering to each other at the bench. "The self speaks, the other self listens and considers. The self proposes, the other self considers. The self makes, the other self evaluates. The two selves collaborate" (p. 140). Diane is in fourth grade and already she has developed an articulate other self.

Greg is seven and he, too, dialogues with his emerging text. I watched him scowl as he reread his homemade book. "This story should go in the trashcan," he muttered. "See, it is a disaster. The kids will have so many questions."

I SAW MY FATHER'S COLLECTIONS. THEN WE LEFT.

"I go through it wicked fast. The kids will say, 'What are the collections? What'd ya see?'" Greg's voice trailed off as he began to squeeze words into the margin of his page. He read the insert to me.

WE SAW BUTTONS, COINS, STAMPS AND OTHER STUFF.

"The kids will have questions still," Greg said, "but at least I got rid of some of them."

Heather, a second grader, reread each page of her book. "I'm having an individual writing conference with myself," she said in a prim, matter-of-fact voice. "On each page I ask myself the questions the other kids would ask me." Then Heather opened her book, "Here I wrote, 'I HAVE A HORSE.' The kids would ask me if I ride it, so I'm going to add 'I RIDE MY HORSE EVERYDAY UNLESS IT'S RAINING.'"

Nine year old Birger paused midway through "The Bottle Story." "In my first story last year, I wrote two stories in one," he said, "and so now I'm always thinking, 'Is this one story?' 'Is this two stories?'" After rereading his story twice, Birger crossed out the title. He explained, "I was going to write about getting 20 cents worth of bottles adding up to a dollar, but on the way my bike was crashed into the wheat field and so I'm going to drop the bottle story." Beside the crossed-out title, Birger wrote "The Wheat Field."

Like most writers, Birger, Heather, and Greg pull in to write, then pull back to reconsider. Closeness and distance, pushing forward and pushing back, creation and criticism: it is this combination of forces which makes writing such a powerful tool for learning. Whereas spoken words fade away, with print we can fasten our thoughts onto paper. We can hold our ideas in our hands; we can carry them in our pockets. We can think about our thinking. Through writing, we can re-see, reshape and refine our thoughts. Smith (1982) explains, "Writing separates our ideas from ourselves in a way that is easiest for us to examine, explore, and develop" (p. 15).

I have always believed that revision is essential to the writing process; that writing becomes a wedge that develops our thinking precisely because it enables us to revisit our first thoughts. But recently I've begun to realize that our alterations and drafts are not the cutting edge—the growing edge—of writing, but the traces of it. Instead, the cutting edge of writing is the interaction between writer and emerging text. The writer asks, "What am I trying to say?" "How does this sound?" "Where's this leading me?" When children learn to ask these questions of their emerging texts, they gain a tool for developing not only their information but also their skills as writers. When Heather has an individual writing conference with herself, when Birger asks himself, "Is this one story?" these youngsters develop not only their texts, but also their thinking and writing skills.

My Changing Concept of How Children Learn Revision

Several years ago, the National Institute of Education funded Donald Graves (1982), Susan Sowers, and me to spend two years documenting the day-to-day changes in children's writing behaviors. In order to do this, we became live-in researchers in a public school in Atkinson, New Hampshire. . . .and it was there that I met Birger, Greg, Heather, and the others (Calkins, 1983). When I began collecting field notes on the children's activities during writing, I recorded voicing behaviors, eye movements, occasional pauses. But that was all. If the children revised, it was only to correct their spelling. Rarely did they even reread their texts. Writing, for these children, was certainly not an interaction with their emerging texts—instead it was an ongoing process of adding on.

Within a few months, however, I was startled to see our case study subjects were drafting and revising. "I've got mounds of drafts!" one youngster announced to his teacher. "Look at how many crossouts I did," another would chime in. I thought Eureka had been reached.

Then I began noticing curious things. Sometimes children's drafts were sequels rather than variations of each other. Often their drafts were copies of each other, with just a line added or a detail changed. One boy learned revision involved cutting and pasting and so he "revised" by carefully scissoring out each word of his story and then pasting them together again—with the only addition being glue and tape. Although most of the children were happily revising, were they rereading, reconsidering, and reexploring their first thoughts? Were they using writing as a tool for thinking? I decided children could learn to sustain work on a piece of writing and to view drafts as tentative, but they probably were too young to interact with their emerging texts.

Kids. No sooner do you begin to understand them than they begin to change. No sooner had I built a tentative description of children's writing than some youngsters began defying the description.

Diane, Greg, Heather, and the others began having those individual writing conferences with themselves. Some children—but not all—began rereading their work and then interacting with their texts. "Is this one story?" "What else should I say?" "Is this really true?" "How else could I write this?" Rather than being age-related, the development of this Other Self seemed classroom-related. It wasn't necessarily the older kids who were having those individual conferences with themselves. Instead, in some classrooms at all levels (K-5), children interacted with their emerging texts, while in other classrooms, children waited for teachers to ask questions, spot problems, or suggest solutions.

I do not have "hard data" about why some teachers succeeded in recruiting children's other selves. But I do have informed hunches. I believe, and our data suggest, that children learn to interact with their emerging texts when classroom environments and teacher-child conferences are structured in ways which help writers assume responsibility and ownership of their craft.

Classroom Routines

When methods for teaching writing and classroom routines and schedules are always changing, children are not apt to monitor their own writing processes, steering their way through a piece. Instead they wait for their teacher's changing agenda. I once assumed "creative" writing required "creative" classroom structures. Each week, my writing class would host new rules, agendas, and approaches. Now I suspect kaleidoscope classrooms keep children dependent on our changing plans. Only when schedules and routines are kept predictable can the unpredictable happen.

In some Atkinson classrooms, children knew they would write each day at the same time. In these rooms, I saw children planning for writing, and writing as if there was a tomorrow. "You need to know you've got all the time you want for a piece of writing," eight year old Susie explains. "Otherwise you're afraid to look back, afraid to see it's not all you could do."

There was not only a regular schedule in these classrooms for when children would write, there was also a predictable flow to each session. Birger, Diane, and their classmates knew each writing class would begin with a brief mini-lesson, followed by a workshop for writing, and conferences, followed by a meeting to share their writing. Some might ask, "Didn't the sameness bore children?" On the contrary, it allowed children to invest themselves in the workshop, making plans, developing their own strategies for writing. Susie began each day by rereading her pieces. Birger often met with several friends to share plans for their writing. Others mapped upcoming sections of their pieces. The simplicity of the schedule gave children a framework within which they could ask, "What am I going to do next?" Like artists in a studio, they discovered that the juxtaposition of a changing craft within a simple predictable environment can free us to make choices throughout the process of our craft.

Teacher-Child Conferences

Now, as I look back I also realize that children learned to interact with their texts in the classrooms where teacher-child conferences became models for child-child conferences. Children internalized the process and began asking themselves the questions which had been asked of them. In these classrooms teachers sensed the impact their conferences could have on young writers. They interacted with children in conferences in such a way that children learned to interact with their emerging texts. They were teaching the writer, not the writing.

Other teachers believed their job was to improve the texts. In conferences, they'd rush in and offer evaluations and solutions, not realizing the lasting effect of such conferences was to perpetuate children's dependence on their evaluations, solutions, and strategies.

I do not blame those teachers. It is so easy for us to take over a child's text, often without realizing what we've done. How easy it is for us to begin a writing conference by taking up the text and thinking, "What would I do if this were mine?" Sometimes I take a draft out of the writer's hands and hold it in my own—what a message! Then, too, sometimes, I take control by eagerly imposing my agendas on a conference, perhaps asking specific questions meant to coax writers to expand on my favorite section, perhaps rushing in with my compliments and criticisms. "Your story is perfect," I say, as if I could know when a piece matches the writer's intentions. How hard it is for us to approach a conference asking questions which return authorship to the writer: "How's it coming?" "How can I help?" "What do you think of it?" "What will you do next?" Our job in a writing conference is to interact with children in such a way that they learn to interact with their emerging text. Our job in a writing conference is to put ourselves out of a job.

The data from our study suggest that when teacher-child conferences are predictable, children are more likely to internalize the temporary structure of a conference. In classrooms where teachers' responses are ever-changing and kaleidoscopic, children do not anticipate their teacher's responses, but instead wait for their changing agendas.

Content Conferences

Several teachers at Atkinson intuitively developed several predictable "kinds" of conferences. Most frequently, teachers focused on the child's emerging subject (I call these content conferences). "Children need to know they are being heard," Currier said, explaining her purpose in a content conference. The pattern in most content conferences was that the teachers listened to the child's evolving subject and then repeated the child's story, as if to say, "I heard you...your meaning is coming through." Sometimes this active listening involved questions which would clear away little snags and tangles which prevented the teacher from hearing what the child was saying, but the focus was on the child's content, not on trumped-up questions asked by teachers who wanted to tug out more information. Ironically, this kind of real listening seems to recruit additional information better than a barrage of questions. The force of listening helps writers see the value of their message and so content conferences often lead youngsters to further develop their subjects—and their confidence.

Because the pattern of these conferences was a predictable one, in their peer conferences first graders and fourth graders alike were soon retelling what they'd heard in a draft and asking questions that could clear away the snags and gaps which clouded the meaning. These peer conferences were later internalized. And so seven year old Greg reread his piece and said, "This story should go in the trashcan. The kids will have so many questions. The kids will say, 'What were the collections?' 'What'd ya see?'"

In her fourth grade classroom, Susie reread her lead:

> I was at a beach in Florida. I pressed my toes in the hot sand. I saw my sister jumping out in the waves with my Aunt. She was jumping around as the waves hit her, she was out deep—I wanted to go and play in the waves but I was too nervous.

Susie reread her lead and then said to herself, "How did it feel? What was it like?" Then she muttered, "I'm realizing my whole first draft is like that—blah." Susie wrote a second draft, adding details:

> I pressed my toes in the hot sand. I wiggled them around. The gritty sand felt good on my sunburnt toes. I looked out over the ocean. My sister was out deep, jumping over the waves with my Aunt. Sometimes the waves got too big and they would knock her over, then my Aunt would pull her up and she'd be dripping wet and they'd start laughing.

Sometimes the teachers' content conferences were directed not only towards learning about the child's subject but, more specifically, towards helping children focus their topic. Whether the writer is a first grader whose stories are a list, a fifth grader who writes without highlighting a specific theme, or a professional writer, searching for the thread of his book, a crucial question we can ask is "What are you trying to say?" This question can be rephrased. "Why did you select this topic; what's the important thing about it?" "What do you want to leave your reader with?" "What's the heart of your piece?" Soon Birger and the others were asking these same questions of their own emerging drafts.

Sometimes the teacher's content conference had a different purpose and a different pattern. If the piece was a skeleton, lacking in details, or if a child had just focused his or her topic and needed to embellish it with more details, teachers geared their content conferences toward helping children expand their information. When Eric narrowed his topic from "All about My Trip" to "The Bunk Beds," he worried that his piece would be awful short. Eric's teacher helped him realize how much he had to say. She did this not with specific questions meant to eke out more details, but instead with general, openended questions meant to tap into Eric's energy. "What exactly happened, Eric?" "How did you feel?" "It's hard for me to imagine what it was like. Will you help me picture it?" The significant thing about these questions is that they leave control in the writer's hands. They don't pull the writer this way and that, distracting him from what he wanted to say. But also, the questions give writers tools which can be used another day, on another piece of writing. They are universal questions, they could be asked of almost any piece of writing. And so it was not long before children were asking these same questions of each other and of themselves.

Sometimes the teachers mostly listened to a child's subject, repeating what they heard to the child. Sometimes they asked questions which helped children select a focus for their pieces. Sometimes they asked questions which drew more detail and more energy from the child. In any case, teachers mostly paid attention to the subject of the child's paper, and so I called these "content conferences." Because the teachers' content conferences were predictable, because their questions were often universal ones, children soon began asking these same questions of each other and of themselves.

Process Conferences

But then something surprising happened. A new kind of conference entered the classroom, and it seemed to come from nowhere. In their conferences with themselves, children began to center on their process of writing rather than on their evolving subjects. Many of the children's questions to themselves were not about the subject at all, but about writing strategies.

> What should I do next? Let's see, I could see if my story goes into parts and then work on each part.
>
> I've got heaps of drafts, I don't know why. . . .This piece was the hardest for me because I wanted to tell exactly what it's like to snuggle with my father, and the words kept being wrong.
>
> I've got five drafts! Now, how are they different?

Along with these surprising new questions, it became clear that the children had an astonishing ability to articulate their process of writing, to select and critically review their strategies, and to consciously guide and control their thinking (Calkins, 1983).

> Birger: Now I'm going to reread my story, trying to make parts longer, like Susie did in her piece. I'm going to add on at this part when I come out of the garage to the accident. I'll tell about when I was walking across the driveway, how I heard sounds, like the vet with the siren, and I smelled the air. It wasn't bad air and I remember thinking, it was hard to believe a part of me had just died, the air smelled so nice and clean. I'm going to put all that in, spreading it out with more details.
>
> Amy: When I write, it's like I have a movie in my mind and the words just come off of me. I'm like a typewriter, clicking them off.
>
> Susie: Usually I put down a sentence that I don't even like. It isn't even going to be in the piece. I just put it down and keep going right through it.

It was not magic which had led these children to such an awareness and control of their strategies for writing. The children's process conferences had not emerged from nowhere. The children were again asking themselves the questions which had been asked of them—this time, not by their teachers, but by the researchers who were observing in the school. How could I have overlooked the impact our presence would have on the children? Day by day for two years, these children had been asked process questions. "How'd you go about writing this draft?" "What new problems did you run into?" "What are you planning to do next?"

All of my efforts not to teach the children had been to no avail. My presence at the child's side, my interest in the process of their craft, and my predictable questions had been a powerful teaching force. Because I continually asked children to put their thinking into words, the children had become exceptionally aware of their intentions and strategies. The children had seen my fascination with their thinking and they, too, began looking at it, asking, "So what am I doing now?" "What kinds of things could I do next?"

Because children were reflecting on their strategies for writing, they were also learning to steer their thinking. Donaldson (1978) writes:

> The point to grasp is how closely the growth of consciousness is related to the growth of the intellect. . . .If the intellectual powers are to develop, the child must gain a measure of control over his own thinking and he cannot control it while he remains unaware of it.

It is not by accident that we learn dance in a room full of mirrors.

I'd meant to observe children's growth, and in doing so, I'd participated in it. I'd meant to study learning, and in doing so, I learned teaching.

References

Calkins, L.M. *Lessons from a Child.* Exeter, New Hampshire: Heinemann Educational Books, 1983.

Donaldson, M. *Children's Minds.* New York: Norton, 1978.

Graves, D.H. *A Case Study Observing the Development of Primary Children's Composing, Spelling, and Motor Behaviors During the Writing Process.* Final Report, Project No. 8-3419-0963. Washington, D.C.: National Institute of Education, 1982.

Murray, D.M. "Teaching the Other Self: The Writer's First Reader," *College Composition and Communication, 33* (May 1982), 140-147.

Smith, F. *Writing and the Writer.* New York: Holt, Rinehart & Winston, 1982.

Reading and Talking: Learning through Interaction

M. Trika Smith-Burke
New York University

> If everybody in the world keeps drinking water, are we going to run out of water some day? I don't mean now, I mean years and years from now?
>
> Why is this macaroni on my plate making steam?
>
> What does gravity look like?
>
> Are there more stars in the sky or in a million cans of chicken and stars soup?
>
> (Lindfors, 1980, p. 248-249)

Children are naturally curious. When given an environment which allows for questions, exploration, and discovery, they interpret their experiences with what they know. For example, after a visit to the hospital to see her dying great grandmother who was 101, Abby (age 4) commented, "Ya know, Dad, the Brooklyn Bridge is pretty old. It's going to die soon!" In her struggle to understand life and death, Abby had made a connection between the Brooklyn Bridge, the celebrations of its centennial and her great grandmother. With Abby's comment even her father understood time in a different way when he suddenly realized that his grandmother was one year older than the Brooklyn Bridge!

A reading tutor had written a story for her student, George, who had never been outside of Manhattan, his home. After they read the story about a boy named David who travelled across the country on a train, the tutor asked, "What did David see from the windows of the train?"

George answered, "Nothin'!"

His tutor probed, "Why?"

George responded, "It was real dark, 'cause the train was underground. An' David, he couldn't see nothin'!"

George's prototype of train as subway was so strong that the information in the story did not modify his concept. It was only after looking at and discussing a picture book on trains during the next session that George broadened his understanding of trains.

Our knowledge continually changes through interaction with people, print, and the physical environment. Adding to our mental store by elaborating what is known and differentiating new concepts is a lifelong process. Frank Smith (1975) proposes that the knowledge which resides in a person's head is a kind of "theory of the world." To comprehend or to make sense of daily encounters, people use what they know to understand and interpret new experiences. To learn is to change what is known in some way, to adjust to the new information which does not fit with what is already known.

Knowledge is often thought of as mental representations, that is, concepts and the relations among them. However, there is little agreement about the nature of knowledge. Some argue that a concept is a collection of exemplars based on common features (Clark, 1973) or attributes (Bruner, Goodnow, & Austin, 1956). For example, in a discussion with her mother's friend, Leslie (age 3) began to modify one feature of her concept of doctor. Because her pediatrician was a man, she insisted that only men could be doctors. When her mother's friend explained that her sister who lives in California is a doctor, Leslie balked, but finally agreed that maybe women could be doctors—in California.

Others (see particularly Rosch, 1975) propose that each concept has minimally a prototypical example, which is largely determined by experience and culture. Differences in individuals' prototypes for a concept sometimes can be the source of misunderstanding or miscommunication. In the example above, George's prototype of train as subway prevented him from fully understanding the story intended by the author.

Research is no clearer about how the connections among concepts are stored, retrieved, used, or changed than it is about the nature of concepts. Different models abound. However, it is generally thought that relations among concepts play a significant role in inferential thinking, allowing the reader or listener to fill in the gaps that are left by an author or speaker. In the following example, Elizabeth cleverly constructs her understanding of the fable:

The Rabbits and the Frogs

> A group of rabbits was very unhappy because it had so many enemies. So they decided to end their troubles by killing themselves. To do this, they went to a lake nearby to jump in and drown.
>
> There were a number of frogs on the edge of the lake, and they were so frightened by the rabbits that they all jumped into the lake. Seeing this, one of the rabbits said, "Life is not so hopeless after all since these frogs are even more unhappy than we are." So the rabbits all went back to their homes.
>
> (Aesop in Adams & Bruce, 1982, p. 4)

Elizabeth explained that the rabbits had returned home because they thought that the frogs were trying to kill themselves, and therefore the rabbits would have fewer enemies and could live in peace. She used the information from the text and added the missing social concepts and relations from her own knowledge to construct a perfectly logical interpretation (Adams & Bruce, 1982). Although children may use the same words as adults, the knowledge underlying their language is often quite different from that of adults.

In order to communicate and do complex higher order thinking, people represent knowledge in language. As Smith, Goodman & Meredith (1976) stated:

> Language may be viewed as. . .an integral part of the personal process of experiencing and knowing. . .the thing is not known until it is named, and its interrelation with other things is not understood until language embodies the idea. If this function of language is accepted, intellectual education is neither the memorization of words and facts, nor the possession of significant experiences, but is the constant interplay of interrelated experiences and language toward knowing. Language is pivotal in a person's knowing through experience. (p. 84)

From this perspective, language becomes the heart of the teaching-learning process. The teacher needs to create a classroom environment full of interesting things, books, and activities which will foster learning through language use and through reading, writing, listening, and talking. Opportunities for children to interact with peers and the teacher are essential.

The Teacher's Role in Classroom Talk

Teachers can easily become effective "kidwatchers" in classrooms where learning occurs through interaction. They can monitor and record children's language and their developing knowledge. Students hazily and mazily verbalize ideas and eventually clarify them during discussion. This may involve adding or deleting attributes or features, changing prototypes, or linking concepts together to relate them in more complex ways. It is through ongoing observation that the teacher is able to orchestrate classroom experiences to help students build on what they know.

The delicate task of scaffolding a discussion among students without imposing (see article by Goodman) is difficult to carry out. As researchers have shown, the usual classroom interaction pattern is teacher question/student response/teacher judgment (Barnes, 1976; Bellack, Kliebard, Hyman & Smith, 1966; Mehan, 1979). Trying to guess the teacher's agenda, children limit their responses, rarely asking questions that might reveal ignorance but which are essential to learning.

However, this type of limited interaction need not be the norm. When children interact among themselves in small groups or in a class discussion led by a facilitative teacher their use of hypothetical language, prior knowledge, and questions increases (Barnes, 1976; Barnes & Todd, 1977; Barr, D'Arcy & Healy, 1976; Cazden, 1982). They test their understanding against other sources and their own knowledge for consistency and truth. During this type of discussion, risk-taking and error-making, both integral parts of learning, occur with feedback in an atmosphere of trust. By focusing attention, posing questions, pointing out problems, suggesting alternatives or providing information at the teachable moment, a teacher can heighten awareness and facilitate learning.

In the next example Vivian Paley (1981), an unusually sensitive teacher and kidwatcher, only enters the conversation to help the children become aware of their findings or potential inconsistencies and problems. She recorded this conversation as her kindergarteners attempted to understand the length and function of rulers. The children were discussing the relative sizes of two rugs for a play which was about to be acted out.

Wally: The big rug is the giant's castle. The small one is Jack's house.

Eddie: Both rugs are the same.

Wally: They can't be the same. Watch me. I'll walk around the rug. Now watch—walk, walk, walk, walk, walk, walk, walk, walk, walk—now count these walks. Okay. Now count the other rug. Walk, walk, walk, walk, walk. See? That one has more walks.

Eddie: No fair. You cheated. You walked faster.

Wally: I don't have to walk. I can just look.

Eddie: I can look too. But you have to measure it. You need a ruler. About six hundred inches or feet.

Wally: We have a ruler.

Eddie: Not that one. Not the short kind. You have to use the long kind that gets curled up in a box.

Wally: Use people. People's bodies. Lying down in a row.

Eddie: That's a great idea. I never even thought of that.

(p. 13-14)

At this point they determined that one rug was a four person rug and the other a three person rug. The next day Eddie decided he wanted to measure the rug again.

Wally: You're too short. I mean someone is too short. We need Warren. Where's Warren?

Teacher: He's not here today.

Eddie: We can't measure the rug.

Teacher: You can only measure the rug when Warren is here?

Jill: Because he's longer.

Deana: Turn everyone around. Then it will fit.

(Eddie rearranges the measurers so that each is now in a different position. Their total length is the same.)

Eddie: No, it won't work. We have to wait for Warren.

Deana: Let me have a turn. I can do it.

Jill: You're too big, Deana. Look at your feet sticking out. Here's a rule. Nobody bigger than Warren can measure the rug.

Fred: Wait. Just change Ellen and Deana because Ellen is shorter.

Jill: She sticks out just the same. Wait for Warren.

Fred: Now she's longer than before, that's why.

Teacher: Is there a way to measure the rug so we don't have to worry about people's sizes?

Kenny: Use short people.

Teacher: And if the short people aren't in school?

Rose: Use big people.

Eddie: Some people are too big.

Teacher: Maybe using people is a problem.

Fred: Use three year olds.

Teacher: There aren't any three year olds in our class.

Deana: Use rulers. Get all the rulers in the room. I'll get the box of rulers.

Eddie: That was *my* idea, you know.

Deana: This isn't enough rulers.

Eddie: Put a short, short person after the rulers—Andy.

Andy: I'm not short, short. And I'm not playing this game.

Wally: Use the dolls.

Teacher: So this rug is ten rulers and two dolls long? (Silence.) Here's something we can do. We can use one of the rulers over again this way.

Eddie: Now you made *another* empty space.

Teacher: Eddie, you mentioned a tape measure before. I have one here.

(We stretched the tape along the edge of the rug and I show the children that the rug is 156 inches long. The lesson is done. The next day Warren is back in school.)

Wally: Here's Warren. Now we can really measure the rug.

Teacher: Didn't we really measure the rug with the ruler?

Wally: Well, rulers aren't really real, are they?

(p. 14-16)

The desire to create a giant's house that is bigger than Jack's house for the play and the disagreement over the relative sizes of the two rugs in the classroom generated the need to measure. As the children discussed the problem, they discovered several ways to measure on their own. But they have not yet internalized the arbitrary abstract convention of uniform units of measure.

The teacher, Vivian Paley, listens to their comments, builds on their understanding and gently asks questions to create a potential alternative which may advance the children to a new level of understanding if they work to solve the new problem. The question about Warren launches them into different attempts to measure the rug without him. Her next question, asking if there is another way to measure with something other than people, is not processed until all the people possibilities are considered and rejected. Like a mirror, Vivian reflected back what they had figured out so far—that the rug was 10 rulers and 2 dolls long. The silence made it clear that no one was satisfied with this solution. Consequently, Vivian suggested using a ruler over again, but met with Eddie's need for continuous, concrete representation of "length." Flexibly she offered another possibility, using the tape measure.

At each step, Vivian watches and brings what the children have discovered to awareness through questions or statements. She only introduces new information when it is called for. The students come to their own conclusions and learn through their actions and discussion. They are not forced to parrot the teacher's understanding.

Reading and Discussion

Reading comprises a substantial proportion of time during the academic day, particularly from fourth grade on when reading becomes one of the major sources of new information for learning. Since the author's meaning is only represented in the print, the reader must infuse the print with meaning and construct an interpretation of the author's message. Readers need to transform the author's symbols into personal meaning. If the reader lacks knowledge or has had different experiences from the author the interpretation of the text may be quite idiosyncratic or fuzzy.

One way to find out what has been comprehended is to share with others, by verbalizing through discussion or writing. Often through this type of actualization readers discover how consistent or inconsistent, complete or incomplete their interpretations of the text are. Through interaction, readers may collaboratively create a more integrated interpretation and learn from the text and the discussion.

In the following example four ten year olds have just read a poem about a boy's grief when his dog dies and are asked to discuss it by themselves.

Rock, Our Dog

He's dead now
He was put to sleep last night.
I was sad,
but I did not cry.

It was not the same
without him here
to prance and
nuzzle his head
into my arms.

Today we were going
to bury him
in the garden.
I helped dig the hole
and then ran off.

Nicholas Hadfield
(Martin, 1976, p. 39)

The discussion began:

J: Um, let's go on to Rock, Our Dog.

S: This one's a bit sad, isn't it.

A: Yeah.

L: It's a sad one.

J: I've got a dog called Pip and it makes me think whether he's going to die.

S: We've got a great big dog...it's an incredible nuisance.

M: Like the dog next door, it's ten now.

S: When our dog next door died...

J: Actually; shall I tell you what I'd do if it were my dog, I'd help dig the hole/and I'd run off.

S: I like the verse um, the second verse.

M: "It was not the same/Without him here/to prance and/nuzzle his head into my arms."

S: That's nice, that one.

L: Yeah. It feels as if he's very, you know.

S: A nice dog.

L: Very happy with you, and he's always comforting you and...

J: Pip does that, ooh I thought she was dead when she came home from her operation, she had her tongue hanging out of her mouth, it was horrible.

S: You know when a dog goes to the doctor's or something and it makes you feel, I hope it comes back all right.

(Martin, 1976, p. 40)

They went on in order discussing things like: when dogs should or should not be put to sleep; how the color in a dog's face changes as it gets older; a child's fear of dogs; a dog that got run over; having puppies; the difficulty of training a labrador, alsatians and on and on. To mitigate the sadness of the poem, they switched back and forth, approaching and leaving the feelings of loss, sadness, and grief.

They finally turned back to the poem when they realized they had lost focus. They had a more critical orientation since they had now explored their own personal experiences and reactions.

L: Let's go back to the poem.

M: Yes, well we're talking about the poem, we're talking about dogs.

L: Well, why did he say he's dead now? Why couldn't they start with he's dead?

S: Our dog...our dog's just died. That sounds better.

L: ...than saying "He's dead now".

S: You could start "Our dog's just died, he was put to sleep last night." That sounds a little better.

M: sounds kinds of, more as if...

S: then "he's dead"...

M: ...more as if he knows the dog...

J: ...no, you get the feeling of it though, "He's dead now/He was put to sleep last night/I was sad/But I did not cry," but I would, I would cry my eyes out if my dog had just died.

L: Yeah, it's probably a boy though, isn't it, it's a boy who wrote it though?

S: Boys don't really seem to cry...

L: Boys don't cry very much, not as...

M: Not over that sort of thing...

L: They don't, not really, the girls are more sentimental and a bit more soppy.

S: No they're not.

M: Some boys are like that, specially if they've known it for a long time.

J: I helped dig a hole, I helped dig the hole and then ran off, and then ran off...

L: Oh, I wouldn't.

S: I suppose he just ran off because he didn't want to see the dog being put into the um...

L: grave

S: grave

J: Yeah.

L: There's the, um, Sizes down the road and they had a dog and it's blind and they, and when it started howling when they were away, and it died, it was dead when they got back and they buried it under, their, their favorite apple tree and they've got it smothered with flowers. It looked ever so pretty.

(p. 40-41)

In discussing this exchange, Martin (1976) commented about how the children constructed the meaning of the poem. They each offered anecdotes about dogs from their lives. Though often implicit, their conversation touched on the major themes and feelings evoked by the poem. Martin argues that it is through these "personal stories" that children are able to comprehend. As Moffett (1983) puts it, "...people fictionalize. They project into invented stories those unobjectified forces of the psychic life that are hard to name or even recognize. Storying is a mode of abstracting..." (p. 48).

In a different context John and Robin, second year students from Walworth School, took turns reading what they had written on India. After Robin read his narrative called "The Destruction of Mohenjo Daro," John read his version of the same event entitled "The Aryans." Then they commented on the writings and reached to extend their knowledge further:

R: That's a good one.

J: Oh, you've described more of the mountains, I've just des...I've just done the battle.

R: Yes, so really, we've just done about the same, because I've described the mountains and you've described the battles.

J: Yes, so in fact we both, it worked out better, didn't it.

R: Yes.

J: Well what do you think type of climate it is in India?

R: Must be all snowy on the Himalayas and when they got down there, you know, it's sunny.

J: Well, it depends, don't it, if they're right next to the Himalayas it might not be so sunny, it might be still a bit cold and wet, 'cause of the snow off the Himalayas.

R: Yes.

J: And you know, as they go, as the monsoon winds go to the Himalayas they might make the snow and it'll snow just before they get to the Himalayas.

R: Yes, and where I put the snowstorm (in the text) that would be right, wouldn't it.

J: Yes.

R: It's blow all the snow up.

J: Yes. And not only that, it might even bring the water in from the...well, it depends what type of year it is, don't it, really.

R: Yes.

J: But they could have, really, because you know the wind blows in, brings clouds in with it and then instead of falling as rain they can't 'cause it's so cold it changes into snow.

....

J: Well, what else shall we read, shall we read...oh I've read that.

R: Where did they come from? I've put they come from Asia.

J: No, Iran.

R: Oh. I put Asia.

J: Well, Asia is in—er, Iran is in Asia.

R: Yes.

J: Asia is a continent, Iran is part of the continent.

(Martin, Williams, Wilding, Hemmings & Medway, 1976, p. 48)

As the boys talked about their writings they genuinely tried on new ideas. John, who was interested in climate, applied his knowledge of monsoons to validate it in another context. He was able to do this by discussing it with Robin and relating what he had just learned in class to what they had written. Later in the conversation the relation between Asia and Iran was clarified for Robin who asked for feedback from his study partner.

Reading and discussing a story several times often helps children begin to see their own learning. Paley (1981) points out that repeated readings are important since each discussion may emphasize different aspects or feelings. When Vivian read Rumpelstiltskin a second time to her kindergarten, Lisa (age 5) shifted her reaction to the little man. After the first reading, Lisa had laughed at him when he destroyed himself. Now she identified with him "as victim."

Lisa: She's really not nice.

Teacher: But he wanted her baby.

Lisa: Why couldn't she just share the baby? Or wish for another one? Because he was really her friend.

Warren: She didn't even know him.

Lisa: If you *don't* know each other you act nice. You don't argue.

Warren: If you *do* know each other you act nicer.

Lisa: Wally and Eddie fight and they're best friends.

Wally: We don't really fight. But if someone is a stranger then you really do fight because you think you're better than him.

Lisa: You don't even bother with a stranger. Anyway Rumpelstiltskin was a friend and he helped her make real gold. He was *lonely*. Lonely! That's why he was stamping and screaming.

Teacher: Lisa, do you remember the first day of school when you didn't want your mother to leave? You stamped and screamed like Rumpelstiltskin.

Rose: You were lonely, right?

Lisa: I was little then. That's why.

(Paley, 1981, pp. 72-73)

Through their talk about Rumpelstiltskin the children tried to understand complicated social rules, and the apparent contradictions. They tried to make sense of their world which in turn helped them understand the story in a new way. Without forcing, the teacher attempted to help Lisa make a connection between Rumpelstiltskin's behavior and his feelings of loneliness and her own behavior in the beginning of the year. Rose's inference was wise beyond her years.

Conclusion

Discussion can evolve from reading stories, poems, or student writings; from science, math, or social studies; or from events outside the classroom. Talk leads to comprehension and learning. As the Bullock Report (1975) stated:

> To bring knowledge into being is a formulating process, and language is its ordinary means, whether in speaking or writing or the inner monologue of thought. Once it is understood that talking and writing are means to learning, those more obvious truths that we learn also from other people by listening and reading will take on a fuller meaning and fall into a proper perspective. (4.9)

It is important to monitor activities continuously to make sure that children are provided with many opportunities to learn through language. To assess the effectiveness of the learning context teachers can pose the following questions:

> How often does a child share his personal interests and learning discoveries with others in the class?
>
> How far is the teacher able to enter such conversations without robbing the children of verbal initiative?
>
> Are the children accustomed to reading to one another what they have written, and just as readily listen?
>
> Are they accustomed to solving cooperatively in talk the practical problems that arise when they work together?

How much opportunity is there for the kind of talk by which children make sense in their own terms of the information offered by teacher or by book?

What varieties of writing—story, personal record, comment, report, speculation, etc.—are produced in the course of a day?

Over a longer span, what varieties occur in the output of a single child?
(Bullock Report, 1975, 12.3)

It is by integrating the language arts for learning that children can become proficient language users and understand more about themselves and their world.

References

Adams, M., & Bruce, B. "Background Knowledge and Reading Comprehension," in J. Langer & M.T. Smith-Burke (Eds.), *Reader Meets Author/Bridging the Gap.* Newark, Delaware: International Reading Association, 1982.

Barnes, D. *From Communication to Curriculum.* New York: Penguin Books, 1976.

Barnes, D., & Todd, F. *Communication and Learning in Small Groups.* London: Routledge & Kegan Paul, 1977.

Bellack, A., & others. *The Language of the Classroom.* New York: Teachers College Press, 1966.

Bruner, J., Goodnow, J., & Austin, G. *A Study of Thinking.* New York: John Wiley, 1956.

Bullock Report. *A Language for Life.* London: HMSO Department of Educational Science, 1975.

Cazden, C.B. "Peer Dialogues across the Curriculum," in Y. Goodman, M. Haussler, & D. Strickland (Eds.), *Oral and Written Language Development Research: Impact on the Schools.* Urbana, Illinois: National Council of Teachers of English, 1982.

Clark, E. "What's in a Word? On the Child's Acquisition of Semantics in His First Language," in T.E. Moore (Ed.), *Cognitive Development and the Acquisition of Language.* New York: Academic Press, 1973.

Lindfors, J. *Children's Language and Learning.* Englewood Cliffs, New Jersey: Prentice-Hall, 1980.

Martin, N. "Children and Stories: Their Own and Other People's," in M. Torbe & R. Protherough (Eds.), *Classroom Encounters: Language and English Teaching.* London: Ward Lock Educational, 1976.

Martin, N., & others. *Understanding Children Talking.* New York: Penguin Books, 1976.

Mehan, H. *Learning Lessons.* Cambridge, Massachusetts: Harvard University Press, 1979.

Moffett, J. *Teaching the Universe of Discourse,* second revised edition. Boston: Houghton Mifflin, 1983.

Paley, V. *Wally's Stories.* Cambridge, Massachusetts: Harvard University Press, 1981.

Rosch, E. "Cognitive Representations of Semantic Categories," *Journal of Experimental Psychology: General, 104,* (1975), 192-233.

Smith, B., Goodman, K., & Meredith, R. *Language and Thinking in Schooling,* second revised edition. New York: Richard C. Owen, 1976.

Smith, F. *Comprehension and Learning.* New York: Holt, Rinehart & Winston, 1975.

Looking at Response to Literature

Janet Hickman
The Ohio State University

"How does Judy Blume ever write so many books?" wonders Sherrie. "Look how *long* they are." It is free reading time in Miss C.'s fourth and fifth grade classroom, a period that stretches into independent and small group work. Cynthia is busy reading *Tuck Everlasting* by Babbitt (1975), for the second time. Janet flips up the cover of her book to show its title, *Fantastic Mr. Fox* by Dahl (1970). "I've read it so many times," she says. "It's really good." Eileen asks Vicky if she is going to read *The Great Gilly Hopkins* by Paterson (1978). Eileen has just discovered the book, has read it almost nonstop, and has discussed it eagerly with her teacher. She goes to the bookshelves to reclaim the room's only copy for her friend. Billy is working on a series of summaries for Cleary's *The Mouse and the Motorcycle* (1965). It is his own idea to report and illustrate the major incident in each chapter and bind these into a book of his own. Johnny labors over a drawing that reproduces one of Mercer Mayer's illustrations for *Everyone Knows What a Dragon Looks Like* by Williams (1976); all the children who stop by his table compliment the success of his efforts. Dawn is writing and painting her own book based on one called *Panda's Puzzle* by Foreman (1978). "But it's not just like it," she says. "Mine is 'The Zebra'."

Response in a Middle Grade Classroom

Dawn and Sherrie and the rest of these nine and ten year olds are responding to literature in a variety of ways. In the process they are revealing information about their levels of development in language and thinking, and something of their progress toward mature understanding and critical appreciation of literature as a form of written language.

Sherrie, for instance, is conscious of the author's role in creating a book; her comment about length suggests a perception that is realistic enough to include respect for the effort involved, but there is no attempt to move from awe to analysis. Cynthia and Janet, as rereaders, represent the intensity of interest that often develops at this age level. But Janet's reasons for returning to a book, or rather her lack of them ("It's really good") show that she has not yet acquired a vocabulary of critical terms that come readily to her when she talks about a book on her own initiative. While the categorical "good" may have specific meaning for Janet, she is not inclined to explain it, possibly because it seems so self-evident to her. Applebee (1976) reported that "good-bad" was one of the basic sets of ideas expressed by elementary students when asked to respond to stories. He also reported (Applebee, 1978a) that children of Janet's age tend to categorize stories according to their own reaction, and then see that reaction as a property of the story itself. As a reader, Janet is not likely to be capable of the objectivity necessary to separate "It's really good because I like it" from "I like it because it's really good." While she may be able to manipulate critical terms in certain contexts, Janet is not ready to shift her focus from personal response to formal criticism.

Eileen, also an intent reader, is quick to offer her reactions to the teacher in a process of confirming and clarifying and sorting out her thoughts. Eileen's impulse to share the story itself with a friend—the inclination to produce the book in fact rather than statements about the book—is an intriguing reminder of the concrete aspect of her thinking. This impulse to share, however, is certainly not limited to childhood. "Have you seen this book?" is common talk for teachers and librarians and adult readers in general, and it may set the stage for a more complex dialogue that includes critical commentary.

Billy's chapter summaries show how well he can organize his thinking and use written language. The ability to summarize stories is not in itself unusual for nine year olds (Applebee, 1978a), but the fact that he chose this task for himself and that he can not only do it but can talk about doing it, with accurate labels and description, indicates to his teacher that Billy is more deliberate and self-aware in his responses than many of her other students.

Johnny's painstaking reproduction of a book illustration that he admires also seems to be fairly typical of middle childhood. Although surrounded by attractive materials and encouragement for creating original pictures, he continues to focus on an image that has greater power for him. He works at recreating the dragon and the plump little man on Mayer's cover, beaming in his success with the same kind of pride seen in younger students drawing their first well-formed letters or numbers. He has been careful to notice the artist's use of watercolor and to strive for the same effects, suggesting that he is very much aware of the illustrator at work in the picture book. Dawn, in making her "Zebra" book, shows equal fascination for a published work, but specifies that her own effort is not a direct copy. She demonstrates some understanding that literature can serve as a model for other writing, a point she is later able to discuss when questioned in terms of the story she is using.

Observations in this middle grade classroom show children on the way toward making their perceptions and understandings about literature more conscious and more formal. To highlight the direction of this growth, we can look at children in an earlier stage of awareness where the responses may be different in kind as well as in degree.

Response in a Primary Classroom

Mrs. K. has a mixed group of kindergarteners and first graders. As in Miss C.'s room, there is plenty of opportunity for children to be with books informally as well as planned times for reading aloud and interpretive activities. There is a play corner, too, where a group of five year olds plan their next moves: "You be the godzilla." "I'm the mother." "Where's the witch?"

Later David and Michelle sit by the shelves, singing nursery rhymes from an illustrated songbook. Michelle, a kindergartener who is not yet reading, continues to carry the book around the room, studying the pages and singing under her breath. David stays in the book corner, reading, tapping on the book from time to time and making other sound effects for the story.

When Mrs. K. gathers everyone on the carpet for a storytelling session featuring "The Little Red Hen," which she has shared previously in Galdone's picturebook edition (1973), most of the children join in on the story refrains the second time through, experimenting with voice changes for the various characters. Wes stands up to offer this comment: "I saw this story on Captain and I remember the pictures. . . .She was doin' all the work. She was so hungry and they didn't help. And that's what happened." The teacher asks, "Why do you think I told you this story and didn't read it?" Bryan says, ". . .when you make the writing and then you don't need it, you rip it up and just remember and you tell it." Then Mrs. K. checks to see if anyone has picked up the term "refrain," which she has used on several earlier occasions. "There were some parts in 'The Little Red Hen' that you heard over and over," she says. "What do you call that?" "That's the chicken," says Bryan.

One of the striking differences between the children's responses in Mrs. K.'s class and those in Miss C.'s group was in the amount of motor involvement and spontaneous activity and comment. The play corner drama with its prototype literary characters, the joining of refrains, the sound effects, and the singing are all acted out responses more characteristic of primary than middle grade children. At this level of unconscious enjoyment and involvement, children seem less aware that they are using literature, a circumstance that adds significance to the older students' more deliberate approach to books.

On the other hand, even this brief bit of classroom data includes evidence of primary children responding in a more objective stance, that is, with talk about a story and their perceptions of it in response to their teacher's questions. Here the contrasts with fourth and fifth graders are of degree. Wes's summary of "The Little Red Hen" may recall Billy's work with *The Mouse and the Motorcycle*, but the first grader has less control of the language needed to show relationship between characters and events. His intent to provide a summary is clear, however, in his explanation "and that's what happened."

Bryan reveals a glimmer of understanding of authorship in his description of storytelling as opposed to reading aloud, "when you make the writing and then you don't need it." Primary children are likely to perceive a story as something written on paper (Applebee, 1978b). Bryan knows that *someone* must make the writing, but his thinking is not flexible enough to account for the possibility that a story might exist with the teller, prior to and apart from its concrete representation. Overall, Bryan's comments show how much he is focused on meaning and making sense, using the information most available to him. In answering Mrs. K.'s question about parts of the story heard over and over, he cites the character who has the most to say. He interprets and deals with the question at its most concrete, human-sense level, in the same way that Donaldson (1979) describes primary children responding to Piagetian tasks.

Gathering Information about Response

In many ways classroom expressions of response to literature function as a showcase where children's language and thinking as well as their literary awareness can be more clearly seen and understood. If such study is to be useful, however, it must include a broad range of evidence as the subject of careful reflection. The examples offered earlier in this chapter are drawn from observations in one elementary school (Hickman, 1981), and their interpretations come from the perspective of one who was familiar with all the children, the immediate history of the classrooms, and the specific context of the reported events. By the nature of their work, teachers share this perspective. They are uniquely prepared to hear a child's meaning as well as his words, to judge the sources of children's satisfaction or puzzlement with a book, to connect today's response with a story read or heard weeks ago. What teachers lack is the luxury of time to attend to responses, time to keep track and compare. Fortunately, literary kidwatching requires no elaborate techniques; familiar and unobtrusive methods will do.

For an overview of classroom responses, a teacher can keep a log or journal which will provide good information. While the entries might not be as detailed as a researcher's field notes, even the briefest notes will serve to document sequence of events and shifts of focus in the group's attitude. Jinx Bohstedt's (1979) running account of the use of folktales in her kindergarten classroom shows what such a journal might include and how it can influence classroom planning. Another approach is to narrow the focus and follow the progress of class response to a single selection. Beaver's report (1982) of her first graders' growing appreciation for the book *Say It!* by Zolotow (1980) upon repeated sharing illustrates the worth of this kind of record keeping.

When children keep track of their own reading in journal form or on cards that provide room for comment, there is built-in opportunity to profile the response patterns of individual students as well as broader patterns within the class. What level of challenge do the choices represent? What are the preferred genre? Are there clusters of books by one author? What do the comments show about the students' implied criteria for a "good" book? What changes are reflected in the course of a year? Hepler's study (1982) of response in a fifth and sixth grade classroom draws many examples from student journals and reading records, demonstrating how this kind of data can be used along with other information to give a more complete understanding of children's progress as readers of literature.

Another source of evidence readily accessible to teachers is children's classwork based on literature—their writing, their art, and various other projects such as comparison charts of related books or board games constructed to follow the plot of a story. Clues to children's perceptions of the story material and their focus of attention within it are implicit in all products of this sort. For instance, watercolor paintings and captions dictated by beginning first graders for the task "Show how Mother Goose would look" demonstrate interesting differences. Sandy's rounded creature labeled "This is Mother Goose. She fell off a wall" shows prior experience with nursery rhymes, but apparently not enough experience to allow for differentiation between Mother Goose and Humpty Dumpty. Suzi's literal "She looks like a goose to me" suggests a focus on the distinction between real and make-believe. Todd's dark picture says "Mother Goose is surrounded by monsters"; it shows the power of monster figures in Todd's concept of story. Personal files of work samples such as these are complementary to reading records and allow for examining response at leisure, with more time to reflect on what the child has done. There are some products that cannot be filed, of course—clay models, dioramas, murals, and such—but these can be recorded with a camera. Photographs have the added value of preserving helpful information about the context in which the work occurred.

Tape recorders can be used in several ways to provide convenient access to verbal responses. Taping a read-aloud session and the discussion that follows helps the teacher keep track of unsolicited comments and reflect on the flow of ideas in the discussion. A reading teacher who recorded fourth graders' discussion of the book *Ultra-Violet Catastrophe! or The Unexpected Walk with Great Uncle Magnus Pringle* by Mahy (1975) discovered, on listening to the tape, that the boy who categorized the book as "dumb" at the outset responded to his classmates' disagreement as well as to the book: "Okay, okay, It's funny. . .it can be funny and dumb at the same time, can't it?" Two girls continued to argue that the book was not "dumb." One said, "The old Pringle guy was havin' fun. Old guys don't have much fun. That's why it's a neat book." While the teacher saw that "dumb," "funny," and "neat" represented an undeveloped critical vocabulary, she also saw that some children's perceptions of the story and its impact went beyond their knowledge of terms. Taping large group discussions seldom provides more than a hint of an individual's level of understanding. However, taping extended discussions or book conferences with a small group of students can provide the data for analysis in depth of their literary development, as Galda (1982) demonstrates in her study of three fifth grade girls' responses to selected books of fiction.

To broaden the perspective for understanding the level of responses in a single classroom, discussions on one book by children at various grade levels can be taped by their respective teachers and shared for comparison. Knowing the differences as well as the similarities in kindergarten, third grade, and fifth grade comments about Sendak's *Outside Over There* (1981) provides more insight for all the teachers involved than simply listening to their own classes. Asking a core of common questions facilitates comparison. The question "Is this a real story or a pretend story?" brought "Real" from a five year old, "A pretend story" from a ten year old, and "I think it would be make-believe" from an eight year old, demonstrating the cautious transition from confidence in the total truth of story to confidence in one's own judgment of the distance between fantasy and reality.

Another way to use a tape recorder is to give it to a single child or a small group of children and ask them to talk over a book on their own. Douglas Barnes (1976) reports using this technique in England to understand how children use language in problem solving situations and in making meaning from the text of a poem. A book discussion not structured by an adult reveals what children know about discussions as well as what they know about books. Four children puzzling over *The Magical Drawings of Moony B. Finch* by McPhail (1978) offered the following

Suzi: Wait a minute, wait a minute. We're gonna have one problem here. Everyone's gonna have to raise up their hand like in a class meeting. Then someone will pick on you.

Bryan: Okay, I got picked....Why do you guys think that he drew pictures with his crayon 'n then they touched it 'n they came alive?

Charlie: It's not really true.

Suzi: I know. It's just a story they made up.

Bryan: ...he always drew pictures. Why did he draw pictures?

Suzi: He likes to draw. . . .

Wes: Well, uh, you see, when he drawed it, it was a magic crayon and he colored it...and rather than makin' it come to life he made it come to a mural, with a dragon.

Charlie: Now—

Suzi: Charlie, sit down so everyone can hear you.

Charlie: Now see, uh, the dragon was here. Here's the big dragon. 'N he got everything off of him without...he disappeared like this. (Charlie moves away from tape recorder, demonstrating disappearance of the dragon.)

Suzi functions as the manager of this discussion, and Bryan plays a questioner role that shows his ability to focus on crucial aspects of the story rather than insignificant details. Wes is caught up in establishing an explanation for the magical happenings of the story, seeing if it will fit with what he already knows about art and dragons. Charlie, however, acts out his meaning, a circumstance lost to the tape despite Suzi's warning to "sit down so everyone can hear you." It is often the case that observation of the taping process provides information complementary to the tape itself. Videotape has obvious advantages if it can be used with a minimum of intrusion.

Looking at response to literature requires a careful ear *and* a good eye. Elementary children's response is nonverbal as well as verbal, and it has social as well as individual dimensions. The more sources that can be used in collecting evidence about children's interaction with books, poems, and stories, the more helpful that evidence will be in guiding decisions on the selection and use of literature.

References

Applebee, A.N. "Children's Construal of Stories and Related Genres as Measured with Repertory Grid Techniques," *Research in the Teaching of English, 10* (Winter 1976), 226-238.

Applebee, A.N. *The Child's Concept of Story: Ages Two to Seventeen.* Chicago: University of Chicago Press, 1978(a).

Applebee, A.N. "Where Does Cinderella Live?" In M. Meek, et al. (Eds.), *The Cool Web: The Pattern of Children's Reading.* New York: Atheneum, 1978(b).

Barnes, D. *From Communication to Curriculum.* Harmondsworth, England: Penguin Books, 1976.

Beaver, J.M. "*Say It!* Over and Over," *Language Arts, 59* (February 1982), 143-148.

Bohstedt, J. "Old Tales for Young Tellers," *Outlook, 33* (Autumn 1979), 31-45.

Donaldson, M. *Children's Minds.* New York: W.W. Norton, 1979.

Galda, L. "Teaching from Children's Responses," *Language Arts, 59* (February 1982), 137-142.

Hepler, S.I. "Patterns of Response to Literature: A One-Year Study of a Fifth and Sixth Grade Classroom," doctoral dissertation, Ohio State University, 1982.

Hickman, J. "A New Perspective on Response to Literature: Research in an Elementary School Setting," *Research in the Teaching of English, 15* (December 1981), 343-354.

Children's Books

Babbitt, N. *Tuck Everlasting.* New York: Farrar, Straus & Giroux, 1975.

Cleary, B. *The Mouse and the Motorcycle.* Illustrated by Louis Darling. New York: Morrow, 1965.

Dahl, R. *Fantastic Mr. Fox.* Illustrated by Donald Chaffin. New York: Knopf, 1970.

Foreman, M. *Panda's Puzzle.* New York: Bradbury Press, 1978.

Galdone, P. *The Little Red Hen.* New York: Seabury Press, 1973.

McPhail, D. *The Magical Drawings of Moony B. Finch.* New York: Doubleday, 1978.

Mahy, M. *Ultra-Violet Catastrophe! or The Unexpected Walk with Great Uncle Magnus Pringle.* Illustrated by Brian Froud. New York: Parents, 1975.

Paterson, K. *The Great Gilly Hopkins.* New York: T.Y. Crowell, 1978.

Sendak, M. *Outside Over There.* New York: Harper & Row, 1981.

Williams, J. *Everyone Knows What a Dragon Looks Like.* Illustrated by Mercer Mayer. New York: Four Winds Press, 1976.

Zolotow, C. *Say It!* Illustrated by James Stevenson. New York: Harper and Row, 1980.

Part Four
Curriculum and Instruction: The Language Learning Environment

Introduction

A major theme developed throughout this book is that context influences language use and learning. In Part Four the writers stress the role played by teachers in creating classroom contexts that support and foster learning.

Harker and Green explore the complexities of classroom communication. They illustrate, through examples of teacher-student interaction, how our own use of language and patterns of working with children can influence their performance. They also describe ways to tap children's knowledge of the social, and often subtle, rules that govern when, where, and how they may talk in the classroom.

In the final article, "Contexts for Language and Literacy," McKenzie shows how language flourishes in classrooms where children have many opportunities to interact with peers and to use language for a variety of purposes. She stresses that teachers need to set up environments and plan experiences which ensure that talking, writing, listening, and reading all play a vital part in the learning process.

When You Get the Right Answer to the Wrong Question: Observing and Understanding Communication in Classrooms

Judith O. Harker
Veteran's Administration Medical Center
Sepulveda, California
Judith L. Green
The Ohio State University

When you get the right answer to the wrong question, things have quickly become very confusing. *You* thought that you said what you meant; they thought you meant what they *thought* you said. You have run up against one of the evident truths about communication: that it is more complex than you usually realize. Insight into the complexities of classroom communication is especially important to teachers who want to understand how miscommunications and also successful communications occur.

In every classroom, the teacher makes a continuing series of decisions about what, when, and how to communicate with children. These decisions grow out of the teacher's evaluation of the nature and quality of the communication that is taking place: "Are they going to understand this? Should I rephrase this question? How can I get Tony or Sue to participate? Who should have the next turn?" This decision making, consciously or unconsciously, is an integral part of every interaction. The roots of this decision making are the teacher's goals, the teacher's knowledge about the nature of teaching-learning processes as communicative processes, and the teacher's ability to assess and understand the student's communications and reactions to the teacher.

Just as the teacher maintains an internal dialogue, the children must also make similar decisions about how, when and what to say: "Do I raise my hand now? Is it my turn? Do I make a noise so the teacher will see me? Do I know the answer? Will Tommy think I'm a showoff if I answer?" The basis for children's decisions are their knowledge about how to use language and their ability to understand the requirements for participation in that classroom. For both teachers and students, these communicative decisions occur minute-to-minute in a largely instinctive or unconscious fashion.

Our purpose is to consider factors which underlie these communicative decisions, and to explore how the requirements and demands of classroom communications may affect student performance. We will present examples of actual classroom events adapted from videotaped recordings. These everyday situations will be discussed from the relatively new theoretical framework of sociolinguistics. Concepts will be introduced which provide a perspective for viewing these events, and teachers will see how they can apply these ideas in their own classrooms.

To begin to develop a sociolinguistic perspective, consider these questions as you read the examples: What is the student expected to do academically and communicatively? How is he/she expected to respond or act? What rules or expectations for actions or talk are being followed by the student(s) and by the teacher? What events signal or cue these expectations?

> A teacher and a single student are seated at a table and are reading a story card containing a story about a peony. When Albert comes to the word "peony," he stops and the teacher intervenes.
>
> T: (points to the "eo" in "peony") Remember the two vowel rule.[1]
>
> A: Peen-y
>
> T: "PE" says...
>
> A: Pē (Correctly pronounces syllable)
>
> T: (points to "on") This says...
>
> A: on (Correctly pronounces syllable)
>
> T: (points to "y") And this says...
>
> A: ē (Correctly pronounces syllable)
>
> T: What's this word?
>
> A: Peen-y
>
> T: (points to "pe" again) This says...
>
> A: pē (Correctly pronounces syllable)
>
> T: (points to "on" again)

A: on (Correctly pronounces syllable)

T: (points to "y" again)

A: ē (Correctly pronounces syllable)

T: Good.

Albert continues reading until he comes to the word "pest" and then he stops again.[2]

The interactions between Albert and the teacher occur when Albert comes to a word he does not know (as indicated by his pause) or makes an error in pronunciation. Then the teacher intervenes to provide help and their conversations focus on what she perceives as Albert's error or problem. In turn, Albert builds on her help by responding to her questions appropriately or following her directions. The previous exchange is directed at helping Albert decode the word "peony" and so is *goal-directed.* The teacher's intervention and conversational behavior established a *frame of reference* (Tannen, 1980; Elkind, 1980; Goffman, 1980) for Albert to use in decoding the problematic word. However, the teacher has verbally ("Remember the two vowel rule") and nonverbally (pointing to "eo") signaled a rule that does not apply here. Albert, who has accepted the teacher's frame of reference, continues to use this frame to guide his interactions with the teacher. The teacher in responding to Albert's appropriate but incorrect pronunciation of the word, proceeds to correct her error (the two-vowel rule) by pointing to each syllable of the word "pe-o-ny" and requesting Albert to say each of them. Her correction of the rule is signaled nonverbally and indirectly, but Albert's behaviors indicate that he is continuing to use the rule that was originally signaled verbally and directly. He does not *read* the new expectations being signaled by the teacher. This is a *frame clash* (Green & Harker, 1982; Elkind, 1980) between the frame of reference which was originally signaled directly and the implicit one to which the teacher has shifted. The teacher appears unaware of the frame clash, and Albert's behaviors do not provide clues for the teacher since he responds appropriately to each demand for performance. He does not, however, infer or read the new expectations from the chain of conversational behaviors provided by the teacher to signal that the rule he should use has shifted. The teacher changes strategies two more times:

Albert continues reading until he pauses at the word "pest."

T: Pest. Do you know what a pest is?

A: Something that bothers you.

T: Uh huh.

Albert continues reading until he mispronounces the word "rodent" and the teacher intervenes.

T: Long "o."

A: Rodent (correcting his error).

T: Good.

Albert completes the story.

T: Now I want to ask you some questions about the story. What was the name of the flower in the story?

A: Pessent...

One way to interpret Albert's response is that it reflects his confusion caused by the earlier frame clash. At the end of this episode Albert is rewarded for pronouncing each syllable correctly, but the goal of decoding the problem word has not been met. Albert never pronounces "peony" correctly, yet the episode is closed by the teacher. This action leaves the goal unmet and a problem unresolved for both Albert and the teacher. Albert later responds appropriately and correctly to the teacher's prompts. However, when the three problems are considered together, Albert's guess, "pessent," seems to be a logical combination of the target words he missed—peony, pest and rodent. Note that "peony" was never pronounced by either Albert or the teacher, but that "pest" and "rodent" were. Albert, therefore, was left with the task of inferring what the correct pronunciation was.

In this example, Albert was shown to be a competent conversational partner. He was able to respond appropriately throughout the instructional conversation, basing his responses on his partner's verbal and nonverbal behaviors. He was also able to extract the directly signaled behavior expectation. Albert's problem was not one of using language for learning appropriately; it was one of *not* reading shifting expectations that were signaled indirectly and nonverbally. Albert's incorrect response to the query about the name of the flower was a "negotiated error"; that is, it was a product of the interactions that occurred during the lesson.

This episode suggests that errors children make during instruction may be due to the nature of the interaction and may not accurately reflect the children's knowledge about content (as in this case, about phonetic rules) or knowledge about participating in classroom conversations. This episode also illustrates the constructed nature of conversations and the consequences of frame clashes. We saw the importance of reading both verbal and nonverbal signals whether signaled either directly or indirectly.

The following example shows how a teacher's knowledge of the processes and consequences of communication can be used to evaluate and guide her decision making. The situation was recorded on a day in the middle of a semester.

> A group of kindergarten children are sitting on a rug waiting for the teacher to begin school. The children are chatting with friends. The teacher enters and sits in her chair. The children continue talking. The teacher looks around and waits for them to get quiet, the expected behavior. The children continue to chat. The teacher picks up her roll book and places it in her lap. All the children stop talking and attend to the teacher.
>
> (Stoffan-Roth, 1981, p. 12)

The teacher, in writing about this episode, indicated that when she entered the area she was surprised that the children continued to talk since her entry was usually a signal to be quiet. This teacher was aware that frames of reference are established for situations and that they are signaled during interactions (Wallat & Green, 1979). She thought that she had established a stable frame of reference; that is, an established norm or signal for beginning school. Her background in sociolinguistics helped her explore possible reasons for the unexpected behavior of the children. She reports that she stopped and asked herself about what she was signaling. In looking about, she noticed that her roll book was on the table beside the chair. She realized that she had completed only part of the signal for school to begin. This observation was confirmed by the children. When she picked up the roll book and placed it on her lap thus completing the signal, all the children stopped talking and turned their attention to her. School has "begun."

This example demonstrates how this teacher used her knowledge to guide her analysis of her participation in the event and to identify factors contributing to the students' apparent lack of compliance with established norms for beginning school.

The ways in which language is used, the ways in which messages are signaled, can contribute to or interfere with appropriate participation in instructional situations. In addition, these examples show that teachers are the orchestrators of instructional events; they are responsible for setting up the rules which signal and guide appropriate participation.

Observing Classroom Communication: Learning to Look Systematically

The teacher reading with Albert did not understand his mistake, nor how her behaviors had evoked it. The teacher in the second situation was able to step out of her role as "teacher" and into the role of "observer" in order to reflect on her behaviors and those of her students in an objective way. Much can be learned by becoming an active, informed observer of communications that occur every day in classrooms.

Triangulation: A structure for looking. Triangulation (Elliot, 1976) requires that three perspectives on an event be considered: those of the observer(s) and two participants. In the Albert example, the observer explored the unfolding lesson by focusing on the *student* within the conversational process (one participant) and then by shifting to the *teacher* (the second participant). By shifting perspectives and exploring the demands on each of the participants to respond, and to participate appropriately, the observer can begin to understand the frames of reference that are used or constructed, the sources of frame clash, and can ultimately better evaluate student ability. The observer, by focusing on Albert's perspective, was able to analyze his incorrect response to the teacher's question. By looking at the teacher's chain of behaviors, the observer could see that the teacher changed from giving a direct signal to giving a series of indirect actions that signaled new rules. The two perspectives when taken together provide a more complete picture of both the lesson and the student's performance.

Teachers can also use this technique. Some form of permanent record is required—e.g., videotape, audiotape, detailed written descriptions of the unfolding events. The value of such records is that they make the conversation visible and that they allow the teacher to explore the consequences of different conversational behaviors (e.g., questions, responses, directions). Having a record permits the teacher to *freeze the conversation* in time and to remember exactly what was said. People can recall what was intended, but often cannot recall the words which were used and how they were received. This may be especially true of young children who attend to meaning more than to form.

Permanent records are essential for clear, careful analyses, but they are not always necessary for this triangulation approach to be effective as the second example illustrates. That teacher was able to step briefly into the role of observer, analyze the participants' behaviors (her own and that of the students) in terms of established classroom rules, frames of reference and signals, and then step back into the role of teacher, appropriately signaling the beginning of the school day.

So far, we have talked about two of the three points of view in triangulation: that of the observer and one participant, the teacher. Let us now consider the point of view of the other participant—the student.

Exploring the student's perspective. Two techniques have been used to obtain information from students about their knowledge of conversational rules. The first example was obtained when children were asked to draw maps of their classrooms and share them with a stranger who wanted to learn what kindergarten classrooms were like. After drawing a map, each child took an observer on a tour using the map. The observer's purpose was to discover what the children knew about appropriate use of language in different areas of the classroom: when, how, and where they were expected to do certain kinds of talking.

> Eric was asked about his map. Initial conversations showed the observer that direct questions were needed in order to elicit information from Eric.
>
> Observer: How do you talk in the block area, in the unit blocks?
>
> Eric: Use inside voices.
>
> O: Inside voices? What's an inside voice?
>
> E: Like this (talks quietly, in normal tones).
>
> O: What's an outside voice? Can you give me an example?
>
> E: Yeah—Ahhhhhhh (said loudly). Like that. You can even yell.
>
> O: So you can't do that in the classroom?
>
> E: Nope.

Eric is aware of differences in how to talk in classrooms and how this talk differs from playground talk in terms of volume. He has also internalized a classroom rule—adjust your voice to the context. Eric is able to demonstrate the differences during the interview although he is unable to define or describe them. This example shows that young children are sensitive to rules of language use and suggests that an interviewer needs to consider the child's level of development and language ability. The interview format and the interviewer's role may be varied depending upon the needs and abilities of the child. The key appears to be establishing that the observer genuinely needs the information the child has. The next two examples further demonstrate these points.

> Alexa, in contrast with Eric, proceeded to take the observer on a tour in a crisp manner with minimum prompting. She moved from area to area providing information as the observer pointed to each area.
>
> Observer: (Points to patchwork rug)
>
> Alexa: You can watch movies there most of the time.
>
> O: (Points to listening center)
>
> A: Four people at a time can play records. There's a special way to play records, first you put the record on the record player, hold it by the edges, then put the record player on. It has to be pretty low.
>
> O: Why does it have to be low?
>
> A: So other people can hear. You can't talk loud either.

Alexa, like Eric, is aware of rules for language use and different communicative demands in various situations and contexts. She demonstrates an ability to describe in detail both overt and tacit rules for participation in the listening center. She is also sensitive to rules for talking and the reasons for talking in special ways in different contexts. She also demonstrates additional awareness of discourse rules that are used in the classroom.

> Observer: (Points to discussion area)
>
> Alexa: You have News and Views and you can have story time. Only one person talks at News and Views. Mrs. M. talks at story time. Then she tells what you can do at work time.
>
> O: (Points to piano) What's the piano for?
>
> A: The signal.
>
> O: What's the signal for?
>
> A: For boys and girls to stop working.
>
> O: Does she play the signal everytime she wants boys and girls to stop working or only special times?
>
> A: Only when work time and arrival time are over.

Here, Alexa shows that she is aware of the rules for talking during discussion time (News and Views); of who talks during which activity; and that demands for talking shift with activity, context, speaker, and time. Much of this knowledge has been gained by observing who talks, when and with whom about what. As suggested earlier, the teacher does not always tell the children directly what the rules and expectations are; rather, they must extract them. This ability to extract rules is evident in Alexa's knowledge of when the signal is used.

The following group of examples was obtained by using a second teachnique for eliciting information from students about their participation in classroom events. A videotape was made of one day in their classroom. The teacher (acting as observer) chose ten children to watch and discuss the events on the tape. She used the opportunity to probe their knowledge about language use in the taped situations. The videotape, like the maps in the previous examples, provided a concrete focus for the children's responses.

> The teacher had explained that the videotape was to be shown and that they were going to discuss what had happened during a story reading lesson.
>
> Teacher: We're going to listen to find out. . .(refers to the upcoming tape)
>
> Stephanie: (interrupting) And nobody talk and you read. . .everybody had to listen and nobody talked and whenever teacher stops and starts again we should be quiet.

Stephanie's response indicates that she was aware of the importance of pauses in a story (a nonverbal, prosodic signal) and that she used this signal to guide her behavior during story reading lessons.

Of course, young children do not always have the same meaning for conversational messages as adults, nor does the fact that they know a rule mean that they will use or follow it.

> The observer wanted to find out about the visual cues teachers give to distribute turns and to call on people. Adam was asked to comment on his performance on the videotape.
>
> Observer: Adam, how did you know you could answer that question?
>
> Adam: I happen to have a children's digest that has the myth Pegasus in it but a different version.
>
> (Adam reads at sixth grade level in kindergarten.)

When we look at the permanent record, the videotape, we notice that the observer's question was somewhat ambiguous. The intent was "How did you know you were supposed to answer that question?" while

Adam's response indicates that he thought the question was "How did you know the answer?" This example demonstrates the importance of having a permanent record to resolve such ambiguities. It also shows that an observer must be aware of children's thinking and that they may use resources not evident in the immediate situation to make sense of questions.

> The teacher and an observer were showing and discussing a videotape of a lesson to a group of children who had volunteered to participate. Two of these children generally behaved as if they were unaware of many of the classroom rules, and often required special discipline procedures. During the questioning both children were able to state the rules for talking during News and Views, for working in different centers, and for using inside and outside voices. Both the teacher and observer were surprised at the extent of knowledge these children demonstrated. Their comments lead to the realization that sometimes children can know a rule but not use it, consciously or unconsciously in a specific situation.

This example shows another aspect of the complexity of communication. Underlying all effective communication is the assumption that cooperation will be obtained from participants in conversations. Appropriate behavior in classroom communication reveals not only knowledge of rules for participation but also an agreement to follow them. Without the interview procedure, the children's knowledge of participation rules would have to be assumed from their classroom behaviors. As we have seen, their overt behaviors in class may mask their actual knowledge. Interviewing and observing children is informative, often surprising, never dull. Gaining an understanding of children's perceptions can provide information about what they know about what is occurring, and also about their ability to extract rules for appropriate communication.

Conclusion

When we unexpectedly get a "right" answer to a question which we did not ask, there are ways to resolve some of the confusions which arise. Using the triangulation approach we can step back from the situation into the role of the observer and review the event. Objectively, what actually was said or done? (The assistance of a permanent record is invaluable for this.) What expectations were held by the teacher and by the student(s) as participants? What cues or signals gave rise to those expectations? What frame of reference was operating for the teacher and for the students? Was there a frame clash? More generally, we (as participants and observers) can explore our own knowledge of the complex factors operating in a particular situation. We can also use various direct and indirect techniques to probe and evaluate students' knowledge of these factors. And we can assist students to clarify and refine that knowledge in order to help them to be more effective participants in classroom life.

Notes

1. The two vowel rule refers to a phonic rule for vowel diagraphs. This rule is frequently taught to children in the following form: "When two vowels go walking the first one does the talking and the second one is silent." This rule holds true approximately 67 percent of the time.
2. This example was adapted from videotape records made by Jerome Harste at Indiana University.

References

Elkind, D. *The Child and Society.* New York: Oxford University Press, 1980.

Elliott, J. *Developing Hypotheses about Classroom from Teacher's Practical Constructs.* Grand Forks, North Dakota: North Dakota Study Group, 1976.

Goffman, E. *Forms of Talk.* Philadelphia: University of Pennsylvania Press, 1980.

Green, J., & Harker, J. "Gaining Access to Learning: Communicative, Contextual, and Academic Demands." In L. Cherry-Wilkinson (Ed.), *Communicating in Classrooms.* New York: Academic Press, 1982.

Stoffan-Roth, M. "Shhhh! The Children are Watching," *Partnership, 6* (Fall 1981), 12.

Tannen, D. "What's in a Frame." In R. Freedle (Ed.), *Advances in Discourse Processes,* Volume 2. Norwood, New Jersey: Ablex, 1980.

Wallat, C., & Green, J.L. "Social Rules and Communicative Contexts in Kindergarten," *Theory into Practice, 18* (October 1979), 275-284.

Classroom Contexts for Language and Literacy

Moira G. McKenzie
Centre for Language in Primary Education
London, England

If we were to take a consensus about our aims in helping children become literate people, we could be reasonably sure that it wouldn't be far from Rosen and Stratta's statement (1979) that

> all children should be made into effective readers, taking to literature with zest, able to grapple with discursive prose and well equipped to detect manipulation through the written word. (p. 28)

Agreement on aims does not mean agreement on practice. Rosen and Stratta go on to say:

> It is their practice which shows them [teachers] to be divided in their assumptions about how children gain mastery over their mother tongue....The sharpest division [is] broadly between those who believe that the use of language can be segmented into separate skills and each of these exercised separately, and those who believe that only the motivated use of language for real and worthwhile purposes can make a significant difference in language development. (p. 28)

Evidence from researchers into preschool language acquisition undoubtedly supports the latter. Children are born into a world in which talk plays a vital part. In the family, children are part of the shared experiences and accompanying talk that are essential for both intellectual and linguistic growth.

As children begin to use the adult system they gradually gain mastery of the forms and structures of their mother tongue as they engage in conversation. Successful conversation entails collaboration between the participants as they negotiate shared meanings, for each participant must listen to the other, and each must encode the meaning she or he wants to convey in language that can be received and interpreted by the conversational partner. Together they must make and maintain a shared frame of reference. Wells (1981) argues that

> collaboration in the negotiation of conversational meaning is both a major part of what the child has to learn and also a necessary condition for learning to take place. (p. 26)

The interactive nature of language development and an understanding of the part played by parents and adults must be of particular interest to us as teachers because there is so much evidence that the nature of the adults' interaction is particularly important. Cross (1978), comparing fast and slow language developers, found that for fast developers a greater proportion of parents' speech was related to what the child was intending to do. Their responses expanded and extended the child's ideas and so made increasing demands on language. Nelson (1973), investigating the effect of different styles of adult interaction on language development, found two aspects of behaviour to be significant:

1. The extent to which the mother was strongly directive of the interaction, and
2. The extent to which she was more or less likely to accept or reject the child's contribution.

She found that an accepting and nondirective style was most helpful, with the acceptance-rejection dimension being more important in the long term. Children who found their efforts, their attempts at language were received and valued, developed the *confidence* to continue.

Children in our schools come from a variety of linguistic and experiential backgrounds which affect their attitudes to life and learning and their general abilities and competencies. Turner, in her book *Made for Life* (1980), draws attention to differences other than intellectual ability. She talks about the child's propensity for learning and stresses the importance of *self-confidence*. She has identified three significant factors:

1. *Efficacy* - the power the child has experienced to have an effect on his environment, a chance to master it, to develop competence, and so self-confidence.
2. *Consistency* - a child's environment is unpredictable if it lacks consistency and this affects the growth of self-confidence.
3. *Opportunity for Communication* between the child and adult where the child's own skills and interests are acknowledged and encouragement given to take them further where it is appropriate.

Research evidence has identified adult strategies and conditions for learning that seem to support general intellectual growth and the development of language. It seems that children's learning flourishes where they are allowed some degree of control over their own actions and where they can interact with adults who are receptive, who are less concerned with rightness and wrongness, and more likely to respond in ways that stretch thinking.

As Wells (1981) puts it

> at each stage, the child also has a contribution to make, stemming from his own interests and directed by his own purpose. The sort of interaction that will be most beneficial for his development, therefore, is that which gives due weight to the contribution of both parties and emphasizes mutuality and reciprocity in the meanings that are constructed and negotiated through talk. (p. 115)

The impetus for learning to speak is functional for it enables learners to do the things they want to do. Halliday (1971) describes the impetus for learning to read and write as functional, too, meeting the learners' needs as they reach out to do more. The notion of purpose and function is not evident in much that goes on in elementary schools where children spend a great deal of time reading reading and writing writing as if reading and writing were ends in themselves. We most often over direct what they should write and make them focus on and practice particular skills long before they get any feel for the purposeful use of written language. Many spend a great deal of time copying either from reading books or the chalkboard and filling in pages in workbooks. Yet, there are school contexts in which teachers acknowledge and use the contribution each child brings to his or her own learning. Within the school curriculum there is room for children to follow their own interests and learn to take a measure of responsibility for their own learning.

Classroom Contexts

The classroom is a context for learning language, spoken and written, alongside the wealth of other learning going on. Literacy skills are established and extended as children use them in purposeful activities. The effective teacher ensures that children learn the specific skills they need to further their own learning. The assumption is that all language is learned in use and that the conditions we set up determine the nature, range and quality of the language used, and that spoken and written language develop alongside each other. The context includes such factors as:

- the whole environment of the classroom and school
- what is happening at a particular time
- the subject being studied
- the books and materials being used
- the ongoing activities
- the participants, that is the teacher (and any other adults) and the children, their roles and their role relationships, i.e. the changing parts they play in interaction.

The teachers' role is powerful for they control the classroom context. They decide the way time and space are organized; how children go about learning; to what extent work is done collaboratively; when, what, and how reading or writing may be done and how long is spent doing it. They respond to students' work, indicating clearly where their values lie. They can influence students' ideas by feeding in good stories, providing experiences rich in potential learning, and allowing children to sharpen their understanding through talk and interaction with them and with peers without feeling in any way threatened. As teachers work with students, observing them carefully, they can make judgments about their understanding, their grasp of principles, their use of skills, their growing ability to read and to write.

I want now to share examples of children and teachers working in two classroom contexts. In the first, the children range from 5 to 7 years and come from a range of cultural and linguistic backgrounds.

Context One: Having Something to Say and Learning to Express It in Writing

Many activities throughout the school year had a strong element of play as children recreated some of their real life situations. At one time the home corner became a hospital. Roles within the play changed as children became doctors, nurses, and patients. As the play developed there was a need to make charts in order to keep check on temperatures and ailments. Story books were written to read to the sick patients. For a long time the classroom post office was kept busy sending letters and greetings cards, as well as ordering stock for the classroom shop, sending out notices and invitations.

If we examine one activity, setting up a cafe, in greater detail, we get some idea of its potential for developing language. There was a great deal of talk as the children planned the cafe, recalling their own experiences and gathering the materials, and making simple food to sell, and the plates and mats for serving. The need for written language arose when the menu was needed in order to inform customers of the possibilities. The special dish of the day was as likely to be "curry and rice" as "fish and chips" or "kebabs," The waiters and waitresses made their little pads for taking customers' orders and adding up the bill. The paper plates became jokes with "Guess what I am eating?" written on them, and delectable items such as "Chips with fried worms" on the bottom. They vied with each other to find the worst combinations. Accustomed to seeing advertisements on TV they, too, decided to advertise. "What do you want to tell people?" their teacher asked. "This jelly is nice," appeared alongside one painting, and "Lovely wobbly jelly," on another. Impatient clients needed something to read while they waited for their food so the one and only edition of the "Daily Planet" appeared full of news stories about current events such as "The three babies that were born to Jack and Jill"—the classroom gerbils (Figure 1). Another story, "The girl that got knocked over," reported the misfortune that had befallen one of the older children in the school (see Figure 2).

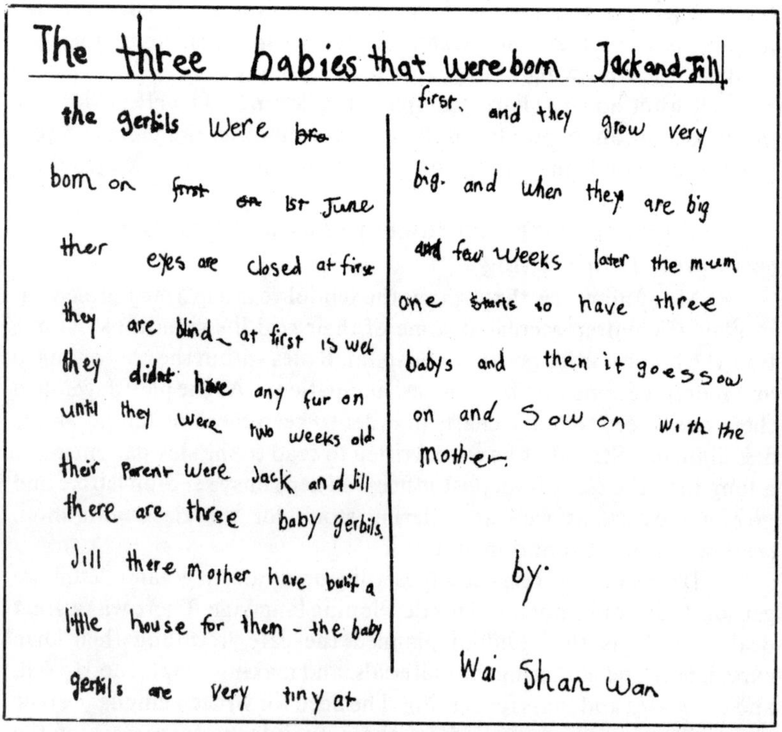
The three babies that were born Jack and Jill

the gerbils were ~~bra~~
born on ~~first~~ ~~on~~ 1st June
ther eyes are closed at first
they are blind at first is wel
they didnt have any fur on
until they were two weeks old
their Parent were Jack and Jill
there are three baby gerbils.
Jill there mother have buit a
little house for them - the baby
gerbils are very tiny at
first. and they grow very
big. and when they are big
~~and~~ few weeks later the mum
one starts to have three
babys and then it goes sow
on and sow on with the
mother.

by.

Wai Shan Wan

Figure 1. The three babies that were born to Jack and Jill.

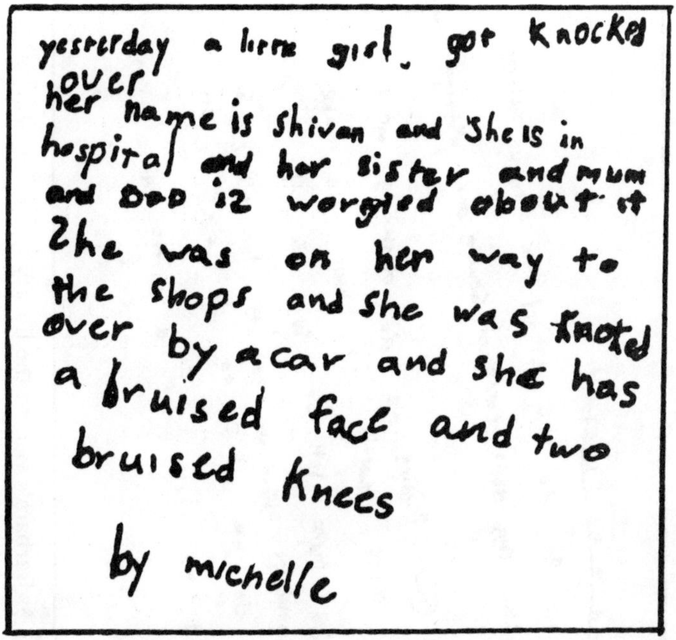
yesrerday a lirrle girl got knocked
over
her name is Shivan and She is in
hospital and her sister and mum
and Dad iz worgied about it
Zhe was on her way to
the shops and she was knoted
over by a car and she has
a bruised face and two
bruised knees
by michelle

Figure 2. The girl who got knocked over.

These examples of writing were no mere exercises. The children's own voices were there informing, reporting, recording, storying, and joking. The teacher accepted their efforts as the best they could do in written language, so children at different levels of learning could take part. There was room for their own experiences from their different backgrounds and different cultures. The teacher determined the context by setting aside part of the classroom for the cafe; allowing time, space, and materials for making the food and carrying on the activity; influencing the modes of writing in the way she responded to the children; and making her own contributions and suggestions to the ongoing work. The focus was on operating a cafe—not on writing, though the teacher would help the children focus on language where it was appropriate.

One further example from this classroom demonstrates writing, arising from need, and being used purposefully. Among the many invitations to write was a book hanging in the class in which children who wished could share their outside school activities with their classmates. Barbara (age 7) wrote about going to the local library (see Figure 3) and brought in a peg doll she had made there.

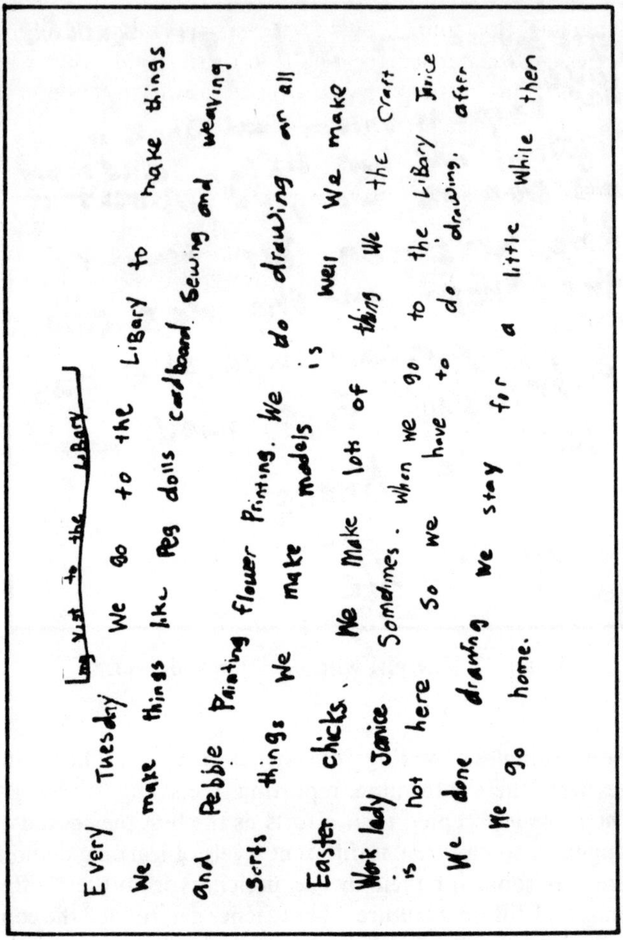

My visit to the Libary

Every Tuesday We go to the Libary to make things
We make things like Peg dolls cardboard. Sewing and weaving
and Pebble Painting flower Printing. We do drawing an all
Sorts things We make models is well We make
Easter chicks. We Make lots of thing We the Craft
Work lady Janice Sometimes. When we go to the LiBary Juice
is not here So we have to do the drawing. after
We done drawing we stay for a little while then
We go home.

Figure 3. Barbara's visit to the library.

The children were fascinated by the peg doll and many of them wanted to make one too. The teacher made the materials available; but as Barbara was the expert, she was constantly being asked for help. You will understand that the need to give instructions clearly, to answer questions, and try to use language very precisely made great demands on her language. She found coping with so many eager doll makers rather trying so her teacher suggested that she might make a book. Hence, a book of instructions, "peg dolls and how to make them" came into being. The first page (Figure 4) reads:

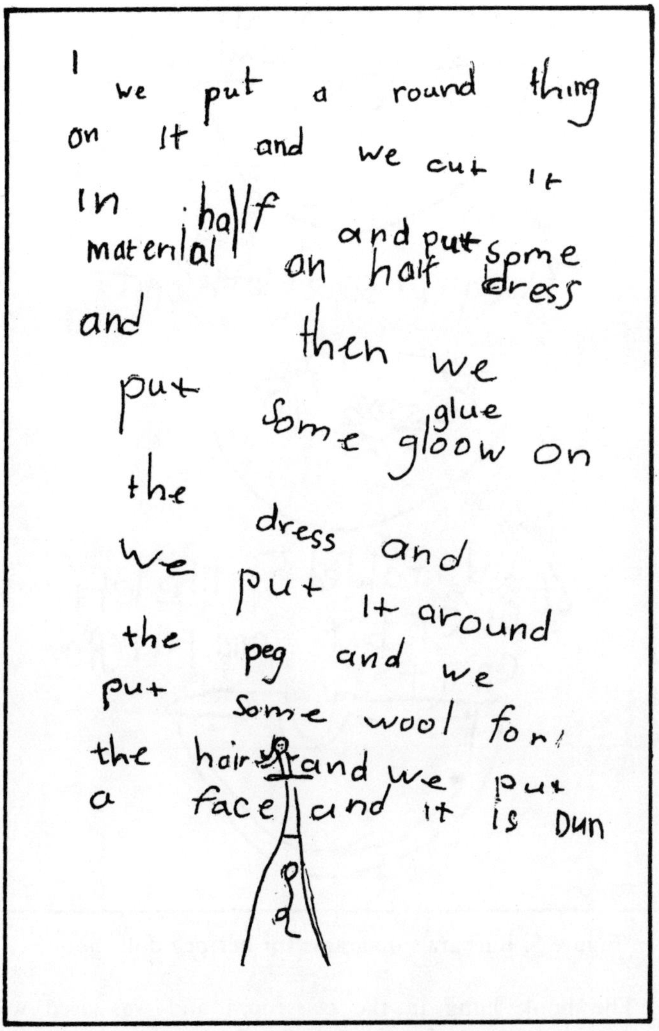

Figure 4. Page from "peg dolls and how to make them."

This was somewhat concise for her readers so her teacher suggested that she might make diagrams as in one of their toymaking books. You can see stages 2, 3, and 4 in Figure 5.

Figure 5. Barbara's diagrams for her peg dolls book.

The book hung in the classroom and was used widely. Information was added when their teacher showed them another way to make dolls. Some children needed help with reading and interpreting the instructions and many of them became aware of the purpose of diagrams.

The great problem for all writers is knowing what to say and how to say it. In this classroom context the children were operating in a world of real experience totally understandable to them. Their work (or play) centered around things they thought to be interesting and important, and the writing they did was part of it. Thus they were helped over the first difficulty of having something to say, and launched into the process of learning how to express meaning in writing. The stories being read to them, the ones they were learning to read themselves, the opportunities they had for telling stories, all contributed to their shift from "talk written down" to using written language structures. The many practical activities going on (cooking, experimenting with magnets, collecting and recording mathematical information, caring for pets, growing seeds and bulbs) meant that children used language for a range of different purposes. They provided visual support for children trying to make their meanings while learning English as a second language.

In the second example, the children are older and the play has become openended drama, through which children explore the issues involved when the needs of large groups of people for water and electricity threaten the lives lived by others.

Context Two: Conflict in Lanesbury

This area of study began after the teachers of two classes of ten and eleven year olds read the story *The Animals of Farthing Wood* by Dann (1979) to their children. The teachers decided that, together with the children, they could create an imaginary village called Lanesbury. The village was planned and maps were made as children determined its layout, worked out the network of roads, decided where the road would cross the stream flowing down from the nearby lake, and so on. They had to decide where to site the church, the pub, and the village store, and who the villagers were and where they would live. There was a wood alongside the village and the children considered what animals and birds would be likely to inhabit the woods and where exactly they would live. The children fell into two groups, animals and villagers and in openended drama each began to forge an identity, deciding who they were and creating a history for themselves. When they were ready they established their identities by writing their own autobiographies. They wrote[1] in very different styles as we see in the following two examples:

Shire Horse

I stand in the fields with all
the freedom walking up and
down, but sometimes I do not
know when I am going to work.
I carn't wait till I see
my owner and sometimes
I pull logs. Sometimes I
turn the mud over. I expect
why they use (me is) because
it is cheaper. Where I live
it is nice and quiet and
plenty of Grass. We can eat
as much as we like any time
any place. I can hear the
water running down the
stream. . . .In the spring
people come and play and
have a picnic.
sometimes they have a county
fair and they decorate
us with pretty things. . . .
I have no enemy's—I like
all the creatures what I
see. . . .

Mole

I am a British mole.
I am six inchs long with a tail of one Inch.
I have broad spade-like front feet.
I am a Small insect-eating mammal
covered with soft black fur like velvet.
I have a sensitive snout and tiny eyes
buried in my fur. one thing my eyes
seem almost usless.
My front feet have almost became spades
which makes it very easy for me to
dig with.
I mostly like grubs and worms to
eat I get them by doing tours of
the tunnels I dig.
I also have a very large appetite.
I spend most my life under ground.
I live in a wood Just outside a
small village, the people in the
village are very nice they leave
scraps of bread so if worms are

scarce I pop up out of my hole
and eat some of the bread.
I have quite a few friends
one of them is dear, also rabbit
and hare and toad those are Just
a few of my friends at the wood
I have to be carful of fox.

Into this idyllic scene came a group of people snooping around carrying files made to look very important by being covered in gold. The animals and villagers were very puzzled and disturbed. See Figure 6 for what Hare wrote later.

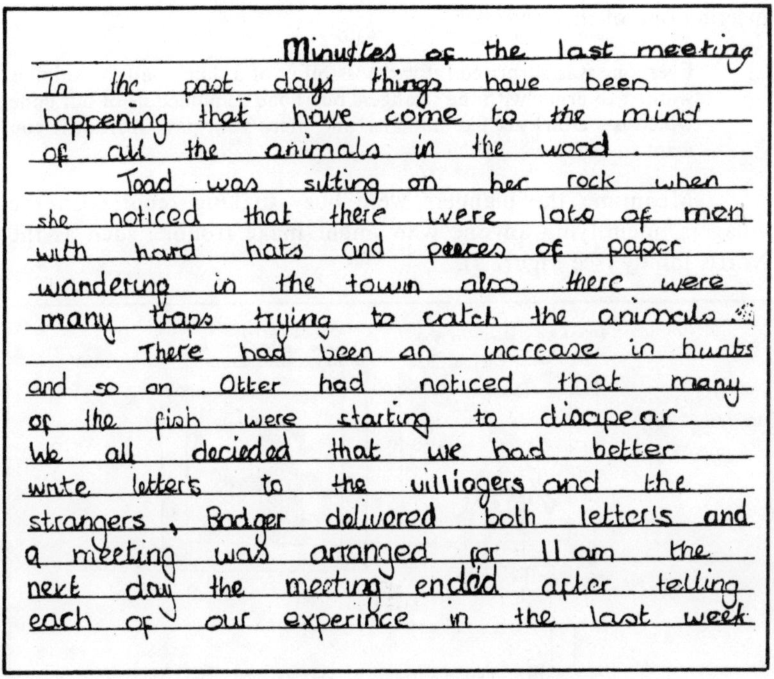

Minuttes of the last meeting
In the past days things have been
happening that have come to the mind
of all the animals in the wood.
Toad was sitting on her rock when
she noticed that there were lots of men
with hard hats and peeces of paper
wandering in the town also there were
many traps trying to catch the animals.
There had been an increase in hunts
and so on. Otter had noticed that many
of the fish were starting to disapear.
We all decided that we had better
write letters to the villiagers and the
strangers, Badger delivered both letter's and
a meeting was arranged for 11 am the
next day the meeting ended after telling
each of our experince in the last week

Figure 6. Hare's minutes of the meeting.

The meeting was called and minutes were kept. One villager began:

> Today the Lanesbury villagers had a meeting with some strangers who are trying to take over the village and make a dam. . . . The reaction of the strangers was appalling. They came trespassing into our village with

> there false letters which they say is from the queen and Maggie Thatcher shouting and arguing....

A report was sent to the local newspaper in which the writer tried to capture the excitement of the meeting. He wrote:

> The meeting had to be stopped now and then because the opposition kept getting over excited. One incedent which was quite disterbing to me, even though I'm a human, was when a villager found a dead worm....

The animals were disgusted at the behaviour of some of the humans, and made their own code of conduct. In a report of the first meeting one of them wrote:

> Everyone was surprised (at the possibility of a dam)—all the animals wanted to argue with the strangers but Toad reminded us of our code which is—Don't act like humans, and place your paw in front if you want to speak.

Meantime the planners were busy making reports on the villagers, identifying anyone who might make trouble, such as the Norris family (see Figure 7).

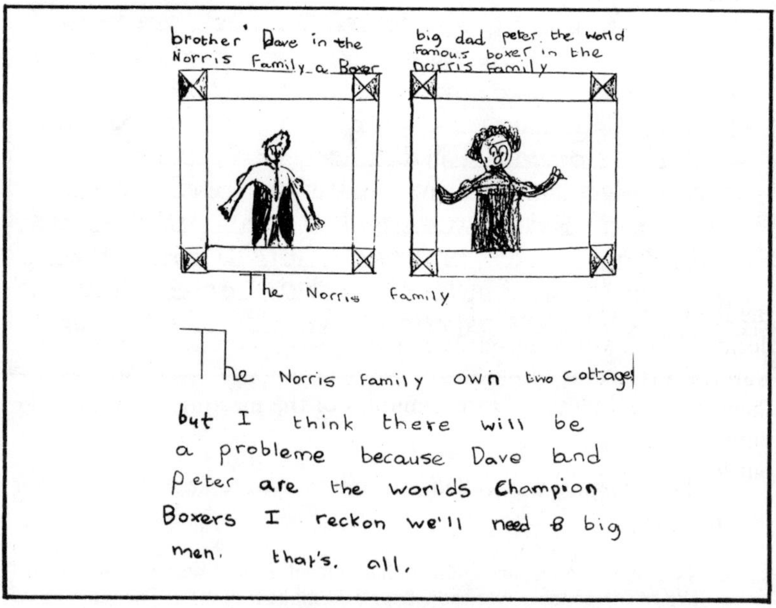

Figure 7. Report on the Norris family.

They wrote profiles of the people likely to be influential such as the vicar and the policeman and noted specially anyone useful for spreading false rumours that would help confuse the villagers. For example Pat Anne Tew (aged 51) was noted.

> She gossips so much so I recommend her to be the first person to be told about a nuclear power plant or air base. . .everyone pops in to the post office for a chat so news will spread like wildfire.

The inhabitants of Lanesbury started a campaign to fight against the dam. They wrote for support to newspapers, the television stations, influential naturalists, and to various societies including the Royal Society for the Prevention of Cruelty to Animals. To the RSPCA they wrote:

> In the village we have been through a lot of things but nothing as cruel as what is happening at the moment. The strangers have thretened to build a dam which will flood the woods and kill the animals. They said there was a place further on down the river where we can live, but the point is we are one big family and the village is our home. . . .

To the newspaper:

> so they can construct a dam in our lake just to supply electricity to their towns. . . .
>
> The naturalist told us he was going to get a petition together. . . .
>
> (at the meeting) they signed their names to stop a dam being built. After about 2 hours, 43 names and pawmarks had been signed. . . .

Emergency plans were made and distributed ready to fight off the enemy. The animals nobly rejected the bribes of biscuits offered by the planners if they would stop resisting what they called "progress."

The planners offered an alternative home in a local spot called the Rookery. The villagers and animals met there and explored it and decided it was worth considering but they wrote asking the advice of the Naturalist (the deputy head) before taking a vote. The Naturalist told them that the Ministry of the Environment insisted the dam must be built. He had visited the Rookery and talked about the new amenities but left the final decision to them.

> I saw a stream running through the middle of it. . .a perfect new home for otter and her family. . . .
>
> you asked for my advice and I have tried to give it but It'll be your decision. I know you'll make a sensible one. Please let me know what you decide.

Voting papers were written and a ballot took place. The majority decided that they would move to the Rookery. Sadly they wrote their postscripts.

Things I remember

I remember my home on the high open place on the hill
I remember my children
I remember when I was a white lively fawn
I remember by parents
I remember the fire on the hill
I remember the stream
I remember the sweet smell of roses blooming
But most of all I remember my friends.

Goodbye to my home

When my home goes
There will be a great rush
The rocks will be carried away
With boulders, trees ripped from the ground.
destroing anything and everything in its path.
Animals will flee from their homes
as the giant monster runs down
the valley
eating everying it sees
crushing animals, people,
dens, homes, any object it wants.
murdering and swooping through the valley.

Setting up the village of Lanesbury provided a context for a variety of spoken and written texts which in turn further shaped the context. Children's feelings ran deep. They were not just doing social studies but coming to grips with the human problems that arose when the basic need for water for a large number of people is set against the destruction of a small community. The issues were brought out and discussed very fully through drama, as the different groups planned their campaign. Books were needed as sources of information and stories about villagers and village life, about map-making, reservoirs, etc., and writing was integral to the whole enterprise, as it served to carry the business on. The children were clear about its nature and its purpose and the different audiences they were addressing. The writing was varied and included reports, plans, descriptions, records, letters, appeals, and poetry. Much of the writing was expressive, personal, and close to the writer, like Shire Horse's autobiography. Some, like Mole's, was more transactional, drawing upon knowledge he had obtained from studying moles in informational books. Much was persuasive asking help from various sources, with some argument as children tried to make their case. Through poetry they expressed their feelings, their love of their village homes, and their regret at its destruction.

In the two classrooms described the teachers were instrumental in determining a context in which the writer's purpose and audience were clearly understood by the children themselves. Of course these children read and write and share good stories; they study authentic documents related to their local history and environmental studies; sometimes they keep very personal diaries, or make nature diaries, using as models books such as Holden's *The Country Diary of an Edwardian Lady* (1977). Some of their writing serves as first drafts to be shared and worked on quite intensively.

In *Primary Education in England* (Department of Education & Science, 1978), a survey done by Her Majesty's Inspectors of Schools, the inspectorate reported that, in writing, considerable effort is made (by teachers) to teach syntax and spelling. They commented:

> It may be that because this work is often based on isolated exercises, the rules are too often forgotten when children write in their own words, as they frequently have the opportunity to do. What is written is often descriptive or narrative in form and, while these forms are important, by 11 years of age more children might be expected to develop an argument or to explore an idea when writing than is now the case. Furthermore, the time spent on writing should allow for the correction and improvement of initial attempts. (8.20)

The inspectors found that children's general educational progress and their competence in the basic skills benefited where they were involved in a broad curriculum, "although not necessarily as separate items on a timetable." They support the notion that when children are motivated to use language for real and worthwhile purposes, it does have a significant effect on its development.

Writing serves children as a means of reflecting, reorganizing, and rethinking their experience. It has a unique function in that it allows writers to see visibly and so become aware of their own thinking. It makes particular linguistic demands as writers make decisions about what they want to say and the way they want to say it.

Functions of Writing

Writing seems to be most purposeful when it is seen by teacher and children as an essential part of life in the classroom. Then writing arises from and relates to current, ongoing interests as children talk, read, and write about what they are doing, making, observing, or imagining.

When children use writing in relation to what they are doing in the classroom, teachers can see how they are taking on different concepts and subject matter, what they are understanding and how they are distilling what they are learning and making it their own. Teachers can see influences from literature both in the way they handle language and in the form or shape they give to their writing. The skill of writing serves the wider purposes of education, in that it leads children to think and to express their thinking more and more explicitly and precisely as they use it to communicate with a particular purpose and audience in mind. In this process they can learn to examine texts and to look both appreciatively and critically at the printed word. They begin to write as readers and to read as writers.

Promoting and Responding to Children's Reading and Writing

Teachers need to set up an environment and a range of experiences that ensures that talking, reading, and writing (and other forms of representation) play a vital part in all learning. They need to talk with children while they are engaged with learning so that they are in touch with the process, not just evaluators of the products. Children need to have opportunities to discuss their work with the teacher and talk about the problems they are meeting. In the Oracle Project, reported by Galton, Simon, and Croll (1980), it was noted that most pupils went home from school having had very little conversation on matters relating to their work. The authors discuss the nature of the teachers' interaction with regard to stimulating thinking and developing independent inquiry. They examined the nature of teachers' questions and statements and categorized them into *higher order* statements or questions (i.e. getting children to think, to investigate and understand particular concepts), and *lower order* (i.e. monitoring and supervising tasks set, asking low-level questions related to literal and factual information).

Just as with younger children acquiring language, the nature of the adult interaction seems to be crucial in influencing children's learning and language development. Could it be that when creating the classroom context there needs to be more understanding of the nature of the interaction, an understanding of the changing role of the participants, the crucial part the teacher plays in allowing the learners to play their part more fully? Perhaps teachers themselves need to experience more opportunities for developing literacy when talk, reading, and writing support each other in taking on specific curriculum learning.

Note

1. The children's spelling and punctuation have been retained in all typed examples of children's writing.

References

Cross, T.G. "Mothers' Speech and Its Association with Rate of Linguistic Development in Young Children," in N. Waterson & C.E. Snow (Eds.), *The Development of Communication.* Chichester: Wiley, 1978.

Dann, C. *Animals of Farthing Wood.* London: Piccolo, 1979.

Department of Education and Science. *Primary Education in England: A Survey by HM Inspectors of Schools.* London: HMSO, 1978.

Galton, M., Simon, B., & Croll, P. *Inside the Primary Classroom: Oracle Report.* Boston: Routledge & Kegan Paul, 1980.

Halliday, M.A.K. "Language Acquisition and Initial Literacy," Paper presented at 38th Claremont Reading Conference, February 1971, Claremont, California.

Holden, E. *The Country Diary of an Edwardian Lady.* New York: Holt, Rinehart & Winston, 1977.

Nelson, K. "Structure and Strategy in Learning to Talk," *Monographs of the Society for Research in Child Development, 38* (1973).

Rosen, H., & Stratta, L. "English as a Mother Tongue," in G.E. Perren (Ed.), *The Mother Tongue and Other Language in Education.* NCLE Papers and Reports 2, Centre for Information on Language Teaching and Research, England, 1979.

Turner, J. *Made for Life: Coping, Competence, and Cognition.* New York: Methuen, 1980.

Wells, G. *Learning through Interaction: The Study of Language Development.* New York: Cambridge University Press, 1981.

IRA/NCTE Committee on the Impact of Child Language Development Research on Curriculum and Instruction, 1979-1982

NCTE Editorial Board, 1983